It all began one sleepless night...

"I tossed and turned for what seemed like hours. I knew I wasn't going to sleep until I made some sense of it all. I needed meaningful answers to the big questions of life. ...

So I decided to look within myself. I closed my eyes, took several deep breaths and reached a calm, meditative state. I asked *my Soul* for some guidance. "If you're real, then help me ... What are the answers to my questions about life?"

Frankly, I didn't expect a response (that only happens in the movies, right?), but within a few minutes I felt compelled to get some paper. Ideas and images began to flow into my mind so quickly that I filled up seven pages with words and drawings in no time. When I stopped to look at what I had done, I was excited and yet at peace. So, I went back to bed and was soon asleep.

When I awoke the thoughts kept coming, and for the next two weeks I wrote and sketched, filling up over two hundred pages before I stopped. I felt guided during the whole process—as if the ideas were coming from a place beyond my normal consciousness. It was a creative marathon unlike anything I had ever experienced. When I did finally stop, I knew I had found many of the answers that would ease my mind. And that is when I decided to write this book and to share with others what I believe my Soul had revealed to me beginning on that sleepless night."

— from the first chapter

"I like to see this book as an essential guidebook for the journey of life. It is the book I wish I had when I was starting out in my life."

Tom Gregory, author of *The Meaning of Life*

This book covers a wide range of topics, including: the creation of our Souls and the universe, karma and reincarnation, children, relationships, sex, work, aging and death. It examines our spiritual nature, presents the model of the "Reality Maker" to explain who we are on Earth, and introduces the "Seven Why Me? Factors" as the reasons why bad things happen to us.

This book is thought provoking and challenges many traditional views. For example, it unites creationism and evolution, offers the "Ten Rules of the Road" as an updated version of the Ten Commandments, and presents a vision of how we might create "Heaven on Earth." *The Meaning of Life* offers a set of spiritual beliefs that promote love, harmony, tolerance and the divinity and interconnectedness of all life.

The
Meaning *of* Life

Spiritual Insights and Practical Advice
On the Big Questions We All Ask

by

Tom Gregory

First Edition

Living Spirit Press, Walnut Creek, California

The **Meaning** *of* **Life**
Spiritual Insights and Practical Advice
On the Big Questions We All Ask

Published by: Living Spirit Press
                  Post Office Box 2455
                  Walnut Creek, CA 94595-0455   U.S.A.

                  http://www.meaningoflife.net
                  http://www.livingspiritpress.com

Copyright © 2000 by Tom Gregory

All rights reserved. No part of this book may be reproduced or transmitted in any form or by any means, electronic or mechanical, including photo-copying, recording or by any information storage and retrieval system without written permission from the author, except for the inclusion of brief quotations in a review.

This book is available in two versions: (1) paperback with black & white illus-trations, and (2) hardcover with color illustrations (*available March 2000*).

Manufactured in the United States of America
Printed on acid-free, recycled paper

0 9 8 7 6 5 4 3 2 1

Publisher's Cataloging-In-Publication
(Provided by Quality Books, Inc.)

Gregory, Tom, 1953-
     The meaning of life : spiritual insights and
practical advice on the big questions we all ask /
Tom Gregory. -- 1st ed.
     p. cm.
     Includes index
     LCCN: 99-90527
     ISBN: 0-9672776-7-1 (pbk)
     ISBN: 0-9672776-8-X (hc)

     1. Spiritual life. 2. Conduct of life.
3. Life--Religious aspects. 4. Natural theology.
I. Title

BL624.G74 2000   291.4'4
                        QBI99-1132

CONTENTS

Contents

LISTS, HOW TO'S and OTHER KEY POINTS
(In order of appearance)

Lists, How To's and Other Key Points

Lists, How To's and Other Key Points

ACKNOWLEDGMENTS

First and foremost, I am eternally grateful to my wife Nancy De-Long Gregory who was my collaborator, editor and unfailing supporter. Her faith in me and in my creative vision was wonderful. Without her, this book would not have turned out as it did, if at all.

I am especially thankful to my brother Pat Gregory. He was an outstanding editor and has contributed incredibly in many other ways to this endeavor. My sister-in-law Ann Gregory was always there too with words of encouragement and creative suggestions.

I am also grateful to the people who read parts or all of the book and provided feedback, including: Rev. Max Lafser of the Unity Church of Walnut Creek, California; Julie Knowles; Lester Brown, President of Worldwatch Institute, and his assistant, Reah Janise Kauffman; Sandy Gregory; my father, Frank Gregory; Jill Brady; Cheryl Storm, who also contributed to the cover design; Susan Piatt; and Michele Gaub.

Special thanks go to: Pete Masterson of Aeonix Publishing Group for his help on book design and production matters; Denise Bazinet and Kristin Prentice for their input on the cover; Susan Miller of the Unity Metaphysical Bookstore for her support and feedback; Andreas Lindarto for his help with the web site; Ron Weber at spaceimages.com for the NASA photos that appear in the book; Andrea Wheeler of the Tiburon Library and the research staff at the Kennedy Library who helped with some of the quotes used in the book; Val Hornstein for his legal advice; and Lyle Mumford and his associates at Publishers Press for their excellent work on the printing of the book.

Many friends and family members were supportive, especially Patricia DeLong, Sandra Reid, Janette Booher-Fulton and Adele Ann Bozza. I also want to acknowledge the love and guidance I felt coming from my mother, Rosemary and grandmother, Nellie, both of whom are in the Spirit World, and the love and companionship of Shubers, Blinkers, and Nellie, my feline kindreds. And last but certainly not least, thank you Harvey for giving me the inspiration for this book and for being my clear inner voice throughout the writing process.

Cover Design: Seat-of-the-Pants Graphics

P.S. I would also like to thank David E. Kelley, producer and writer of *Ally McBeal*. I don't know him personally, but his show provided some great lines that I use in a few places in the book.

DEDICATION

For Nancy, my best friend and life partner,
with eternal love and gratitude.

My Search For Meaning

"The Thinker" – by
Auguste Rodin, 1880

> Who, or what, am I? Do I have a Soul?
> Where did I come from? Is there a God?
> What is the meaning of life? What is the
> purpose of *my* life? Did I exist before?
> What happens to me after I die?
>
> Why do some people have all the luck,
> while others struggle or suffer so much?
> And how can I make my life better?

> Humans have been asking those ques-
> tions for thousands of years. No one can
> know for sure what the answers are, but
> this book presents a view on life and the
> beyond that you might like.

We are an inquisitive species. We like to solve mysteries and to explain the inexplicable. We want to know the "who, what and why's" and to make sense of it all. It's a trait that distinguishes us from other animals. We are especially perplexed by the paradoxical nature of life —that so much beauty and joy can coexist with so much pain and suffering. Whether we are young or old, rich or poor, we're all looking for answers that will help reduce the pain and bring more passion and fulfillment into our lives.

Our ability to ponder the meaning and mysteries of life is a blessing and, at times, a curse. It drives us to explore and learn and thus to grow, but it can cause us to be anxious too. When life seems particularly confusing or unfair, our inquiring minds can be so active they won't let us sleep. And that is exactly what happened to me a few weeks before my forty-third birthday and what led me to write this book.

My Soul "Spoke" To Me Late One Night

It was past midnight, and I was lying in bed thinking about a lot of things. Earlier, I had been out gazing at the stars and was struck by the vast and incredible nature of the universe. How did we fit into this cosmic picture? Are we just a fluke of evolution, or did a supreme being put us here on purpose *and* for what purpose?

Then I wondered if there is a "God" at all. I had serious doubts —especially about the kind of God that might exist. Why would a *benevolent* God create a world filled with natural disasters, disease, war and senseless accidents? Watch the local news or read a history book, and you can't help but think that no one is looking over us. We must be on our own.

Other thoughts were keeping me up that night as well. I was questioning the very goodness of the human race! Of course we can be loving and compassionate, but we have also demonstrated an innate ability to be hateful, greedy and selfish. Many millions of lives have been lost or ruined because of human actions, not because it was God's will. And I wondered why we live as we do—so fast-paced, materialistic and superficial. If there is a God, this is certainly not what He (or She) would expect of us. Our behavior does not reflect well on our species.

As I stared at the ceiling I also thought about my own life. I wasn't sure where I was headed. I even found myself second-guessing some of my past choices. I was living well and had been successful to date, but I wanted more—not more things, but more joy and contentment. I knew I wasn't fully utilizing my gifts, and I wasn't even sure I knew exactly what they were. I also felt that too many of my goals and dreams from earlier years were unfulfilled. I was middle-aged now, and time was going by way too fast.

Finally, I was thinking about friends and family members who had died, and I wondered if their Souls lived on and if they could "hear" my thoughts. I missed them very much, and I realized that my own journey would also end—perhaps sooner than later. I wondered if God was going to "call me home" before I had a chance to live the life I really wanted.

And so I tossed and turned for what seemed like hours. I knew I wasn't going to sleep until I made some sense of it all. I needed meaningful answers to the big questions of life.

> Without knowing what I am and why I am here, life is impossible.
> Leo Tolstoy – Russian writer; 1828–1910

 One can make it through life without caring about philosophical or spiritual matters, but the journey can be better if we know at least some of the answers. However, where could I go at one o'clock in the morning to find the meaning of life?

At that point I got out of bed and went looking for wisdom. I grabbed one of my favorite books—*The Great Thoughts* by George Seldes—and started reading. Before long I was feeling worse! I found that many of the great minds, especially of the recent past, didn't think too highly of mankind or of God.

A deaf, dumb and blind idiot could have made a better world than this.
> Tennessee Williams – American dramatist; 1914–83

Human life must be some kind of mistake.
> Arthur Schopenhauer – German philosopher; 1788–1860

(We are) the supreme clown of creation.
> H.L. Mencken – American editor, critic; 1880–1956

Man is cosmically unimportant, and ... a (God), if there were one ... would hardly mention us (in a history of the universe).
> Bertrand Russell – British mathematician, philosopher; 1872–1970

There is no reason for life and life has no meaning.
> W. Somerset Maugham – British writer; 1874–1965

Our world is ... a practical joke of God.
> Franz Kafka – Austrian writer; 1883–1924

This wasn't a promising beginning to my search, but considering the fact the people I quoted lived during some of the worst wars of human history, I could understand their perspective. I wanted insights that would not only help explain life but that would also be hopeful and optimistic. I wanted to be inspired.

Next, I thought about religion and some of the positive teachings I had learned as a child. (I was raised as a Catholic, but I am not currently an active churchgoer.)

My religion taught that God loves me, there is life after death, Heaven is a great place (if you can get in), and we should treat others with love and kindness.

That made me feel better, but I also had some major issues with my religion. I felt the message of love was overshadowed by what I call the teachings of *negativity, punishment* and *intolerance.* Instead of telling us that as children of God we are basically good people, we're told we are all "sinners" and that we were born that way. Is it really necessary, or even effective, to fill our minds with images of a vengeful God or of a place where people will burn forever? And am I really supposed to believe that someone who follows a different religion is destined for the "spiritual dumpster?" What if he or she is a wonderful person leading an exemplary life? I didn't like or accept these beliefs when I was child and I still don't. They make us feel bad about ourselves, and they separate us from each other. (I devote a full chapter to this subject later in the book.)

Some Religious Ideas That Trouble Me

A famous evangelist said, in effect, to the talk show host (who is Jewish) — "Heaven is only for those who believe in the divinity of Jesus. Sorry, my friend, it is not for you."

Heard on a religious radio show — "The whole universe is so corrupt that God is going to destroy it and start over. Only those who accept the Bible as is will be saved."

A priest said on a television show — "If you are a good Christian in this, your only life, your dead body will be raised by God. Otherwise, you will cease to exist." (So, hasta la vista nonbeliever!)

 And what about the notion that women are supposed to be subservient to men? That's not nice. In fact, it has caused great harm over the ages. I can't believe God supports such beliefs.

At this point I thought some of the "new age" books I had read over the years might be helpful. They emphasized our divinity and great potential, and they spoke to our spiritual connection with each other and with all living things. The message was one of empowerment, mutual respect and tolerance. But then I thought about the other parts of this not so new spirituality that bothered me such as placing all of the blame for a person's difficult life circumstances on them—as if we all get what we deserve. It seemed to me that in trying to make sense out of life's complex mysteries, we are sometimes willing to accept concepts that are incomplete and not always fair.

Over-Simplified Explanations

- There are **no** accidents.
- I create **all** of my own reality.
- It is **all** part of God's plan for me.
- It's my "karma" from a past life.
- Where I am is where I need to be

It was now after three o'clock, and I thought I would be up all night. I had made some progress, but I wasn't satisfied. So I decided to look within myself. I closed my eyes, took several deep breaths and reached a calm, meditative state. I asked *my Soul* for some guidance. "If you're real, then help me make sense of all this. What are the answers to my questions about life?"

Frankly, I didn't expect a response (that only happens in the movies, right?), but within a few minutes I felt compelled to get some paper. Ideas and images began to flow into my mind so quickly that I filled up seven pages with words and drawings in no time. When I stopped to look at what I had done, I was excited and yet at peace. So, I went back to bed and was soon asleep.

When I awoke the thoughts kept coming, and for the next two weeks I wrote and sketched, filling up over two hundred pages before I stopped. I felt guided during the whole process—as if the ideas were coming from a place beyond my normal consciousness. It was a creative marathon unlike anything I had ever experienced. When I did finally stop, I knew I had found many of the answers that would ease my mind. And that is when I decided to write this book and to share with others what I believe my Soul had revealed to me beginning on that sleepless night.

I know that may seem presumptuous, but I was excited by what I had learned. I felt this had all happened for a reason. I understand why some people may find it hard to believe that my Soul was talking to me. Still, I think the information presented in the book is meaningful even if one doesn't accept my story.

 This book is both conceptual and practical in nature. It has the "big picture" view and some "how to's."

I realized during those first two weeks that what I was really doing was creating a guidebook, or an "operator's manual" for the journey of life. It provides explanations for the big questions (the who, what and why's). It also includes suggestions as to how we can make better choices and improve the quality of our lives.

Of course, not every concept in this book is original. Indeed, I found that I was integrating the best of what was already in my head (from the learning I had done throughout my life) with the wisdom that was coming from within me—or from beyond this realm. What excited me was how all this knowledge fit together so well.

My Truth Comes From Many Sources

Religion	Philosophy
"New Age" spirituality	My Soul, or "inner voice"
Science and logic	Common sense
Psychology	Imagination

And FAITH is the "glue" that holds it all together.

I found meaning from all of the above.

When I told my father I was writing this book he asked if I had done a lot of research. I told him I had not because I wanted to stay true to my own vision. But during the actual writing process I did get valuable insights from several books and from speakers I heard —and I am grateful to be able to include their words of wisdom. I have also used quotations throughout the book, a number of which came from Seldes' *The Great Thoughts*. While I feel I have put forth some fresh ideas, it is clear I am just another voice in a chorus of many trying to explain the mysteries of life.

> Nothing is said nowadays that has not been said before.
> Terence – Latin playwright; 190–159 BCE
>
> [I would like to think there are a few new ideas in this book. But who knows, maybe my Soul was sending me ancient wisdom.]

Some of the ideas in this book will seem pretty fanciful, but isn't that true of most spiritual concepts?

At times I felt like I was doing more creative thinking than channeling a vision from the Spirit World. But I believe our Souls do speak to us and often through our imaginations. I was willing to accept some seemingly far-fetched ideas but only if I thought they were plausible and didn't contradict what we know to be scientifically real. Plus, it was essential the ideas be positive in nature. If a concept inspired me to live a better life and to be hopeful about our future, then I included it.

I wish I could prove all of the ideas in this book, but I can't. Indeed, no one can know for sure what the truth is, unless they receive divine revelation. And even then, we might doubt whether it really happened. When it comes to spiritual matters we have to take a leap of *faith* and be willing to reach some conclusions without having the material evidence we desire. Although I can't prove what came to me that night, I believe it could be true.

> A wise man may think he understands the handiwork of God, but he doesn't really.
>
> Ecclesiastes 8:17; (paraphrased)
>
> The gods are laughing at those who believe they know what the Truth is.
>
> Albert Einstein; (paraphrased)

I am not saying that what is presented in this book is the absolute truth, just that it works for me. It satisfies my own emotional, rational and spiritual needs and thus is *my* truth. Perhaps some of it will resonate with you as well. I can only ask that you be willing to reexamine some of your long-held beliefs and consider some new spiritual concepts.

> Whatever satisfies the soul is truth.
>
> Walt Whitman – American poet; 1819–92

> Just a brief comment on this quote — A person can believe emotionally and fervently in something, but that doesn't mean his or her Soul does too. If a belief leads us to be intolerant or to cause harm, then it is safe to assume our Soul is quite distressed by that belief. The truth that satisfies our Soul is that which helps us to be more loving and compassionate and to lead more fulfilling lives—not to be harmful or judgmental.

> Doesn't the Bible, the Koran, the Vedas, the Tao Te Ching, and other sacred texts already tell us what the truth is?

Billions of people believe that the holy book of their religion is the truth, and I respect that. While I have not studied these texts in detail, my basic feeling is this—there are words of God in all of them, but not every word is divine. Any book produced by man (including mine) is affected by the personal prejudices of the author(s) and by the mores of the time and place in which it was written. While I have found the Bible, for example, to be profound, I have also been frustrated trying to read it. I am stymied by passages that are obscure or archaic or that are overly negative.

My goal was to write a book that looked at the mysteries of life from a modern perspective and free of the dogmas of any one religion. I wanted a book of "practical spirituality" which included ideas from both Eastern and Western religions and which honored the teachings of many guides, such as Jesus, Buddha and Muhammad. This book is my attempt to respect the wisdom of the ages and to make it more accessible, at least to myself.

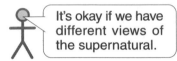
It's okay if we have different views of the supernatural.

The existence of a supreme being or Creator, whom I prefer to call "God," is an essential part of my belief system, for reasons I discuss in the next chapter and in the *Big Picture* section of the book. Feel free to substitute the name or word that describes your view of whoever, or whatever, created and rules the universe. If you don't believe in such a Being or force, that's fine too. Many of the ideas in the book are useful even if there is no God.

I Will Be Putting Words In God's Mouth

You'll see Me throughout this book expressing the thoughts and feelings that Tom believes a **kind** and **loving** God would have.

Not only do I accept the idea of a supernatural power, but I also find it helpful to imagine what God would say on various subjects if He (or She) spoke directly to us. I know many people feel God has already spoken, and His messages are recorded in the Bible. There may even be those who will feel I have been blasphemous. Nevertheless, I believe a God of *love* would most likely support and agree with what I have said in His (or Her) name.

Although this is not a book of any one religion, I do consider it to be a religious book of sorts—but not in a righteous or preachy sense. Instead, this book stresses the values of love and compassion, personal responsibility and tolerance. It focuses on our spiritual mission and how each of us can reconnect with our Soul and with God. This book also shows reverence for the divine within all of us.

There Are Many Paths To God. Who's To Say Which Is Right?

The concept of "God" is beyond anyone's comprehension and descriptive abilities. We can only imagine what the truth is about such a powerful Being. And we can either accept a particular religion's view of God or develop a model that feels right for us. I have chosen the latter course, and I now see God in a different light than I did when I was growing up.

It Is the Illustrated Book on Life

There are a lot of pictures in the book because that's how my Soul chose to communicate with me.

I have always been a "visual" person. I like to draw and would rather look at pictures than read a lot of text. So, I was not at all surprised that the original inspiration came that night more as images than as words. It is also why I have structured the book so that the illustrations are presented before or beside the accompanying text. I suggest you look at each picture first and then read the words below it, or next to it, as the case may be.

It's a good thing a picture is worth a "thousand words" because I cover a lot of ground in the book. My goal was not to explain every spiritual or psychological concept in detail or to write exhaustively on the practical issues of living in this world. Rather, I wanted to present enough information to convey the essence of my Soul's vision and to provide a framework for how one could make better choices in life.

I should also tell you there are times when I editorialize and offer my views on sensitive subjects like population control, sexuality, and the environment. Again, I feel my views are in line with what a loving God would say and are quite pragmatic. Still, I realize there are other perspectives which are valid and meaningful.

If Only I Knew Then What I Know Now

I wish I had a book like this in high school or college—when I was just starting my journey.

Most of us don't get enough in the way of "life tutoring." We hear truisms like, "If you want to get ahead, study and work hard." So, we learn about the art of living primarily by observing how other people live, especially our parents. We get some direction from our schooling and religious training (and from our peers), and the rest we learn through personal trial and error. Unfortunately, it's not the most effective way to approach life.

While it is my hope this book will be of value to readers of all ages, it would please me the most if teens and young adults find it helpful. I think back to when I was growing up, and I am amazed at how little I knew about the meaning of life or how to make wise choices. It would have made a world of difference if I had started my journey better prepared.

Please Talk Amongst Yourselves

 We could all benefit from a respectful discussion of the topics in this book, especially parents and children.

I know my parents did the best they could, but I do wish I had received more guidance from them. So, I think it would be great if parents were to discuss the questions of life with their children. It is my hope that this book might provide a vehicle for that process. The range of subjects I have covered can provide a framework for a series of give-and-take discussions.

Each generation passes down certain values and beliefs to the next one. So it is only appropriate to examine whether we are perpetuating views that are harmful or not particularly useful. And we can ask what values and beliefs would help a child to become a better and happier person, to be more loving, and to create a new and improved world for themselves and others. We could also encourage our children to be *freethinkers,* who are willing to study various religious beliefs and then come to their own conclusions.

It is my hope this book will also be of value to "baby boomers" (like myself), who are now thinking about the meaning of life and about their own mortality—especially as we watch our parents and our friends pass on, as we reflect on the choices we have made to date and as we consider how we want to live the second-half of our lives. Finally, it would be gratifying if readers of my father's generation (and older) found meaning and comfort in this book too as they wonder what comes next.

Life is not a problem to be solved but a mystery to be lived.
Thomas Merton – Trappist monk and author; 1915–68

We each look at life and the realities of the world through our own lens. We won't (and don't need to) agree on everything. Moreover, there will always be unsolved mysteries. Even if one thinks he has it all figured out he is going to discover, if and when he finally meets God, he still has a lot to learn. So, I offer this book not as *the* answer to the questions posed at the beginning of the chapter, but as one perspective. I hope you will find it thought provoking and helpful. Thanks for taking the time to read it.

Here Is A "Road Map" For the Rest of the Book

So you will know where we are headed, this is how I have organized the subject matter:

> **The key question**: Is there a God? – The reasons why I say "yes, there is" – How I picture God and the benefits of believing.
>
> **The Big Picture:** The Spirit World – The birth of our Souls – The creation of the wondrous universe – The nature and essence of our Souls – Values and Beliefs to live by – Our spiritual mission (the purpose of our existence) – Evolution – Reincarnation – Kindred Souls – Karma and other cosmic laws.
>
> **Down to Earth:** Incarnation explained – Who we really are – The power of love – Why we're not perfect (and a look at bad Souls) – Becoming a powerful "reality maker" – Creating the life our Soul dreamed of – Family and friends; life partners; sex; and children – Communities and home; our calling and money – What it takes for us to be happy – Being creative – Choices and consequences – What else affects our reality (and how we respond to bad events) – Forgiveness – What else we can expect on our journey – What death means and what happens to us after we die.
>
> **We're All In This Together:** How we can create Heaven on Earth – Spirituality and religion (and finding common ground) – A vision of the future (and why the best is yet to come, or why it could be).
>
> **Epilogue:** A brief summary of the key points in the book.
>
> I would also encourage you to read the appendix, where I acknowledge the people and books I found most helpful and interesting.

Approach this book as if it were a "buffet" of spiritual insights and practical advice.

Because this book is intended for a wide audience, some of the material may not be of interest to you or relevant to your life. And you will, undoubtedly, have different views on many of the subjects. So, I encourage you to pick and choose what you find most appealing and agreeable. Also, because there is so much in the book, I suggest you not read it all in one sitting. Of course, I hope you will be so engrossed that you can't put the book down. And while I think the material is a "quick read," it probably makes more sense to only take in several chapters at a time.

Some Final Comments On What Lies Ahead

I mentioned that I use quotes from other people throughout the book. My inclusion of their words doesn't mean they would necessarily agree with what I have written. For example, statements from several scientists appear in the early chapters. These quotes, which I found in other books, support aspects of my story, but that is not to say my views are validated by those scientists.

About My Little Friend ...

Sometimes when you see me I'll be speaking for Tom; other times I'll just be some person asking a question or making a point. It will be pretty obvious who I am.

I use the *stick-man* a lot, so I hope you like him. I use him to emphasize key points, to indicate a transition to a new subject or to save the space that regular text would take. At times, he seems to have a mind of his own, but of course, I assume full responsibility for all the words that come out of his mouth.

Finally, allow me to emphasize again that what you are about to read is just my (and my Soul's) viewpoint. I don't regard it as the absolute truth, even though I called the book, **The** *Meaning of Life*. Rather, it is a collection of insights and suggestions that have brought more meaning and understanding to my life.

Actually, there is one more thing—regarding grammar. I've chosen to mostly use the pronoun "we" throughout the book—instead of "I" or "you." Neither one of those seemed appropriate. As a rule, "we" in this book is referring to us as *individuals.* Consequently, I use words of a singular nature in many sentences that contain a "we," such as "we might ask *ourself.*" Of course, there are times when I use "we" in the plural sense to refer to all of us or to people in general. But it should be obvious when I have switched to that perspective. Lastly, regarding the word, "their": It may not be totally proper, but I sometimes use "their" instead of "his or her" when those words are too awkward in a sentence.

It was my intent to maintain an informal tone in my writing. To that end, I might bend the grammar rules on occasion. Please don't report me to my former English teachers.

Is There a God?

I believe in God, whom I understand as Spirit, as Love, as the Source of all.

Leo Tolstoy – Russian writer; 1828–1910

How Can There Be a God When Life Includes All This?

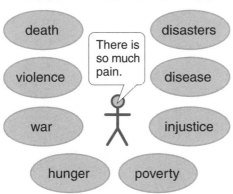

There are many reasons for us to doubt the existence of God or at least to wonder what sort of God would let these awful things happen, especially to good people. But, the fact there is so much misfortune does not mean there is no God or God is unkind. It means we have to look much deeper to find the meaning of it all.

Seven Reasons Why I Believe In God

1. The wonders of life—such as the beauty and diversity of nature, the existence of humans and animals, and conception itself—are too astounding to be just an accident.

2. The universe is so vast and incredible. It apparently had a beginning and came out of nowhere. It seems to have been pre-planned and calibrated so that stars and planets, and life itself, could exist.

3. The emergence of life on Earth several billion years ago may be inexplicable as anything but a miraculous event.

4. There are many things we can't see which are real.

5. Many of us have had signs that a Spirit World exists.

6. The Bible and other holy books contain many divinely inspired words, and they describe a multitude of amazing happenings.

7. The existence of a God means that I do have a Soul, and it puts my life in a broader, spiritual context.

> ... all of nature cries aloud that God does exist; that there is a supreme intelligence ...
>
> Voltaire – French philosopher (paraphrased); 1694–1778

God's handiwork is all around us. When I see the glorious blue sky, a breathtaking sunset, vibrant flowers, or the majestic redwood tree I just "know" God is real. These and the many other marvels of nature are the creative expression of a divine being who is not only powerful but who also has an exquisite sense of beauty.

Also, the fact you and I are alive is a profound testimony to the existence of a supreme intelligence. As "biological entities" we are so intricate, and our ability to create a new life is so amazing, that I can't imagine we are merely the result of an evolutionary process. The initial design or blueprint for life must have come from a source beyond our physical reality. When I consider our capacity to think and choose, and to make our dreams come true, I can believe that we are the reflection of a supernatural being. Finally, whenever I see a newborn child and think of the promise he or she brings to the world, or experience the joy and healing power of love, I feel there must be a God.

> It is the heart (not reason) which experiences God.
>
> Blaise Pascal
> French philosopher; 1623–62

The subjective "proof" is enough for me, most of the time. And when I'm being a "doubting Thomas" I can turn to other evidence that points to the existence of God, most notably of which is directly overhead. Looking at the stars and planets through my telescope always leaves me humbled and awestruck. And whenever I contemplate the vast and incredible nature of the cosmos I am certain God is real. For example, the universe came into being 12 to 18 billion years ago, and it contains at least 10 *billion trillion* stars!

Putting the age of the universe in perspective —

If you were to start counting—at the rate of one number each second and each number represented one year of history—it would take you only 1 minute and 40 seconds to cover the twentieth century. But it would take you nearly **500 years** of nonstop counting to reach the mid-range estimate of the universe's age, or 15 billion.

Putting the number of stars in perspective —

One person could count all the stars visible to their "naked eye" under the darkest of skies in less than one hour, assuming they could count one star per second. But it would take every person on Earth (all six billion of us) simultaneously counting one star every second over **50,000 years** to count the 10 billion trillion stars that are really out there! Or look at it this way—there are far more stars in the universe than there are grains of sand on all the beaches on Earth.

We can't understand the universe in any clear way without the supernatural.

Allan Sandage – astronomer

Not only is the universe old, huge and really complex, but most scientists say there was a time when it didn't exist at all. There was an event, known as the "Big Bang" (12 to 18 billion years ago), that created all the energy and matter which would eventually become you and me and everything we see. I will cover this in the next chapter; but for now suffice it to say there is an ongoing debate in the scientific community about the Big Bang and its cause.

The "Big Mystery"— Who or What Made the Universe?

Was it ... (A) a **spontaneous creation** that just happened all by itself, without any external influence; or was it ...

(B) a **conscious choice** by a supernatural power, who said "Let there be ... light ... and stars and planets and life"?

... when the world's greatest minds are put to the task of finding a way to propose a universe without a Creator, they find the task impossible ...

Fred Hereen, author of *Show Me God*

Our Home In The Universe Was Made Perfectly For "Life"

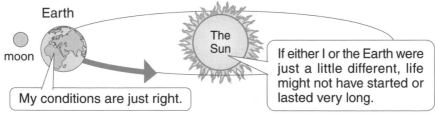

Earth

moon

The Sun

My conditions are just right.

If either I or the Earth were just a little different, life might not have started or lasted very long.

There are so many characteristics of our planet and Sun which allow life to exist—including how big each is and how far apart they are, the degree to which the Earth tilts on its axis, the composition of the Earth's atmosphere and core, the availability of liquid water, and even the presence of our moon, to name just a few—that it all seems too incredible to be just a coincidence. And that doesn't even take into account the inexplicable emergence of the first living cell on the Earth. That by itself could be seen as a miracle.

Even if our existence on Earth were the amazing result of a myriad of chance events, the fundamental state of the universe points to the handiwork of a supreme intelligence. Basic forces, such as gravity and subatomic charges, are so precisely what they need to be for us, or anything else to exist, that it is, to some of the greatest thinkers of our time, unexplainable unless one includes the possibility of a God. The odds of the universe being as it is just as the result of randomness are beyond comprehension.

... the "constants of nature" ... have exactly the values that allow stars and planets to form ... The universe, it seems, is fine-tuned to let life and consciousness flower.

Edward Kolb – physicist

The remarkable fact is that the values of these numbers seem to have been very finely adjusted to make (life) possible ...

Stephen Hawking – physicist

... these circumstances indicate that the Universe was created for man to live in.

John O'Keefe – astronomer

The universe in some sense must have known we were coming.

Freeman Dyson – physicist

The Big Bang, the most cataclysmic event we can imagine, on closer inspection, appears finely orchestrated.

George Smoot – physicist

I found these quotes in *Show Me God*, by Fred Hereen. Although I don't agree with all of his conclusions, I highly recommend this book if you'd like to study the scientific evidence for the existence of God.

God

Even Albert Einstein tried to explain the universe without including Me, but he couldn't. In fact, he became a believer and said he wanted to know **how** I created the universe, not if I did.

Something Can Exist Even If We Can't "See" It

Visible Light	ultraviolet radiation	X rays	gamma rays	cosmic rays

Increasing rates of vibration ⟶

Human Body	Human Mind	Our Soul	GOD

This is not to imply God is like cosmic rays, but that many things exist at levels higher than either visible light or the human body.

When it comes to matters of spirituality, some people say: "If I can't see it, or touch it, it can't be true." There is so much we cannot see in the physical world that is real. Why should it be any different for the spiritual domain? In *Secrets of the Night Sky*, Bob Berman offers this description: "Our eyes detect just a narrow part of the energy that echoes throughout the universe ... hidden parts of the energy spectrum [including radio and television waves (and) infrared radiation] differ from visible light only in wavelength: they vibrate at too high or too low a rate to stimulate the receptors in our eyes." Even though we can't see most energy, he points out that we can see or sense the *effects* of that energy. We hear music on the radio, we see pictures on a television, we can feel the heat of infrared radiation, and our skin burns because of ultraviolet energy.

Everything in existence is formed of energy and vibrates at a particular rate. The energy originating in the spiritual domain operates at a much higher frequency than the "normal" energy we experience on Earth and in space. We can't directly see the energy of our Soul or of God, but we can certainly see or sense their effects, for we can see the reality of life.

There Are Signs That The Spirit World Exists

Many of us have felt the presence of the dearly departed. And some people say they have "seen the light."

If there is a dimension beyond our physical reality, where some part of who we are resides after we die, then it makes sense God could be real too. While no one has brought back postcards from the "other side," there have been many people who have returned from "near death" experiences with similarly profound descriptions of what happened. Some people dismiss this as nothing more than a chemical reaction in the brain, but I believe those who have "seen the light" have experienced something real.

There are other phenomena pointing to the existence of a non-physical reality—namely, communication with "spirits" (and with God), psychic readings, and the recollection of details from "past lives." Even if we can disprove most claims of such paranormal abilities, there would remain numerous cases which are inexplicable, unless we accept an otherworldly perspective. Finally, many of us have experienced the spiritual realm in a more personal and subtle way. On quite a few occasions, I have sensed one of my departed loved ones near me. I didn't hear voices, but I *knew* they were there—just as I did when I felt the presence of my own Soul.

> Doubt is not the opposite of faith; it is one element of faith.
> Paul Tillich – American theologian; 1886–1965

The Holy Books Were Divinely Inspired

I may not believe or agree with everything in the Bible, but I do accept that it speaks to the reality of God.

The Bible is full of miraculous events, including of course, the resurrection of Jesus. I have my doubts as to whether *all* the stories are true, but we know that many aspects of the Bible are historically accurate. So, I am reluctant to dismiss every account of a divine action as mere fiction. Even if just a few of those miracles or the ones recorded since then are accurate, then either there is a God or we ourselves have powers we don't yet understand—or both. (I believe both are true.)

Was Jesus *the* Son of God, sent to save us? Frankly, I'm not sure. I think it is possible. At a minimum, Jesus is a very enlightened Soul whom God sent to show us how to love and be compassionate and to teach us that we are inherently good. God has sent other Souls, such as Buddha and Muhammad, for the same purpose. In any case, I believe we are all children of God, our behavior means more to God than what we believe, and Jesus would want us to be more concerned about his message than whether others see him as the Son of God.

It is more important that you act like Jesus or one of the other enlightened Souls, then it is for you to know or to accept what is Jesus' true identity.

If There Is a God, What Is He (or She) Like?

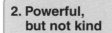

1. Both kind and powerful

2. Powerful, but not kind

God

3. Kind, but not powerful

4. Neither kind nor powerful

One of these four descriptions should apply. By a "kind" God I mean one who is **willing** to end suffering and eliminate evil; and a "powerful" God would be **able** to do it.

If God is like #1, why do we still have so much misfortune?

According to George Seldes, editor of *The Great Thoughts,* this question about the nature of God was first raised, at least formally, by the Greek philosopher Epicurus around 300 BCE. Seldes felt it was one of the greatest questions of all time, and he included many quotes from those who doubted God's benevolence (and existence), some of which I presented in the prior chapter.

However, I believe God is both kind and powerful and She would eliminate evil and misfortune if She thought it was in our best interest as spiritual beings. It is not God's Will that we suffer in life. In fact, I imagine God is really quite sad about the overall condition of humankind—like a mother (or father) who is disheartened because her child is hurting, especially if the child is doing it to him or herself by making bad choices in life.

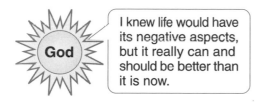

God

I knew life would have its negative aspects, but it really can and should be better than it is now.

Natural disasters and other calamities don't occur because God is punishing us. Some of the pain and suffering comes with the territory. It is the price of admission to our physical reality. But the amount of anguish we experience on Earth is not what God intended or hoped for, and it doesn't have to be as bad as it is.

The misfortunes of life are testing our faith in God, but they're also a challenge as to how we see ourselves. If we accept our interconnectedness and common spiritual heritage, and look within to see why misfortune exists, we will be able to create "Heaven on Earth." And that would show God *we* are both kind and powerful.

God Left It In Our Hands

I set everything in motion, but I want you to finish My work there on Earth—because you and I are "co-creators."

The Earth speaks ...

Think of me as a "work-in-progress." And God is looking to you to get rid of the needless pain.

That is not to say we are on our own. God did send Jesus and other very special Souls to show us how we can reduce the suffering. And we can ask for help from those in the spiritual domain, including God. Ultimately, the state of the world, is in our hands—or more accurately, in our *hearts and minds*.

The Lord God is subtle, but malicious He is not.

Albert Einstein; 1879–1955

... we ourselves have produced all the wickedness.

Tatian – Syrian-Christian heretic; 2nd century AD

I am convinced that the universe is under the control of a loving purpose. And that in the struggle for righteousness, man has cosmic companionship. Behind the harsh appearance of the world there is a benign power.

Dr. Martin Luther King, Jr. – civil rights leader; 1929–68

The world into which we are born is brutal and cruel, and at the same time, one of divine beauty.

Carl Jung – Swiss psychiatrist; 1875 –1961

I See God As the "Spiritual Sun"

... because, like our own sun, God is power and light, and we could not live without Her. She is a radiant being.

For thousands of years, mankind has tried to represent the likeness of God in some human or physical form. Of course, no one can know what God really looks like, and we are constrained in our efforts by the limits of pictures and sculptures. Still, we're inclined to come up with some visual symbol for the Being who gave us the gift of life. The metaphor I prefer is that of God as the "Spiritual Sun," which is why the "sun" appears on the cover.

I See God As Our Spiritual Mother

You can call Me "He" or "She." I am both masculine and feminine. Still, it's nice to be referred to as "She" for a change.

God is beyond gender as we know it.

God *the Father* has been the predominant depiction for a long time, at least among some religions. I don't mean to upset the apple cart or to be controversial by referring to God as our Spiritual Mother. I just like to think of God as a loving, compassionate, forgiving, nurturing and creative Being—especially in the sense of giving birth to the universe and our Souls.

As a man I would like to think I possess those qualities (except the "birthing" part), but I consider them to be more *feminine* in nature than masculine. Of course, neither "He" nor "She" can adequately describe God. We need a new pronoun that encompasses both genders and then some. Still, for me, thinking of God as my Spiritual Mom gave me a warm and comforting feeling. So, I will use "She." If you prefer another view of God, then please substitute "He" (or what ever word works for you) where it is appropriate.

> Reexamining one's conception of God is a noble tradition. Throughout history people have changed how they see and refer to their deities. Plus, various societies in the past have seen God in the female light, and many people still do.

Does It Matter What Name We Use?

Allah	The Father,	Yahweh
Brahma	Son and	Shakti
Yu Huang	Holy Spirit	Almighty

No one can know My real identity, so call Me whatever you like. But most of all be respectful and tolerant of each other's views.

All views of God are an interpretation of a force that is beyond the understanding of *any* human mind. Also, I would imagine that if there is a Being that created the universe, (He) She (or It) would not care what we called Her. Instead, She would want us to respect each other's right to believe in the "God" of his or her choice. She would be very disappointed with us if we judged or harmed others because they saw or experienced God in a different way.

We are like artists, each with our own depiction of the super-natural. In my creative expression, there is a supreme Being, or God, who made the universe and us—with each of us having a unique Soul. Still, there are many people who believe in a spiritual reality but who don't accept the existence of a Creator or of individual Souls. And lots of people believe there are multiple gods.

In my mind, any view that puts a person on the path of *love,* for themselves and for others, is fine. Maybe someday we'll hear directly from God in such a way that no one doubts Her existence or nature. Or, someone will prove scientifically what God is really like. Until then, and even afterwards, let's look to the quality of a person's *be-havior* and not just to his or her spiritual beliefs. Besides, even if God did appear before us and spoke, we probably wouldn't all have the same interpretation of what She said.

> A God we can comprehend is no God.
> Dio Chrysostom – Greek scholar (paraphrased); 40–120 AD

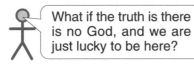

What if the truth is there is no God, and we are just lucky to be here?

Maybe we are deluding our-selves—believing in God and our eternal Souls to help us cope with the harsh realities of life. Could it be the universe created itself, we are not children of any God, this is our only shot at life, and once we're dead, we are gone for good? It's not a pretty picture, but it might be true. Even if it were, there are still other reasons for us to believe.

> I admit that the love of God ... would make it possible for human beings to be better than is possible in a Godless world.
> Bertrand Russell – British philosopher and non-believer; 1872–1970

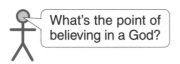

What's the point of believing in a God?

Even if life is full and satisfying, most of us want there to be more to our existence than just this physical reality. To believe in God, and in a spiritual domain, is to see our time on Earth in a broader context—as an *episode* in our Soul's journey. Of course, our faith in God also gives us hope that we will eventually transcend the absurd and tragic aspects of life.

Believing in God gives us a spiritual incentive for our personal growth because then we can act as if there is someone *very* important who cares about what we do and who has certain expectations of us. The prospect of receiving God's approval and reward (or possibly being punished if we act badly) empowers us to meet our challenges and to become better people. Believing in God also gives us the feeling of having a parent who provides support and guidance and uncon-ditional love. The alternative—of being a spiritual orphan—is not very appealing.

Besides, it is so much more interesting and expansive to think we, and all the cosmos, were intentionally created by a supernatural being. By opening our hearts and minds to the possibility of a God, we can discover our own divinity. We can come to realize and appre-ciate that each of us is capable of so much more than we previously thought imaginable.

I know it's hard to believe, but I really do exist. I made you, and I love you.

I do believe—because of what I see around me; what I see above me; what I can't see (but I know is real); what others have claimed to see; and what I hope to see some day (namely, my dearly departed loved ones, my own Soul, and of course You).

Part I – The Big Picture

To understand the mysteries of life and to appreciate the grandeur of our existence, we need to look way beyond our everyday reality. If we can be expansive and think about the creation of our Souls and the nature of the universe, and consider why God made us and how we can accomplish our "mission," then we can put this lifetime into a broader spiritual perspective. That is what we will do in this part of the book.

The story you are about to read will probably conflict with some of your current beliefs. But go ahead and have fun with it. You might just find that you like some of these concepts better than what you learned growing up. I know I do.

This is a photo from the Hubble Space Telescope of the "Pillars of Creation"—one of billions of places in the universe where new stars and planets are being born, and where our Souls might one day choose to live. (photo: J. Hester and P. Scowen AURA/STScI/NASA)

God

As you read these chapters, think of yourself as more than just human. Imagine you are a wondrous spiritual being.

P.S. This part of the book combines insights from my Soul with science and a dash of imagination. It is a spiritual tale based on the assumption the universe had a specific and intended beginning. While this is a common belief, it is not held by everyone. Still, let's proceed with my story.

In the Beginning ...

Before There Was Us or the Universe, There Was ... God

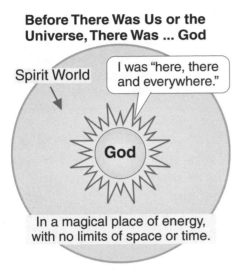

Spirit World

I was "here, there and everywhere."

God

In a magical place of energy, with no limits of space or time.

Everything in the universe, including you and me and the Earth and Sun, had a beginning. But God and the domain in which She lives did not. In fact, before the beginning of time and all we know, there was only God, in a place known as the *Spirit World*. God always was and always will be.

No one can accurately describe what a supernatural being or spiritual reality is like. Still, I like to visualize God as pure love and light. While I see God as the Spiritual Sun, I doubt She has any specific shape or form. She is probably limitless energy. The "place" that God lives in has no boundaries either. It is eternal and full of energy. The Spirit World is a place of inexpressible beauty.

I'm going to use a little astronomy and a few technical terms to tell this part of the story. But don't worry. There's not much of it, and there won't be a quiz at the end.

The "Cosmic Glossary" — Part I

Matter is the stuff that occupies space as a solid, liquid or gas, and it can be perceived by one or more of our senses.

Energy is not as easy to comprehend. It is defined as the capacity to do something, and it comes in different forms such as heat, electricity, magnetism, or chemical energy. There is energy of some kind contained within all matter. The energies I have just mentioned exist here in our physical universe.

In the Spirit World, where there is no matter, a special form of energy exists—it is the capacity to love and to make desires come into being. It is the reality of consciousness and thought.

How I "See" an Omnipresent God

To get a limited sense of what it might be like to see God's energy "here, there and everywhere" close your eyes tight, and cover them with both hands (after you've finished reading this, of course!). Wait a few seconds until you see nothing but blackness. Then, while looking in the direction of the sun or a very bright light, take your hands off your eyes, but leave your eyes **closed.** You will see a golden or white light in all directions. Again, keeping your eyes closed, move your head up and down, then left and right. You will "see" the light everywhere. There are no boundaries, just limitless energy.

I don't think the Spirit World is just light. I envision it sort of like the "holodeck" on the starship *Enterprise* (from *Star Trek – The Next Generation)* where one can create the image of an object or place by merely thinking of it. A simple thought of "Let there be ... " brings whatever one desires into existence, but it would be an *energetic* representation, not one made out of matter.

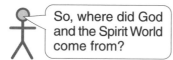

So, where did God and the Spirit World come from?

I was hoping you wouldn't ask that question, because I don't know. This is where faith really comes into play for me. Without having any proof or explanation (except that time does not exist in the Spirit World), I choose to believe God always was. What I find more curious, is what was God doing all by Herself in the Spirit World? Granted, it's an incredible place, but wouldn't She be lonely? Sometimes, I entertain the notion there was (and is) more than one God—maybe a nice family called the "Divines." Basically, I'm content to believe there is just one God and She found a *creative* solution to Her desire for companionship.

It is too quiet here in the Spirit World. I'd like to hear the sound of little Souls.

Acting from the same impulses we have when we want to have children and be a parent, God decided to make a new form of spiritual being—the *Soul.* God did this not just for the company, but because She wanted to share the glory and wonder of the Spirit World. She also had other creative ideas that would call for the existence of Souls. So, after careful consideration as to what these Souls should be like, God thought "Let there be ... *My children.*"

The Creation of Souls
An Event Known as the "Big Kaboom"

Spirit World

Let there be ... lots of little Me's.

you ○ **God** ○ me

You're each unique and very special.

God made "billions and billions" of Souls in a sudden burst of creativity.

You and I have Souls, and they came into being *before* the universe that we now live in as humans ever existed. Unlike the holodeck images I described previously, our Souls are "alive." As spiritual beings, they have "consciousness" or an awareness of their existence. Although they probably don't have a specific form, I envision our Souls as balls of energy, which emanated from God and which contain the very essence of God.

Our Souls were created from God's own divine energy, and so, as spiritual beings, you and I (and everyone else) are *immortal*. We can't say our Souls always were, but we can say that like God, they always will be. Also, the fact we all came from the same source—the same parent, if you will—means you and I (and everyone else) are *spiritual siblings*. We are all part of God's family of Souls and so, we are "simply divine."

As any act of procreation should be, the making of our Souls was an act of love. We weren't created just to be God's companions. We were made in such a way that we could grow and become powerful beings in our own right. Like a child, who comes from *and of* his human parents, each Soul begins its existence in an undeveloped state. Only by learning to make its own wise choices, can a Soul become a loving, joyful and creative "adult."

The need for our Souls to mature and to bring forth our divine essence is at the heart of our mission in life. After we were created, we discovered that even though the Spirit World is fantastic and hanging out with God is a real thrill, the spiritual realm wasn't the best "place" for us to become wise Souls. We needed to be exposed to a different and much more challenging environment in order to grow.

Once I had children, they needed a place where they could play and learn.

So, God decided to create a new reality—a new realm to complement the Spirit World and where our Souls could "get physical." It would contain exotic and beautiful places for us to explore, and it would have the ingredients necessary for "biological entities" (such as humans) to develop. This new place would give our Souls the means to experience *physical* life.

A long, long time ago ... there was an explosion. It was the beginning of the universe. It actually created "space" where none existed before. It also was the beginning of time itself.

God — I made the Big Bang happen. It was another "Let there be ..." thought of mine.

The
Big Bang!
12 to 18 billion years ago.

All of what makes up you and the entire universe was once packed together in a single point smaller than the period at the end of this sentence. The pressure and heat were great enough to cause an incredible cosmic explosion. It truly impressed your Souls.

To tell the story we need some more definitions.

The "Cosmic Glossary" — Part II

Stars are tightly compressed balls of gaseous matter (mostly hydrogen) that produce energy (heat and light) through the process of nuclear fusion. The star that we see during the day is the "Sun."

A **Galaxy** is a whole bunch of stars traveling through space together. Our Sun is in a galaxy called the "Milky Way." It contains more than 200 billion stars and stuff like comets and black holes.
By some estimates, there are at least 100 billion galaxies which together are home to the 10 billion trillion stars mentioned before.

Planets are bodies of matter (solid, liquid or gas) that revolve around stars. They don't generate their own light; they reflect the light coming from the star. There are nine planets, including the Earth, going around our Sun. There are trillions of planets in the universe.

The **universe** is the collection of everything listed above and then some. It contains all the matter that exists and all the energy that is not of a spiritual nature. (Let's call it "universal energy.")

> I will use the term "Physical World" to describe the universe (even though not everything in the universe is purely physical) as a way of contrasting it with the Spirit World (where nothing physical exists).

The beginning of the universe was an expression of God's active and creative imagination. She had a vision, and with just a simple "Let there be ..." She made it real. That miraculous act of creation together with the Big Kaboom (the making of our Souls) demonstrates why we call God *omnipotent*—for She is all powerful, without any limits or constraints on what She can do.

There are whole books on the Big Bang. So, I would like to make just a few points that are relevant to our story and help put the scope of God's creative act into perspective—

1. Matter, universal energy, time and space did not always exist. All of it apparently came out of nowhere.

2. My answer to the Big Mystery (of who or what made the universe) is that God was the *cause* behind this most incredible effect.

3. Before the Big Bang, God figured out what the parameters of the universe needed to be to allow stars etc. to form, and to support life—and then She made it so.

4. The diversity of people and things on the Earth, and throughout the universe, is wondrous, but we all came from the same single point (the one source). So, we and all that lives are spiritual *and* universal siblings.

5. One of the words that best describes the universe is *change*. From the first instant, everything has been in motion. The universe was infinitesimal at first, but it has become huge and is getting bigger every second.

> **Putting the size of the universe into perspective** — The closest star to us (after the Sun) is more than 24 trillion miles away. It would take the space shuttle over 150,000 years to reach it. The farthest stars are 5 to 6 billion times more distant than that!

> Put three grains of sand inside a vast cathedral, and the cathedral will be more closely packed with sand than space is with stars.
>
> Sir James Jeans – English astronomer; 1877–1946

6. The universe has been going through a remarkable transformation since "day one." All that we see around us today did not begin in its current form. It took billions of years of *evolution* on many fronts before the Sun and Earth could exist—and even longer before our Souls could incarnate as human beings.

After the Big Bang ...

there was a "primordial soup" of universal energy and the basic elements of matter ...

... then clouds of hydrogen gas developed and trillions of stars formed ... and then all the stars came together to make billions of galaxies ...

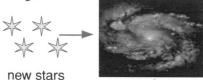

new stars   a galaxy

... later, in those galaxies, new stars formed with planets around them – so our Souls would have places to experience "life." New planets are still forming.

The Spirit World is the safe, peaceful, nurturing home our Souls share with God. Here in the Physical World, the planets are like *public schools*—where we go to learn the lessons that will help us become wise and mature Souls (or so God hopes). Planets are beautiful and exciting places for our Souls to live on, but they have quite a few negative aspects as well. It is on planets where we must cope with pain and the decline of our physical bodies.

We are all familiar with our planet, the Earth. But in this wondrous universe there are trillions of planets—billions of which might be hospitable to life. The conditions of the Earth and our Sun seem miraculous, but the odds favor the scenario that God performed the miracle more than once.

> If it is just us, it seems like an awful waste of space.
> From *Contact,* by Carl Sagan – astronomer; 1934–96

For two thousand years or more human beings thought that the Earth was at the center of the universe. But the Earth wasn't even formed until about 10 billion years *after* the Big Bang. So, our small planet is a relatively new kid on the universal block.

Putting It All Together on The "Cosmic Timeline"

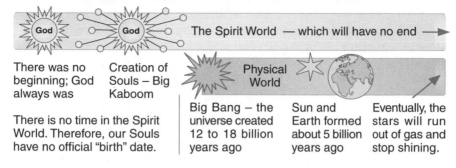

There was no beginning; God always was	Creation of Souls – Big Kaboom		Physical World	

There is no time in the Spirit World. Therefore, our Souls have no official "birth" date.	Big Bang – the universe created 12 to 18 billion years ago	Sun and Earth formed about 5 billion years ago	Eventually, the stars will run out of gas and stop shining.

The Universe Is Huge, But The Spirit World Is Way Bigger

There is spiritual energy around us all the time because the universe is contained within the Spirit World.

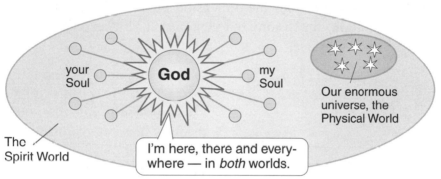

Our Souls can explore the universe and experience life on the planets, but their primary residence is in the Spirit World.

The two worlds are distinct but interwoven. By this I mean the Spirit World permeates the universe, but it also extends *far* beyond the "boundaries" of the universe. Imagine a room with four glass walls and a source of light somewhere outside of that room. Everything outside the room is touched by the light plus the luminescence extends through the glass and into the room. But here's the catch— it is an invisible light, at least to us inside the room. (We humans have the innate ability to see the light and other manifestations from the Spirit World, but only a few people have developed that gift.) With respect to God, She is *beyond* the universe (She had to be otherwise She could not have created it in the first place), and God is also *within* the universe—just like the light I described. God is all around us.

> To make sense of this view (that the universe was designed), one must accept the idea of **transcendence**: that the Designer (God) exists in a totally different order of reality or being, not restrained within the bounds of the Universe itself.
>
> George Ellis, cosmologist

The two worlds are on different "planes" of existence with very different natures. The Physical World, with its matter and universal energy, is denser—with rates of vibration (remember, everything is vibrating) much slower than that of our Souls or of God. Here on Earth, we experience the passage of time and the decline of our physical bodies. In the Spirit World there is no need for clocks, and our Souls never wear out.

In the Physical World we have at least four dimensions—the three dimensions of *space* plus the dimension of *time*. The Spirit World also has multiple dimensions, but they exist at a higher level than the reality of this universe.

It's a nice place to visit, but I don't need to live there forever.

A Soul coming home after "life" on a planet   The universe

The human body and mind exist within the confines of the Physical World, but the Soul's primary home is, of course, the Spirit World. When we die, our Soul doesn't go "up into the sky." It just returns to whence it came to continue its spiritual existence. Our Soul was alive before we incarnated, and it lives on afterwards. (When we're experiencing physical life our Soul doesn't leave the Spirit World completely. I will return to that point in the first two chapters of Part II of the book.)

> Life without a body is the Soul's normal state.
> Aristotle – Greek philosopher; 384–322 BCE

When our Soul does "come home," it brings with it new and improved manifesting skills together with memories of its earthly adventure. In the Physical World we spend a lifetime learning how to turn our thoughts and dreams into reality. It is this lifelong effort that hones our Soul's creative abilities. When we're back in the Spirit World we can recall the *essence* of the earthly realities we enjoyed most (the essence of a reality is stored in our Soul's memory), and we can create *energetic* versions of those realities. It's not the same as the physical experience, but it is very pleasurable.

As spiritual beings, our Souls also have the ability to explore the universe and to observe without being seen what is happening on any given planet. When we are involved in an episode of life (such as we are now), our Soul is always observing our behavior from its higher perspective. Other Souls are not watching us like our Soul does, and especially not when we are involved in intimate activities. They're not voyeurs. Generally, if a Soul wants to see something in the Physical World, it just thinks of a specific place of interest (such as on Earth), and a "window" opens into that part of the universe. It's like tuning into a channel on a *really* big television screen.

Are There Multiple Universes?

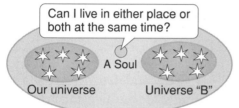

Maybe the Big Bang wasn't a unique event.

Some people say we are leading "parallel lives" in multiple universes. Others claim that everything we see and experience in the Physical World is really just an illusion. Well, it all seems real enough to me, and I am quite content to focus on this one universe and this one life for now. I have got my hands full already.

Now, before we conclude this chapter, let's take a quick look at our very special star, the Sun, and at one last astronomical concept.

The Sun Is the "Sustainer of Life"

God gave us the gift of life, but we can't live without the Sun. It keeps us warm, causes rain to fall and makes plants grow. And it's powerful too – creating enough energy in 1 second to meet the needs of the United States for 7 million years.

It is not surprising that past civilizations worshiped the Sun as a God. It plays a vital role in our lives, even though it is just an average star as stars go. The solar energy from the Sun and the divine energy from within our Souls are keeping us physically alive. As I wrote in the previous chapter, I see God as the "Spiritual Sun" (I *don't* see the Sun as a god). God has more brilliance and power than all the 10 billion trillion stars put together. Instead of radiating visible light like most stars do, God is projecting love and spiritual energy. And unlike stars in the universe, which only have so much gas to burn, God's supply of energy is infinite and eternal. She will never die or fade away. God will shine forever.

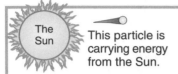

The Sun

This particle is carrying energy from the Sun.

Like all stars, our Sun sends out its radiant energy in the form of **photons**. These fantastic particles have no mass, can exist forever, and travel really fast (at the speed of light, which is 186,000 miles *per second)*. At that speed, we could make the round trip between New York and San Francisco thirty times in just one second! And we would have no sense of the passage of time. It would seem like we were here, there and everywhere all at once. We could be in Tokyo at say 1:03 p.m. and then be in Paris at exactly 1:03 p.m. (just by thinking of the Eiffel Tower.) We would never be late or early. We would always be "on time" because it would *always* be "right now."

God Is The Spiritual Sun ... and We're Like Her "Photons"

God

you

me

As energy, our Souls can be anywhere in an instant. We can illuminate wherever we are with the love inside each of us.

You and I came from the same divine source and are "emissaries" sent forth by God to bring the light and power of love to all corners of the universe. At the moment, the planet Earth is the center of our attention, but as we shall soon see, this is not the only place we can or will live. When we are not in physical form, our Souls are out and about exploring. Like photons of sunlight, we can be anywhere in the Spirit World, or the universe, instantaneously just by wanting to be there. You might say we can travel at the "speed of God." And yet, God can keep track of where all Her children are and continue to provide each of us with the love and energy we need.

Give me the splendid silent sun with all (Her) beams full-dazzling!
Walt Whitman
American poet; 1819–92

We Are All Children of God

The decisive question for man is: Is he related to something infinite (and divine), or not?

Carl Jung
Swiss psychiatrist; 1875–1961

When we look in the mirror we don't see ourself as a photon or as a "ball of energy." We see only our physical form—a human body that is mortal. But we are so much more than that. Our true identity is that of a spiritual being created by God. Within each and everyone of us is some of Her divine energy. It is an essential part of our Soul.

When we see ourself as a child of God, we take the first step on a path of personal transformation and empowerment. We begin to change how we look at our whole life when we really believe we are not "only human." Acknowledging our Soul's existence is not enough, however. We also need to understand its true nature, so we can appreciate the full extent of our potential.

Our Wondrous Souls Are More Than "Balls of Energy"

Every Soul has three incredible elements.

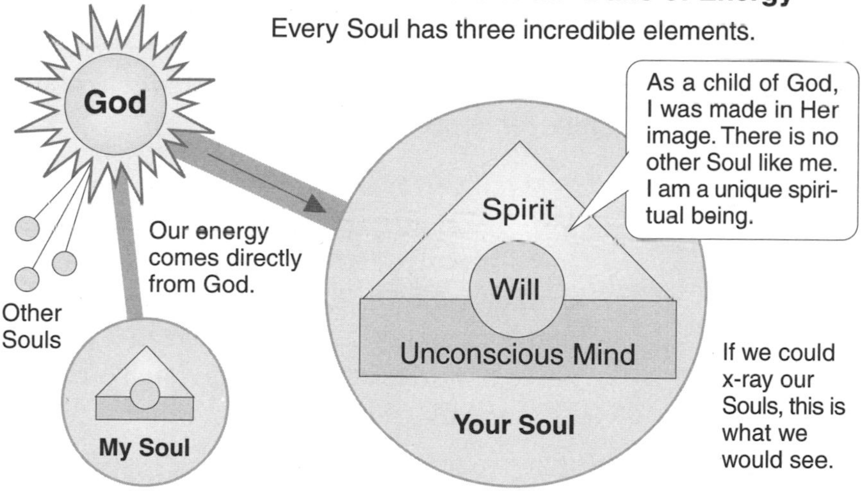

God

As a child of God, I was made in Her image. There is no other Soul like me. I am a unique spiritual being.

Spirit

Other Souls

Our energy comes directly from God.

Will

Unconscious Mind

Your Soul

My Soul

If we could x-ray our Souls, this is what we would see.

Because we possess some of God's energy, even the most infinitesimal amount, we are *like* God. We are like God not in the sense we can do what She can (or anywhere even close to it) but because we have the capacity to be *loving, joyful* and *creative*—which is the very essence of God.

> I'm not saying I am God. But I am saying, like most Eastern thought believes, we are one with God and God is in all of us.
>
> Carl Jung – Swiss psychiatrist (paraphrased); 1875–1961

I will return to the subject of our divine abilities in a minute, but now let's take a look at the three elements of every Soul.

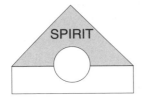

First, there is the **Spirit**. The Spirit is God's actual energy and our Soul's vital force. It sustains our spiritual and physical existence. The Spirit brings the "spark of life" to our human mind and body. It is also the source of our Soul's consciousness or self-awareness. Many people use the word "Spirit" to describe their complete Soul, but it is just one part of the picture.

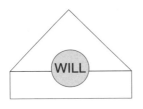

Every Soul is also equipped with its own **Will**. The Will is the faculty by which we *choose* the course of our existence. It is referred to as our "free" Will because God put no constraints on the choices we could make. That does not mean, however, we should make any choice that pleases us. In fact, God did define what good choosing is, as we shall see in the next chapter. With a Will, we have the ability to create our own reality, for better or worse.

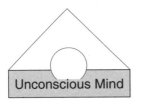

God also gave each Soul an **Unconscious Mind**. Among its many powers are the ability to "talk" with other Souls and to retain all the memories of our existence. It helps us solve problems and to develop new, creative ideas. It also communicates with us through our *intuition*. Its abilities go far beyond those of any human mind.

These three incredible elements form the *trinity* of the Soul. Together, they make you and me viable spiritual beings with amazing powers. And while you and I have the same three parts, we are unique and special to God. Also, every Soul is on its own path of growth and maturation. We're all learning how to use our innate abilities (especially our *free Will*) so we can bring the light of God's energy to the Physical World.

(I will go into more detail on the three elements in the chapter *Who We Are On Earth*, because it is here in the Physical World where our Soul is currently expressing its powers.)

Godliness Is In Our Genes
Because Her energy is part of us

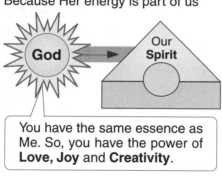

You have the same essence as Me. So, you have the power of **Love, Joy** and **Creativity**.

If we could use only three words to describe God's nature they would be *love, joy* and *creativity.* We can also characterize our Soul using the same three words because we were made by *and of* God. Every Soul has the ability to give and receive love, to enjoy life and be happy, and to make dreams come true.

Love is the deep feeling of affection our Souls feel for each other and much more. It is the fundamental force of the universe which brings meaning and passion to our spiritual and physical lives. Love also has the power to cure all that ails this world. When we love ourself and other people, and all of God's creations, we have found the best way to proclaim our divinity.

Joy is the feeling of pleasure and satisfaction that is inspired by something wonderful, whether it be the laughter of a child or the gift of life. Joy is the state of supreme well-being and good spirits that comes naturally to our Soul but which many of us need to rediscover here on Earth. Souls are optimistic by nature; they tend to be exuberant and expansive in their outlook.

Creativity is the Soul's ability to transform thoughts and desires into realities we can experience. But it is not just about the creation of material things. We also use our creative energy when we raise children, when we bring harmony to a stressful situation, or when we change the world with a new idea. When we contribute something *positive* to the world—which helps people to be more loving and joyful, or to feel less pain—we're being creative in the *divine* sense of the word. We are acting like a child of God.

This is the essence of our Soul

Please say it with Me: *"Let there be ..."*

The power of our creative energy is brought forth with the most divine of utterances, which is "Let there be...". Those are the sacred words God said, or thought, when She made us and the universe. As children of God, we also possess the ability to take a "Let there be ..." vision and to make it so—that is, to bring it into our reality. Of course, there are limits on what we can do. We are not *so* like God that we can create other Souls or a new life (on our own), or make physical matter materialize out of nothing. Still, our creative powers are far more extensive than we currently realize.

> The will is free.
> Strong is the Soul, and wise, and beautiful.
> The seeds of godlike power are in us still.
> **Gods are we ...**
>
> Matthew Arnold
> English poet, critic; 1822–88

Joy is not the only feeling I experience.

Our Soul's natural state is to be joyful, but it can feel other emotions too. For example, our Soul can be sad and disappointed if we're deliberately harming others or not doing our best to make the most of our ever so brief physical life. Our Soul feels the greatest joy when we're doing what we love and using our talents to help others.

God Gave Us Unique "Gifts"

I made each of you with special talents. No one can do exactly what you can.

I'm at my creative best when I can discover and use my gifts on Earth.

The essence of our God-given talents is "encoded" in our Soul.

It was God's desire that each and every Soul would have the opportunity to excel in one or more creative activities and to feel the passion and satisfaction that comes from doing so. To achieve this, She configured each Soul differently and in such a manner that we would be attracted to certain avocations. We would also have what it takes to succeed at them. It was Her hope that we would discover our talents and apply them in a way that would not only help us evolve but be of value to other Souls too.

The activity that uses our special talents is called our "calling." That particular pursuit might not be the same as our paying job. It could be expressed through one of our hobbies, or being a great parent could be our calling. Once we discover our gifts, we develop them by taking on creative challenges. Also, our Soul can acquire new talents if we're inquisitive and willing to expand our interests. Finally, we develop these gifts across lifetimes—bringing into each new life the cumulative effect of all our prior experiences.

Our Souls Are Connected To God and Each Other
We share love with our Spirits; we talk with our Unconscious Minds

And there is "universal wisdom" all around us that we can access.

God

Our spiritual network makes the "internet" look very archaic.

our love connection
our telepathic link

Your Soul

My Soul

On Earth we tend to live with a sense of separateness from one another, but from a spiritual perspective we are all connected. Not only do we come from the same source and thus share a love for each other and for God, but we're also linked by the power of the Unconscious Mind. With our telepathic capability, our Souls can communicate easily with each other. On Earth we use this same faculty whenever we pray to God or send our love to others. Just by thinking of another person, whether they be alive or one of the dearly departed, we can transmit our thoughts and feelings directly to his or her Soul. So we are never truly alone in the universe.

Our connection with God is very special. Even though we are unique and distinct spiritual beings, we stay linked to Her with a sort of "spiritual umbilical cord." No matter where we are, we continue to receive God's love. It flows to us unconditionally, but we need to be open to receive it. When we believe God cares for us, and we send Her our love in return, we realize a stronger connection with all other Souls—and we greatly enhance our self-love too.

Each of you can have a personal relationship with Me. Even if we have not talked in a long time I'm always ready to hear from you.

We are connected with God in the Spirit World, and while we are on Earth too. We can talk with Her, or "phone home," anytime we like by having Her in our thoughts and by praying. But that is not the only way we can connect with our Spiritual Mom. We can sense or *"feel"* the presence of God in everyone and everything around us. What is most important is that we see God as a loving, supportive and nurturing parent, who is also very forgiving.

As spiritual beings, we're also connected to an energy field called the *Universal Knowledge.* Think of it as God's cosmic library, which contains all of the spiritual and physical laws of the universe. It is also a storehouse of creative ideas that can have immense value to us in the Physical World. All of this wisdom is "out there"—floating through the Spirit World, like radio and television waves permeating our earthly atmosphere. A Soul receives the knowledge through the power of its Unconscious Mind.

Our Souls have easy access to this information. But when we're on Earth in human form and subject to the lower vibrations of this world, we have a hard time tapping into the Universal Knowledge. It is not impossible though. Indeed, throughout the ages, quite a few people—such as Newton, Edison and Einstein—have been able to check out some very important books from the cosmic library, and we have all benefited from their insights and inventions.

Still, one doesn't have to be a genius to make a connection with the Universal Knowledge. Any of us, if we're pursuing our Soul's calling, or when we're in a focused or meditative state, can open a channel to the Spirit World. We might get an answer to a question we've been thinking about, or we could receive an unsolicited inspiration. This happens a lot. For example, composers at times just "hear" a song (even while they're sleeping), and many writers have been moved to write a particular book. Anyone can be more creative and make wiser choices if they listen for their "inner voice."

We contain within us all universal truths, all universal knowledge. Everything that is, is known to us. Our Soul ... has limitless capacity.

Machaelle Small Wright
author of *Behaving As If The God In All Life Mattered*

God Created a Nice Variety of Spiritual Beings

All Souls are made of the same divine energy, but we've been given different abilities. We have unique roles to play and we're on different evolutionary paths. None is "better" than another.

Up until now, the story has focused on the creation and nature of Souls like ours. You and I are children of God, and so we are very special indeed. Some humility is in order, however. We are not the sole, or even the prime, recipients of God's energy or love. As children of God, we have many "spiritual cousins."

There is some of God's energy in everyone and *everything*—not just in beings like us. She created more than one type of Soul, because She knew a universe as incredible as ours would most certainly bring forth many different forms of life.

Many of us believe we have Souls and that Angels exist, but we are probably less willing to accept that animals have Souls. We are even more reluctant to believe that trees or plants do, not to mention the Earth, which many people view as an inanimate object. But all creatures and things do have a spiritual essence. There is more "consciousness" around us than we, in these self-oriented and consumptive times, realize or appreciate. It is our lack of reverence for *all* life that is causing us to be very harmful.

If The Earth Could Speak

I possess God's energy too; and I'm aware of how you're treating me.

We must realize that we do not live in a world of dead matter, but in a Universe of living Spirit. Let us open our eyes to the sacredness of Mother Earth, or our eyes will be opened for us.

David Monongye – Native American elder; 1902–82

Obviously, not all Soul types are the same. Souls like ours have very different abilities than the Souls who inhabit the physical form of an animal or a tree. Your Soul and mine have capabilities well-suited for the human body and mind. For example, the nature of the human brain supports our ability to make moral judgments and to create intricate realities. But that doesn't necessarily make us better than other Soul types. The other kinds of life in our Physical World possess abilities that we don't have and which are amazing in their own right.

Some people believe (in part because of statements in the Bible) that our Soul type is in charge of all other forms of life—that we were given dominion over the world. I prefer to think we are all part of a "web of life" and are interdependent and connected to each other. Humans have evolved over time to a position where we have the power to control the earthly fate of the other Soul types and to seriously affect the state of the Earth itself. This doesn't mean we exist at a higher level than the other Souls, but it does mean we have a greater *responsibility* than they do.

> I want to realize brotherhood or identity not merely with beings called human, but ... with all life, ... because we claim descent from the same God, and that being so, all life (in whatever form it appears) must be essentially one.
>
> Mohandes Gandhi – Indian leader; 1869–1948

> If God could make angels, why did (She) bother with (us)?
>
> Dagobert D. Runes – American writer; 1902–82

> Souls like ours bring life to human beings (and to similar species on other planets). Angels were made to help God and to aid us, which they can do best by being free of the need to experience physical life. We are not inferior to the Angels; we're just different and with our own purpose. Who knows, maybe Angels wish they could be like us so they could see the Physical World the way we can.

The key point is God made us in Her own image and we are each a unique spiritual being. We are *all* children of God.

Your Soul

By the way, this is not how I really look in the Spirit World. I inherited God's good looks, if you can imagine that.

God's Values and Beliefs

Will: I'm the part of you that makes **choices**. So, the quality of your Soul's journey is in my hands.

(Note: at times, I will show just one of the elements of the Soul instead of all three.)

God created a vast number of Souls to live with Her in the Spirit World and to periodically experience life on planets throughout the universe. And each one of those Souls is free to choose as it pleases. This freedom is a wonderful gift, giving us the power to create our own reality. But that reality can include pain and misfortune for us and others if we don't make wise choices.

God: All newborns need direction so they can know right from wrong and make the most of their lives. That is why I gave your Souls the same guidelines that I follow.

It is God's wish that we live together in harmony and that we be happy Souls. To help us achieve that state, She felt it would be best if we were guided by the same moral principles She lives by. She also wanted us to be aware of certain spiritual truths that would put our life and role in the universe into the proper perspective. These principles and truths are known as *God's Values and Beliefs*, and are presented on the next two pages.

These Values and Beliefs can also be viewed as "universal laws"—in the sense that they prescribe a way for us to behave that will help our Souls grow as spiritual beings and that will improve the quality of our lives here on Earth. Our Souls were given these Values and Beliefs before humans received the *Ten Commandments*, which of course are very important too. Indeed, I will close the chapter with a few words about them.

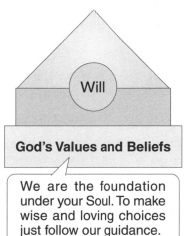

We are the foundation under your Soul. To make wise and loving choices just follow our guidance.

Some of God's Favorite VALUES	 God	Live by these ideals and principles and your life and the world will be far better.

(These are written as if God were speaking to us.)

Love – accept yourself as you are; cause no harm to others; cherish your family and friends; be accepting and supportive

Joy – find pleasure by living in the moment; have fun in life

Creativity – use your gifts and "Let there be ..." power to add something positive to the world; follow your bliss

Freedom – for you and others to make your own choices and to pursue your dreams; aim to be free of needless fear and worry

Responsibility – for what you choose and what you create

Kindness – treat others as you would want to be treated; be nice

Empathy – try to understand the other person's situation and feelings

Compassion – reduce or eliminate the needless suffering of others

Tolerance – allow others to have their own opinions and practices

Forgiveness – recognize the weaknesses inherent in being human and live without persistent anger or resentment

Harmony – live "in balance" with yourself and with nature; find paths to mutual understanding among you and your neighbors

Service – use some of your time, energy and resources to help others in need, without expecting anything in return

Stewardship – take good care of all I have created, and leave the world better off for future generations

Faith – believe in yourself, in the goodness of others and in Me too

Courage – to choose and act wisely in the face of fear and temptation; to overcome the personal shortcomings you can change

Growth – do your best to improve yourself ... body, mind and Soul

Gratitude – appreciate your life, the beauty of the world, your loved ones, and your ability to choose a new reality

Honesty – be truthful, sincere and honorable in all you say and do

Humility – keep yourself in perspective, individually and as a species; (you're *very* special, but you are not at the center of the universe)

Some of God's Favorite BELIEFS

God

I find these spiritual truths to be self-evident, and it would be good if you did too.

(Again, these are written as if God were speaking to us.)

Each of you is an eternal spiritual being. You were created by Me and with My energy. Therefore, you are divine—and you can be loving, joyful and creative.

Animals, plants and trees, and the Earth came from Me too. All Soul types are to be treated with basic love and respect.

Life is a gift. It is a chance to enjoy the sensations of being physical and to become a better chooser and creator. So, life should be savored and appreciated every day. (I want you to help those who are suffering and not enjoying life.)

You have the power to create you own realities. Bad things will happen, but you can choose how you respond to them.

People should not be judged for how they see Me or for how they look or act (as long as they are not causing harm.)

All Souls have the universal right to make their own choices, but they must live with the consequences. (No offense, but "human Souls" could make better use of their free Will.)

Every Soul, regardless of prior choices, can change. You can become a more evolved person. (That is what I expect from each of you.) A "lost" or "bad" Soul can return to the light.

The real joy in life comes from learning to live simply, by living "in the moment," and by sharing love with family and friends. It does not come just from having material things.

Doing what you love, and loving the people you are with, are the best ways to make yourself, your Soul and Me happy.

Life is best experienced with a sense of awe, wonder and discovery. Go about life with a child's curiosity. (The universe is more spectacular than you can imagine. Trust Me, I know.)

Each Of Us Had to Decide What Kind of Soul We Would Be

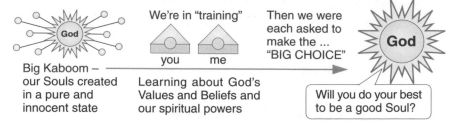

Big Kaboom – our Souls created in a pure and innocent state

We're in "training"

you   me

Learning about God's Values and Beliefs and our spiritual powers

Then we were each asked to make the ... "BIG CHOICE"

Will you do your best to be a good Soul?

God asked each of us if we were going to be "with" or "against" Her. That is, would we live in accordance with Her Values and Beliefs, or would we become a wayward Soul, or even a spiritual delinquent?

When we were first created, we had to get our bearings and get up to speed on what was involved in being a Soul. We were spiritual neophytes. Like a human baby, who must learn the basics (walking, talking etc.) and the ways of the world, we also needed instruction. So, we were tutored by the Angels in sessions similar to Sunday school classes. We learned the spiritual "facts of life"—including how our Souls worked and how to make choices and create realities with our "Let there be ..." power. We also got a preview of what life would be like in the Physical World.

When all this training was done and we had a sense of our abilities, and of the challenges and opportunities we would encounter out in the universe, we were asked to make our first *Big Choice.* God wanted to know if we would stay in the company of the "good Souls," or choose to join the "Organization of Souls Headed for Trouble?"

Not All Souls Are "Good"

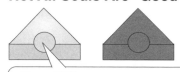

Free Will means we can make bad choices. Look at him—he said "no" to God and the "light" left his Soul.

It doesn't mean I have stopped loving him. But, I'm sad and disappointed.

Why would any Soul, at this early stage, choose not to be with God? Well, there were relatively few that did forsake Her. These wayward Souls were overly impressed with themselves and were seduced by the prospect of having lots of power in the Physical World. It is hard to believe a "child of God" could become a harmful Soul, but God knew that was a possibility when She gave us a free Will and said— "You decide how you will exist."

We learned during our "orientation period" that as eternal Souls we would be making an infinite series of choices, the hardest of which will occur while we are in the Physical World. We also learned that the Big Choice (are we with or against God) can be revisited at any time during our existence. Good Souls might give into the temptations of the Physical World and have a *change of Will*. And bad Souls can change too. They can become good again. We're lucky that God believes in second chances, and third chances, and so on.

> If you prefer not to use the terms "good" and "bad," you could use "in the light" and "in the darkness." Personally, I think if a Soul is deliberately hurtful it is okay to say they are "bad" or, at least, "acting badly."

"Conscience" Is The Voice of the Spirit

The Will is the part of us that makes choices. When we're on a planet like the Earth, trying to cope each day with a myriad of challenges, the Will can lose its way. So, it falls to our *Spirit* to keep us on the moral path. When we hear a "little voice" telling us that what we're about to do or say is not a good idea, it is our Spirit speaking. If we go ahead and do the wrong thing, it is our Will that will feel the pangs of guilt.

> Never do anything against (your) conscience ...
> Albert Einstein; 1879–1955

God is *not* a strict disciplinarian, who is sitting in judgment or waiting to punish us. But that doesn't mean we can be bad and get away with it—at least not in the Spirit World. When we act in harmful ways our Soul's energy is diminished and we move further away from God. She still loves us, but there is a loss of trust and intimacy—which we can regain *if we change*.

How can I be "free" if I pay a price for my poor choices?

The "freedom of speech" has certain limitations. For example, we can't yell "fire" in a crowded theater. The same logic applies to our Souls. It is not appropriate for one Soul to behave in ways that will adversely affect the ability of other Souls to make good choices or to enjoy their lives. So, to say our Wills should follow God's Values and Beliefs is not to make them less "free." It is making it possible for all Souls to live with *more* freedom. When everyone is living in accordance with God's Values and Beliefs, we won't have to worry about someone deliberately hurting us. Without that particular fear, we can lead more fulfilling lives.

> A free Will and a Will subject to moral laws are one and the same.
>
> Immanuel Kant – German philosopher; 1724–1804

God Is Almost, But Not Quite Omniscient (a "Know It All")

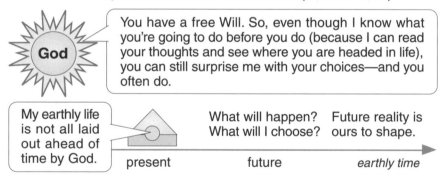

You have a free Will. So, even though I know what you're going to do before you do (because I can read your thoughts and see where you are headed in life), you can still surprise me with your choices—and you often do.

My earthly life is not all laid out ahead of time by God.

What will happen? What will I choose?

Future reality is ours to shape.

present   future   *earthly time*

God knows far more than we could ever imagine, but She is not *omniscient*—at least not in the sense She knows everything we are going to say or do. She knows us better than we know ourselves, but we can still surprise Her. If God already knows what choices we are going to make, then what is the point of Her trying to influence our behavior by giving us Values and Beliefs or The Ten Commandments? We were given those guidelines because the future is uncertain and we can become better choosers. Finally, our lives are not totally planned. God may have made arrangements for certain events to occur during our lifetime, but She did not write an entire script for us. We are not just a character playing out a role with no ability to improvise.

God has been trying to influence our choices for a very long time. She has sent advanced Souls to live as role models, and She gave us laws that supposedly were "cast in stone." But if you read all of the "commandments" given to Moses—and also read the Bible's description of God and why we're supposed to follow those laws — it makes you wonder if something was lost in the translation.

The Eleven Commandments – from Deuteronomy 5:6-21

1. Thou shall have no other gods before me
2. Thou shalt not make thee any (sculpted) image, or any likeness of any thing that is in heaven above, or that is in the earth beneath, or that is in the waters beneath the earth
3. Thou shall not bow down thyself unto them, nor serve them: for I the Lord thy God am a jealous God; visiting the inequity of the fathers upon the children unto the third and fourth generation of them that hate me
4. Thou shalt not take the name of the Lord they God in vain: for the Lord will not hold him guiltless that taketh his name in vain
5. Keep the sabbath day ... and thou shall not work on that day
6. Honor thy father and thy mother
7. Thou shalt not kill
8. Neither shall thou commit adultery
9. Neither shalt thou steal
10. Neither shalt thou bear false witness against thy neighbor
11. Neither shalt thou covet thy neighbor's wife, house, servant, etc.

Note: the first and second commandments were later combined so there would be a total of 10.

Why we should obey the commandments, according to the Bible —

(For the Lord thy God is a **jealous** God) ... lest the **anger** of the Lord thy God be kindled against thee, and **destroy** thee from off the face of the earth. And the Lord commanded us ... to **fear** the Lord our God, ... that he might preserve us alive ...

(From Deuteronomy 6: 15 and 24)

I'm sorry; I just can't believe a God of love would be jealous, or get angry enough to destroy us, or would want us to be fearful. I think some of the strict paternalism of the times was interjected into the Bible by the authors.

It is not presumptuous to question the tenets contained in a holy book, even if doing so will offend some people. Having faith in God doesn't mean we must have "blind faith" in the *human* interpretations of God. People are fallible, so it is alright to question what we are told. We can ask if it sounds like what a loving and compassionate God would say. In any case, I present the following for your consideration. These are the guidelines I prefer (and try) to follow.

The "Ten Rules of the Road"

1. Be tolerant of any view of the supernatural that places people on the path of love for themselves and others.

2. Look for the good in other people, and treat them as you would want to be treated. Honor the divine essence that is in all of us and in all things on Earth.

3. Accept responsibility for your choices. Don't blame or swear at God for the bad realities you or we created.

4. Be grateful (more than once a week) for the three big gifts given to us by God—our Souls, the universe, and physical life. Give thanks for all the good people and things in your life.

5. Show respect for your parents, and expect it from them. Care for your family members. Love and support each other.

6. Don't murder anyone or needlessly harm other forms of life.

7. Don't have sex if it will cause you or your partner, or anyone else, emotional or physical harm or if it might result in the birth of a child when you're not ready to be a good parent.

8. Don't take things that don't belong to you. (Help those who feel that stealing is their only way to survive.)

9. Tell the truth, and don't make up false stories about others.

10. Don't be so envious of others that you hate them or yourself or ruin your life trying to keep up. Focus on what is right and meaningful for you, and make your own dreams come true.

My Soul

If I live by God's Values and Beliefs—and follow the "rules of the road"—I will be on a path of spiritual growth.

And that brings us to the next chapter, which looks at what every Soul is trying to do here in the Spirit World and especially there in the Physical World.

Every Soul Has a Mission

God made our Souls so we could share the wonders of the Spirit World and universe with Her. We were created in Her image, so our innate abilities are truly amazing. But like all children, we began our journey in an undeveloped state and in need of a goal. So, God sat us down and told us what She expected of us.

The "Mission Statement" – What God Expects Of Each Soul

God

Go forth and **expand your spiritual energy** – because that will bring out the godliness in you, and it will bring you and Me closer together.

And this is how you accomplish the mission –

(a) Use your Will to make wise choices (which means they are in accordance with My Values and Beliefs);

(b) Express the essence of your Soul – which is love, joy and creativity – in all you say, think and do;

(c) Develop your special gifts, and use your "Let there be ..." power to create positive realities for yourself and others;

(d) Learn and grow from day to day; become better than you are now, at least from a spiritual perspective;

(e) Face your fears, and do your best to respond in a positive way to the challenges of the Physical World.

Each Of Us Can Become a More Radiant Spiritual Being
— As we make wise choices, our energy expands and our Soul shines brighter.

At the Big Kaboom   This occurs during and across lifetimes

The more energy we have, the more loving, joyful and creative we can be – and the easier it gets!

As the "godlike" Soul we can all be. (We'll use a small "g.")

> It is man's goal to grow into the exact likeness of God.
> Plato – Athenian philosopher; 428–348 BCE

Sorry Plato, you can't be exactly like Me. But all of you can get a lot closer than you are now.

Given how difficult life is for most of us, it is hard to imagine we could ever become "godlike." Just getting through life without being hurt too badly or causing harm to others is challenging enough. While we might wish otherwise, we should not expect to reach our full potential in just one lifetime, especially when the conditions on Earth are so difficult. For example, our Souls must cope with the limits of the human mind and body. As a species, humans haven't been in existence very long, and we have got some inherent weaknesses. Of course, as Souls, we have been around for eons; but even so, we still have a long way to go in our spiritual development. Indeed, we have only begun to use our divine powers. So, all in all, we are just getting started on our mission.

Still, unless our current life situation is so bad that mere survival is the best we can do, God expects us to make meaningful progress toward our goal. Each new moment in our life, especially if it involves other people, is an opportunity for us to act in a way that would reflect well on our divine heritage and which would expand our energy.

I don't expect perfection. But I want you to do your very best to learn and grow.

> I do the very best I know how—the very best I can—and I mean to keep doing it so until the end.
> Abraham Lincoln – American President; 1809–65

One can only imagine what it will be like when we fulfill our mission. Our capacity for love will be unlimited, and we'll be joyous most of the time. Our creative abilities will be miraculous. I see this level of godliness that our Souls aspire to as the spiritual equivalent of the *Gold Medal*. But unlike the Olympics, where only one person or team can stand on the top platform, we can all "win the gold." *Every* Soul has the capacity to become "godlike." It is just that some of us need more time than others to do it.

This is not a competition. Don't compare yourself to others. Focus on your own spiritual growth. And don't sell yourself short. You can be magnificent!

We are not in a race to see who can accumulate the most energy the fastest. Each of us is at a unique point in our spiritual development, and we will accomplish the "mission" in our own time and in our own way. Finally, regardless of what has happened in our life so far, we still have the capacity to grow. Our past has placed us where we are now, but it doesn't limit what our Soul can become. What matters the most is our willingness to change and our commitment to do what is necessary to become a better person—because that will result in God sending more energy to our Soul.

We Go To The Planets To Live Because They Are . . .

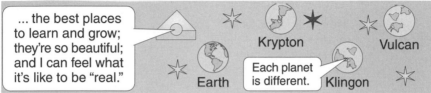

... the best places to learn and grow; they're so beautiful; and I can feel what it's like to be "real."

Krypton

Vulcan

Earth

Each planet is different.

Klingon

Our Souls are mostly full-time residents of the Spirit World, and in that domain they can do a lot of learning and growing. We are drawn to the planets for our advanced studies. If a Soul accepts the "mission" (which it doesn't have to), then it must learn how to make wise choices and to express its godliness here in the Physical World. This is where our Will is really put to the test. Choosing Earth, with all of its challenges, as the place to develop our Will is an act of real courage. Life is not easy here. To borrow another term from the Olympics, Earth has a high "degree of difficulty."

> If I can choose well there, I can choose well anywhere.
>
> From the cosmic musical, *Incarnate, Incarnate!* It is sung by Souls coming to Earth, and it has the same melody as *New York, New York*.

Each habitable planet offers a special set of circumstances for us to face. It's like there are different "school systems" throughout the universe. The one we're all enrolled in now (the Earth) was designed to teach us how to grow in spite of—(a) physical and emotional pain, and (b) the temptations of selfishness and materialism.

Souls come here to develop their logical side.
Vulcan

On me, Souls learn to live in peace and how to "talk" with animals and plants.
Harmonia

Our Souls are currently focused on their earthly studies, but during the course of our existence we will live on many other worlds and develop abilities rarely seen on this planet. After we learn these new skills, we can bring those abilities with us to the next planet and help "raise the consciousness" of its inhabitants. Indeed, there are people on Earth with certain "gifts"—such as psychic healing or the ability to communicate telepathically with other species—who might have lived previously on a more enlightened planet, such as Harmonia.

It's the Element of Our Soul That Affects Our Energy Level

Will — Regardless of which planet I live on, I still have to learn how to make godlike choices.

The *quantity* of our Soul's energy is determined by the *quality* of our choices. As we become better "choosers," we become more energetic. This is such an important spiritual reality that I will devote much of Part II of the book looking at the kinds of choices we can make, at the consequences of our choices, and how we can make better ones.

We Must Contend With FEAR

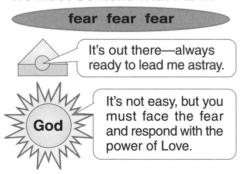

fear fear fear

It's out there—always ready to lead me astray.

God — It's not easy, but you must face the fear and respond with the power of Love.

In the Spirit World, where "love is in the air," it's easier for the Will to express its divinity. But here in the Physical World, there are negative forces around us —the most potent of which is **fear**. This negativity exists not because God is mean but because it is something we have to overcome as part of our spiritual development. When we finally learn to make godlike choices in the face of fear, we will be ready to "graduate" from this *universe-ity*.

> The education of the **will** is the object of our existence.
> Ralph Waldo Emerson – American philosopher; 1803–82

We Are All In This Together – Our "Collective Mission"

 This is the greater cosmic plan. When you achieve this mission, it will show you have really grown as Souls.

Your Soul   My Soul

Our goal is to create **"Heaven on Earth,"** which means:

(a) We have used our "Let there be ..." powers to minimize the pain and suffering experienced in the Physical World;

(b) We have created a reality in which all people can meet their basic needs and most are able to lead a long and fulfilled life;

(c) We are living in harmony with our fellow humans and with the Earth and other Soul types (the animals, trees, etc.);

(d) We have left the world better off for the Souls who will come after us (including ourselves when we come back again).

Each of us is concerned with our own well-being and spiritual growth, and that's fine. However, God reminds us that we're also part of a team. There is a "group assignment" that we need to make a real contribution to before our Soul can graduate and take its place close to God. We don't have be a world leader or a full-time charity-worker. The requirement is *simply* this—at some point in our Soul's journey, whether it be in this life or a later one, we need to live in such a way that we are a "beacon" of love, joy and creativity to the people around us. And we need to help at least one other Soul who is having a hard time, so they can accomplish the mission too. Then, we can look God in the eye, and say—"I did my best to help create Heaven on Earth, at least in my little corner of the world."

... while we are just a grain of sand in the great flow of time, we are, each of us, unique and necessary to the fulfillment of some cosmic plan.

Kathleen Brehony – author of *Awakening at Midlife*

 As I said before, you and I are co-creators. I made the Earth, and now you have to make it as close to paradise as you can.

Would we all be in the "Garden of Eden" right now had Adam and Eve not chosen to eat the forbidden fruit?

Are we trying to *recover* the paradise that was ours and then lost, or are we trying to create it for the *first time?* The Souls of our earliest ancestors arrived on an Earth that was, and still is, a "work-in-progress." God gave us the raw materials, with the expectation we would use our spiritual and human abilities to create Eden for ourselves. Besides, if God just handed us paradise, we wouldn't have the chance to grow.

Why Wasn't Everything Made Perfect From the Beginning?

The universe   Souls   Biological beings

God wanted the forces of nature and our free Wills to determine how we and the Physical World would evolve.

God is like the affluent parent who could give her children anything, but who wants them to work so they can learn the value of money and even create their own prosperity. God thought it would be best if we earned our energy the "old-fashioned way"—by learning how to make wise and loving choices. And in doing so, we would come to appreciate our true power.

As a Whole, Are We "Human Souls" Moving Away From God?

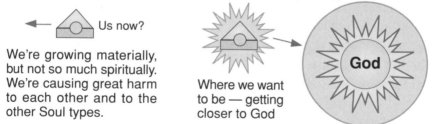

Us now?

We're growing materially, but not so much spiritually. We're causing great harm to each other and to the other Soul types.

Where we want to be — getting closer to God

God

Almost all of the people on Earth have good Souls. We came to this planet to expand our spiritual energy and to move closer to God. And there are many people who are actually doing that. They are growing as individuals and helping others as well. But it seems like many of us have lost sight of our spiritual mission. For example, we have gone overboard in our pursuit of material pleasures, and we haven't done all we can to prevent or eliminate suffering. We have also made it even harder for us to contend with fear and selfishness by overpopulating a world that has limited resources. God knows physical life is not easy, but She also knows we can get off this undesirable track and head back in Her direction.

If enough of us focus on the "mission," we'll have the collective power and Will to finish the job God started.

We are a long way from creating "Heaven on Earth." I don't expect it to happen in my lifetime, but it doesn't need to take forever. If we were to redirect our creative energy and set new priorities, we could eliminate hunger and poverty and many other causes of suffering within a generation or two. Of course, we won't solve every earthly problem, because some misfortune will always exist. But we have the power, if we choose to use it, to create a reality that is very close to Heaven on Earth. And that would fulfill our mission.

We're Not Alone In Our Quest
All Soul types are trying to get closer to God, and we need each other's help to fulfill our mission.

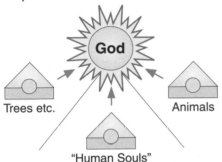

Even if God gave us dominion over the others, She didn't give us the right to wantonly destroy the physical forms that the other Soul types inhabit here on Earth.

If our human Souls are moving towards God, then it must be happening very slowly —mostly because we're letting so many people suffer needlessly, and also because we're treating the other Soul types with such disrespect. We're all on a "mission from God," and we're supposed to be working *together* to create Heaven on this and other planets. By disregarding the welfare of our "spiritual cousins," we're impeding our own growth—and putting life itself at risk.

How Do Plants and Animals Grow Spiritually?

Every Soul type can express love, joy and creativity but in ways that are unique to the species it inhabits in the Physical World. Animals, for their part, can't write a book, but they can be healers, helpers, rescuers, teachers and companions. Trees and plants can't drive a car, but they can clean the air, provide medicines, feed us, brighten our life with color, and in some cases, live for thousands of years. These other Soul types also have the ability to become better at what they do and thus expand their energy. We can help them in that effort.

(There is more on the next page)

There is a place in Scotland called the Findhorn Community, where a real connection was made between humans, plants and God. Receiving telepathic messages from the Spirit World, a few ordinary people were told how to prepare the soil and to tend their garden so vegetables would grow larger and more nutritious than their normal state. I have talked with people there, so I believe it is true. In my own home, I have seen our cats become more loving over the years as my wife and I have made an effort to connect with them. The point is all Soul types have the capacity for growth, and we can help each other to lead better lives.

All humans and Soul types are interconnected. The child dying from hunger, the species about to go extinct, or the rain forest that's burning, might have been able to make a major contribution to the mission. Now, we'll never know.

We Have Got Great Potential

Human Souls can become nearly angelic, but you have only just begun to grow. You are now using less than 2% of your spiritual power.

We can look at the current world situation, or at our own life, and think that the "missions" are a lost cause. We might even believe the people who say we are just "sinners" and that God should start over. But none of that is true or very helpful. We were made in God's image, and so we are inherently good and powerful. She set such high expectations for our Souls because She knew we had it within us to meet them.

The short version of your personal mission is –
Let there be ... love, joy and creativity throughout your life—because that will expand your energy and make you more like Me.

The short version of your collective mission is –
Make it so all people and other living things can use their gifts and express their love, joy and creativity.

Neither one is a "mission impossible." It's mostly a question of Willpower and having faith in ourselves. If we don't accomplish them in this life, we will eventually *if we keep on doing our best.*

Evolution and Wise, Old Souls

Certain things had to evolve before I could pursue my mission in the Physical World.

The Spirit World

Our universe

It took several billion years before I was ready for you.

Once our Souls learned about God's Values and Beliefs and were told our mission, most of us wanted to get right to work. But we couldn't go live on the planets yet, because they didn't exist. The Big Bang had produced a universe that at first, and for some time thereafter, contained no solid matter or any signs of life. There was just gas and lots of energy.

God created a Physical World that would *eventually* contain the ingredients necessary to form the Earth and our bodies. As noted before, the parameters and forces of the universe were set perfectly for the emergence of stars, planets and life itself. However, the reality we now see all around us and in the heavens above did not come into existence overnight. It took billions of years of transformation, occurring throughout the universe. God set everything in motion, and then "evolution" took over. Evolution is the process by which something develops into a new form that is usually more complex or better. It generally happens very slowly and is the result of natural forces. Finally, as essential to our existence as evolution was and still is, it is only part of the story. At key points in the history of the universe, God chose to intervene and to make things happen.

Stars Had To Evolve First

The early universe did not contain most of the substances we are made of. They came into existence when some of the big, early generation stars ran out of gas and blew up. These special stars "died" and ejected vital new elements into the universe.

When a star explodes, producing new types of matter, it's called a "supernova."

We're all made of "star dust."
The iron in our blood, the calcium in our bones and the oxygen we breath came from a star that exploded in our part of the galaxy. The cloud of gas that would form our solar system was "floating" through space at the time, and so it got filled with these essential elements. [That supernova was most likely a natural event, or was it God's handiwork?]

Our "home" is born.

When that star exploded about five billion years ago, it created the matter now inside us, and it triggered the formation of our solar system.

Then, getting from that point to where Earth could support life involved many critical events. If any one of them didn't happen, we almost certainly wouldn't be here today. Was this process entirely natural, or did God nudge it along? I believe in God partly because the Earth seems too incredible to be just the result of random events. Even if God did sit back and watch, because She was confident everything would turn out alright, I am still left believing in Her—if for no other reason than the processes of stellar and planetary evolution are so miraculous.

Many solar systems got the right elements.

Our Sun and its "siblings"

The cloud of gas that made our Sun (and its planets) most likely produced other stars too. So, if we got the elements needed to support life from the supernova, then the other members of our "stellar family" probably did as well. Also, supernovas and the formation of "later generation" stars like our Sun occurred throughout the universe, and it is still happening. That's why it is so hard to believe the Earth is the only place where life can exist.

"That (Earth) is the one and only planet where life has emerged would be a ridiculous assumption ... it is presumptuous to think that we are alone."
Harlow Shapely, astronomer

Where did life come from in the first place?

Could the emergence of life on the planets be a miracle? Without the theory of *divine intervention* it is hard if not impossible to explain how the first living cells came to be on Earth. Indeed, the odds of life developing on its own and so quickly after the Earth was formed are *way beyond* minuscule. So, it is reasonable for us to believe that life exists because God put it here—or that She at least made it possible for living cells to emerge.

"Seeds of Life" Were Planted Throughout the Universe

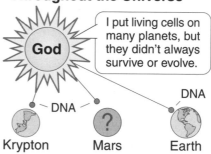

I put living cells on many planets, but they didn't always survive or evolve.

God

DNA

Krypton   Mars   Earth

DNA gives a cell its genetic traits and reproductive abilities. Did God put the same DNA on all habitable planets? We don't know, yet. [God might have used comets as the "delivery vehicle" to bring the cells to Earth and elsewhere.]

An honest man, armed with all the knowledge available to us now, could only state that in some sense, the origin of life appears at the moment to be almost a miracle, so many are the conditions which would have had to have been satisfied to get it going.

Francis Crick – co-discover of DNA; cracked the genetic code

A common sense interpretation of the facts suggests that a superintellect has monkeyed with physics, as well as with chemistry and biology ...

Fred Hoyle – astronomer

We Can Thank God That Life Began At All. And It's Amazing That Humans Ever Appeared.

"life" appears below the surface and deep in the oceans

I will rule the Earth forever.

And how long will we humans last?

time

| 4 billion years ago | billion of years of random evolution; billions of species | 65 million years ago, a comet hits; the dinosaurs die | the evolution of the ape proceeds and leads to us |

Billions and billions of years after the creation of the universe, "human beings" finally stood up to take their place on Earth.

Rudimentary life appeared on Earth early on, but it took a very long time before it evolved into who we are today. And it was by no means certain the *human* body would be the form our Souls would come to inhabit. To assume God orchestrated the emergence of human beings would mean She sent that comet to deliberately kill off the dinosaurs and most other forms of life. That's not like Her. God began the process of biological evolution when She placed those first living cells on Earth and elsewhere, but then She let the forces of nature mostly determine what would develop. God knew intelligent life would eventually exist in the universe, but She was willing to be "surprised" as to *how* and *when* it would appear and in *what form* it would finally emerge on various planets.

The dinosaurs may have already been headed for extinction due to disease and atmospheric changes. The comet impact was the coup de grâce. Had they lived, one of their kind might have developed higher intelligence, and we would now be called "**dinoman**" instead of human! On other planets, perhaps the reptile species did progress and produce E.T.'s (extraterrestrials) with hairless skin and lizard-like eyes.

Our Evolutionary Turn Came Just A Few Million Years Ago

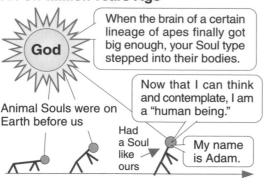

God

When the brain of a certain lineage of apes finally got big enough, your Soul type stepped into their bodies.

Now that I can think and contemplate, I am a "human being."

Animal Souls were on Earth before us

Had a Soul like ours

My name is Adam.

The earliest humans were very primitive and still learning to walk upright, but their Souls were just like yours and mine.

Man has reached his present state through the process of evolution. The last great step was the (doubling of) the size of the brain ... It is this change that permitted ... learning ... (and) communication ...

Linus Pauling
American scientist,
Nobel Prize winner;
1901–94

The first Souls to inhabit the new human bodies were pioneers, who were probably handpicked by God. They paved the way for the rest of us to experience life on Earth. At that time, their mission was mainly just to survive and to learn how to play with fire.

When we think about human life, it's appropriate to be both humble and proud. We were not here first, and we haven't been here that long. Dinosaurs ruled the Earth for nearly 160 million years whereas our oldest direct ancestors existed only four million years ago. It might have been only ten *thousand* years ago that humans began living in primitive societies, making rudimentary tools and learning to be civilized (something we're still working on). On the other hand, we have used our "Let there be ..." power to create great works of art and architecture, write inspiring music and books, unravel many mysteries, and develop intricate social structures. We have come a long way in a very short period of time.

The evolutionary process was *and is* occurring throughout the universe in unique ways on those planets where the "seeds of life" took hold. It is unlikely it happened here first because Earth is not *that* old. Also, there are probably billions of planets where life has not yet evolved far enough for our Soul type to get involved.

Your Soul

By the way, I wasn't really "waiting" for biological life to evolve because there is no time in my world. Besides, there was plenty for me to do before I "got physical." It was like spending my first years of childhood at home before going off to school.

Adam

But the Bible says the Earth and stars, and Eve and I, were made 6,000 years ago in just six days by God.

The theory of evolution has been controversial since the days of Charles Darwin, in part because people feel it excludes a "divine creation" of the universe or any other form of intervention by a higher power. But the existence of God and the concept of evolution are *not* mutually exclusive. I believe God is real and that we wouldn't be here if it weren't for Her. However, I am also convinced by the archaeological and astronomical evidence that evolution is real too. Indeed, our current reality is a *combination* of divine action, evolution and the choices we and our ancestors have made. Those who believe the Bible is the literal truth say that God "planted" the fossils of dinosaurs and early humans, and made the starlight look like it was billions of years old, to basically fool us. I'm sorry, but I find that harder to believe than anything I have written so far.

God

The divine creation of life in the universe and the reality of evolution can both be true.

If a single cell, under appropriate conditions, can become a human child in the space of a few months, there can surely be no difficulty in understanding how, under appropriate conditions, a cell may have, in the course of untold billions of years, given origin to the human race.

Herbert Spencer – English philosopher (paraphrased); 1820–1903

Can Souls Evolve Into a Different "Types"?

A Human Soul

If I work hard and expand my energy can I become an Angel? Or, could an animal Soul become like us? And what happens if I make really bad choices and lose a lot of my energy?

I believe there is some sort of impermeable boundary between Soul types. Still, it's fun to think we could get a halo and wings and the Souls of my cats could come back in human form. So, we will leave the door open a little for that possibility. Even if it isn't in the cards, it doesn't mean one Soul type is better than the others. All Souls can grow (far beyond where they are now) and attain the "gold medal" in their particular "category." And what happens when we lose our spiritual energy? We move away from God. (There will be more on that later.)

Our spiritual and biological sides are both evolving. From the start, Souls like ours have been trying to make the basic nature of the human being more positive.

Our Souls join up with one type of life form on any given planet, and each situation presents us with a different set of challenges and opportunities. Here on Earth, we have been lucky enough to get a mind and body that can excel at being creative and which have the capacity to be very compassionate and emotional. But the human form is also prone to bouts of negativity, such as greed and violence. So, in our effort to become more godlike and to expand our energy, our Souls must work hard to overcome these harmful tendencies. Ultimately, our Soul type is going to raise the state of the human form so its negative side (which will always exist to some extent) will no longer play a significant role in our behavior. This will happen the more we learn to—(a) see ourselves as spiritual beings, and (b) use our free Wills to make choices that are in accordance with God's Values and Beliefs.

The Earth speaks ...

Now more than ever, it is essential that you focus on raising the state of human nature. For you have gotten to the point where you can adversely affect the course of my evolution. You could even bring your own existence to a premature end.

Now, let's briefly return to a question that was addressed in a previous chapter—when were our Souls created? It's an important issue in the context of this chapter, because if your Soul and mine are brand new (and we get only one chance to live), how can we evolve? How can we get progressively better if we have no past, or no chance to face the Physical World again?

The traditional Western view is that Souls are created "as-needed." When a new life or baby comes into being, God creates a new Soul. So, this life is the first one for me and the first one for you (and our only one).

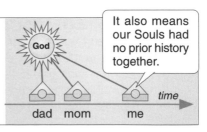

It also means our Souls had no prior history together.

When Were Our Souls Created? — Here are two other possibilities:

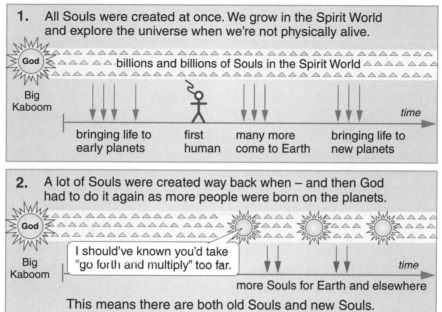

1. All Souls were created at once. We grow in the Spirit World and explore the universe when we're not physically alive.

billions and billions of Souls in the Spirit World

Big Kaboom

time

bringing life to early planets

first human

many more come to Earth

bringing life to new planets

2. A lot of Souls were created way back when – and then God had to do it again as more people were born on the planets.

I should've known you'd take "go forth and multiply" too far.

Big Kaboom

time

more Souls for Earth and elsewhere

This means there are both old Souls and new Souls.

As you already know, I believe in the *preexistence of Souls*—that is, our Souls were alive in the Spirit World before our human bodies were even conceived. I also believe God made our Souls a long time ago, before She created the universe. We have lived before, and we will "get physical" many more times. In this way, we have the opportunity to learn and grow and to bring the benefit of our prior experiences back into the Physical World.

Still, maybe God did underestimate how prolific we'd be in the area of procreation, and She had to make more Souls (again, God is not quite a "know it all" when it comes to our choices). These newer Souls will be just starting on their journey of spiritual growth and development. One thing I am certain of is there are Souls among us who have been "around the block" quite a few times. These Souls have evolved through their efforts here and in the Spirit World to the point that they are now *"wise, old Souls."*

And Which One Are You?

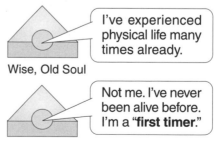

I've experienced physical life many times already.

Wise, Old Soul

Not me. I've never been alive before. I'm a **"first timer."**

You become a "wise, old Soul" by living multiple times and by learning and growing as a result of each experience. That's the subject of the next chapter. But first, here are some further thoughts on My role in the Big Picture.

Obviously, God has been the central figure in this story so far. I have said She is responsible for the creation of our Souls and the universe and for the origination of life. After setting this incredible drama in motion, She then left its outcome primarily up to evolution and the other forces of the Physical World and to our free Wills. But God is not a "hands-off" observer. She still gets involved at key moments in the unfolding of the universe and in our individual lives. Only, we cannot know for sure when or why She will intervene. And there are times when we wish She would intervene, but She doesn't. God loves us and cares very much about our well-being, but She is like a parent who is expecting Her children to develop their own "Let there be ..." power.

Needless to say, these views are not shared by all. Some people claim the universe created itself and that the Big Bang occurred within a physical realm that always was. Others believe life also appeared on its own and feel no need to bring a divine being into the story. Even if such theories were true, it does not preclude the existence of God. If there can be a Physical World so astounding that it could create itself and spontaneously generate life (not to mention intelligence and consciousness), then it makes it *easier* for me to believe God is real. The more amazing the reality of this Physical World is, the more believable the spiritual becomes.

Now, let's return to the story and look at another controversial topic, "reincarnation." Even many of the people who believe in it are troubled by the notion. We Souls know that reincarnation is not only real but also a good thing.

This and Other Lifetimes

A Soul enters a body so it can experience life in the Physical World. This is known as "incarnating." (It is from the Latin word *incarnatus*, which means "to become flesh.") *Reincarnation* is the re-birth of the Soul into a *new* body (after the previous one has died of course) so the Soul can experience life all over again.

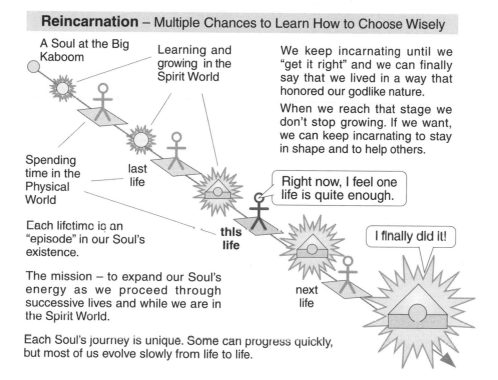

Reincarnation – Multiple Chances to Learn How to Choose Wisely

A Soul at the Big Kaboom

Learning and growing in the Spirit World

We keep incarnating until we "get it right" and we can finally say that we lived in a way that honored our godlike nature.

When we reach that stage we don't stop growing. If we want, we can keep incarnating to stay in shape and to help others.

Spending time in the Physical World

last life

Right now, I feel one life is quite enough.

Each lifetime is an "episode" in our Soul's existence.

this life

I finally did it!

The mission – to expand our Soul's energy as we proceed through successive lives and while we are in the Spirit World.

next life

Each Soul's journey is unique. Some can progress quickly, but most of us evolve slowly from life to life.

There are times when I think to myself, "Life is too hard. Why would anyone want to go through this again? There is so much pain." (My life is really a walk in the park compared to what billions of people have to endure.) So, to have us come back *again* seems like a cruel joke, not a gift. But God is not out to make us suffer. From our Souls' perspective, the pain will not last forever, and reincarnation is actually proof of God's love and compassion. She is giving us a chance to learn from our mistakes and to evolve because no Soul can "get it right" in just one lifetime. And for those who got a bad deal this time around, they get another shot at a good life.

One Lifetime Couldn't Be the "Whole Shebang," Could It?

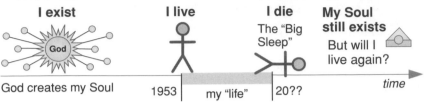

Why would a God who could make immortal Souls and a glorious universe that will last for billions of years limit us to just one lifetime?

We are learning how to be more loving, joyful and creative; and just as a child on Earth can't complete his or her education in one school year, so it is with our Souls. We *need* multiple lifetimes in order to grow and to "graduate." Also, it seems too incredible to think that with all of God's power, and given the eternal nature of our Souls, we would have just one opportunity to live. In the big picture, a single lifetime of say 100 years (if we're lucky) is not even a drop in the cosmic bucket.

Putting Our Time On Earth Into Perspective

Imagine that people on another planet could watch a movie that showed the entire 5 billion years of Earth's past. Also assume that for each <u>hour</u> of viewing they would see 1 <u>million</u> Earth years.

At that rate, they will have to be in their seats for over **6 months** to see the whole show. But get this – they won't see our modern human ancestors on the screen until the last 10 <u>minutes</u> of the movie. With only 10 <u>seconds</u> left, they will see the pyramids being built in Egypt. Jesus will arrive when there are only 7 seconds left in the movie. The entire history of the United States will occur in the final second. And our lives will flash by in the last two-tenths of one second. If they blink, they won't even see us! Surely, our Souls deserve (and will get) more "screen time" than that.

 What were billions of Souls doing before the Earth's population got as big as it is now?

 As I said before, there was plenty to do in the Spirit World, and we lived on other planets.

It is not sensible to claim that we have all lived many lives here on Earth. There haven't been enough bodies on the planet to date for that to be true. But that doesn't refute the reality of reincarnation. Indeed, our Souls were able to keep busy while they "waited"

for the "baby boom." Besides, to focus on how many earthly lives we might have had in the past is to miss the point that we're near the *beginning* of the reincarnation process and the best is yet to come —*if we can change some of our harmful choices.*

Many More Lifetimes Lie Ahead Than What Came Before
Humans have really only begun their time on Earth (or so we hope).

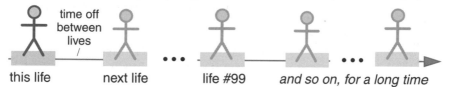

| this life | next life | life #99 | and so on, for a long time |

If we don't destroy ourselves or the environment first, the human race could live another 35 million years (or more) before the Earth is hit by another comet or asteroid (of course, it might happen sooner). In 35 million years, we each could have thousands of lifetimes (not that we would need that many to fulfill our "mission"). Of course, not all of our lives would have to be on Earth.

It Takes Only a Small Leap of Faith

If you can believe in Me, the existence of Angels and Souls, life after death, and Heaven, then why is it so hard to believe that a Soul can live more than once?

As a child, I was led to believe that reincarnation was a strange, Eastern idea. Actually, it has been accepted by all sorts of people for thousands of years, and it's even in the Bible. It was part of the early Christian faith until it was suppressed in the sixth century. Still, a lot of people have a hard time accepting reincarnation, even if they readily believe in God and other mystical concepts.

If You Believe in Reincarnation, You're in Good Company

> The education of Souls is continued in successive (lifetimes).
>   Origen – eminent Christian theologian; 185–254
>
> ... (after death) ... we start a new earth cycle again.
>   Thomas Edison – American inventor; 1847–1931
>
> [Edison also believed the Earth was not the first or only place where life emerged, and he said "there is life in things which we used to regard as inanimate."]

more on the next page

It is no more surprising to be born <u>twice</u> than once.

> Voltaire – French philosopher; 1694–1778

I believe that we ... will come back again ... (and we can) utilize the experience we collect in one life in the next. (Genius) is ... the fruit of long experience in many lives. Some are older souls than others, and so they know more.

> Henry Ford – American businessman; 1863–1947

<u>Each</u> <u>time</u> we die we gain more of life. Souls pass from one sphere to another ... (and they) become more and more bright ...

> Victor Hugo – French author; 1802–85

I live in the hope that if not in this birth, (then) in some other birth I shall be able to hug all humanity in friendly embrace.

> Mohandes Gandhi; 1869–1948

The soul is an emanation of the Divinity ... a ray from the source of light. It comes from without into the human body, as into a temporary abode, (and then) it goes out of it anew; it wanders in ethereal regions (the Spirit World), and it returns to visit (the earth, where) ... it passes into (another body) ... for the soul is immortal.

> Ralph Waldo Emerson – American philosopher; 1803–82

I know I am deathless, ...
Believing I shall come again upon the earth ...

> Walt Whitman – American poet; 1819–92

These quotes are from the book *Reincarnation in World Thought* – compiled and edited by Joseph Head and S.L. Cranston

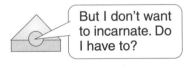

But I don't want to incarnate. Do I have to?

There is no cosmic law that says a Soul must incarnate. Like everything else with our existence, it's a matter of choice. Given all the pain and suffering that exists on Earth, it's understandable why a Soul would want to stay put in the Spirit World. However, most Souls do choose to incarnate, and to reincarnate, because they know "getting physical" is a great way to learn how to make wise choices.

Of course, personal growth isn't the only reason why we incarnate. There are "perks" too—including the ability to experience human emotions, to enjoy the sensations of the body and to transform dreams into reality. These and many other pleasures draw us to the Physical World, in spite of the pain that exists.

So, we are all here in the Physical World because we *want* to be here, not because God made us do it. That does not mean we all got the kind of lives our Souls had hoped for—because the nature of each life is dependent upon the choices made by the Souls who incarnated before us (e.g. our parents) and by other factors such as fate. We will look more closely at this subject in the chapters *What It Means to Get Physical* and *What Else Affects Our Reality.*

> What happens to a Soul who chooses not to incarnate or to sit out physical life for awhile? Nothing bad happens. Indeed, they can learn and grow in the Spirit World. But Souls like ours really do need to experience, at some point, the realities of the Physical World. Only then can we make a "hands-on" contribution to the "collective mission." It is also how we can become a spiritual mentor who can say to other Souls—"I understand what you're going through."

Each New Life Builds Upon the Prior Ones

last life next life

I need to work some more on my self-love, and I want to put my gifts to better use.

We continue to work on lessons from life to life. Chances are the issues we are struggling with the most have been a problem for several lifetimes. We also bring into each new life unresolved issues that we have with other Souls. This is because each time we incarnate we do so with many of the same "cast of characters." Also, each lifetime is an opportunity for us to develop our special talents. Of course, it can take awhile before we rediscover what those gifts are and find the courage to use them or to do what we love.

The goal is not to be perfect. While we can aspire to be far more godlike than we are now, we can't be just like God—especially here in the Physical World which will never be completely free of pain or temptation. God's expectation is for us to eventually live in such a way that we are motivated by love, not fear; each of us is pursuing our creative interests; and we're feeling joyful, *most of the time.*

Even "enlightened" Souls, like Jesus and Buddha, had a hard time on Earth. So, do your best, and be kind to yourself. It's going to take several lifetimes.

We Play a Different Role In Each Life

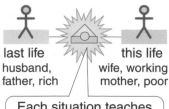

last life
husband,
father, rich

this life
wife, working
mother, poor

Each situation teaches me something new.

Each new life offers a unique set of challenges, which can help us to become a well-rounded Soul. Also, we really can't tell by looking at the state of someone's life, including our own, what the true nature is of his or her Soul. Just because someone has lots of money, power, or prestige does not mean he or she is a wise, old Soul near the end of the reincarnation process. They might actually be near the beginning. Conversely, if our life is especially harsh or challenging, it does not mean we're a spiritual neophyte—or an undeserving Soul who did something bad in a prior life.

Don't put off until the next life what you can do in this one. Be a "here and now" kind of Soul, and do your best to grow in this life.

God wants us to be kind and patient with ourself, and She also wants us to live each life to its fullest. She is asking us to do our best to overcome those personal shortcomings that are most persistent—and are harmful to our emotional or physical well-being and to others. In that way, we can move on to new challenges and opportunities in the next life.

Still, life is not just about striving to be better. We can grow without all the pain and struggle. In fact, learning how to enjoy life and how to grow through acts of love, joy and creativity are a very important part of our Soul's lesson plan.

A wise, old Soul who has fulfilled the mission says ...

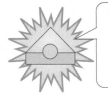

When I incarnate now it's mostly to help others reach a higher state of godliness.

When we finally become a wise, old Soul we won't stop coming to the Physical World. We will want to stay in shape and continue to experience the pleasures of life. The main reason we will come back is to help others. We will endure the pain and suffering all over again so we can share our wisdom and show others how to be loving and compassionate—and that will bring us even closer to God.

Earth – "been there, done that"

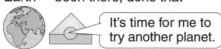

Earth is wonderful and a great place to learn, but we won't spend every lifetime here. Just like human children, who go to different schools for their education, we will seek out different environments, teachers and classmates. That we can sample the diversity of the universe is one of the key benefits of reincarnation. There is so much to see and do and learn that it would be a shame if we were restricted to just one lifetime.

When we're born into a new life, our prior experiences are screened from our conscious awareness. Even though it might be helpful to know what happened before, the human mind, in its current state of evolution, is not equipped to handle that information. Most of us would "short-circuit" if all the details of the past and present coexisted in our brain. This self-protection mechanism allows us to focus on the realities of *this* life.

Still, the conscious recollection of past lives is not unheard-of. For example, Tibetan monks knew the current Dalai Lama was the reincarnation of their spiritual leader because of his ability to identify specific people and objects from his previous life in that role. This is not an isolated story. Other cases of past life recall have pointed to the reality of reincarnation.

Finally, we all have unconscious memories of our prior lives. They can reveal themselves in the way we are attracted to certain people and physical places, by our preference for particular creative interests, and even for specific types of food or music. Our Soul keeps everything from our past in its Unconscious Mind, but it doesn't give up its secrets easily. Even hypnosis doesn't usually reveal many details from our previous adventures.

It is nature's kindness that we do not remember past births. Life would be (more of) a burden if we carried such a ... load of memories.
Mohandes Gandhi; 1869–1948

Looking back at how our ancestors lived, and considering how hard life still is, it's no wonder reincarnation might be seen more as a burden than a bless-ing. In fact, "nirvana" is defined, in part, as the end of the Soul's need to experience physical life.

There will always be sickness and unfairness, accidents and natural disasters, aging and death—regardless of how godlike we all become. That is the nature of the Physical World. So, perhaps it is appropriate to see our escape from the pain and suffering as the ulti-mate goal. However, we have another option and that is to trans-form our personal and global reality so we don't have to fear the prospect of reincarnation, but we welcome it.

Do your best to make this lifetime such that you would say when it's over – "all things considered, I would like to come back and do it again." When that can be said by most, if not all people, you will have achieved your "collective mission."

We can't eliminate all the misfortunes that befall mankind, but we can make Earth a place that our Souls would be eager to come back to, after resting up in the Spirit World of course. We can make it so each of us feels that in spite of life's inevitable travails the journey was, on balance, well worth it—and worth doing again. Many people feel that way now; but there are far too many that don't. Changing that reality is at the heart of our mission.

I'd like to get away from earth awhile
And then come back to it and begin over.
                    Robert Frost – American poet; 1875–1963

Now, let's take a look at the Souls who have become our best friends in the Spirit World and with whom we share the experience of life.

We All Have Kindred Souls

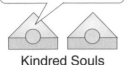

> I'm drawn to you. I like your energy. Let's be eternal friends and help each other grow.

Kindred Souls

We were all created by God and are part of one incredibly large spiritual family. But over the eons we have each gravitated towards certain other Souls with whom we have similar interests and who can help us with our mission. We have become part of our very own "spiritual tribe."

Most Souls are amicable in the Spirit World, but Kindred Souls *really* like each other. They are supportive, nurturing and loyal, and they accept each other as they are. "Kindreds" tend to incarnate together—because they like the companionship, they enjoy creating physical realities together, and they can help each other become better Souls. From a spiritual perspective, their mutual intent is always constructive, never harmful. They have each other's best interests in mind.

Our Kindreds Are Here and There

Some of them are with us on Earth, and many more are still in the Spirit World.

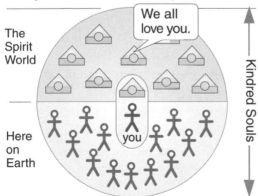

Everyone has Kindred Souls. They exist in the Physical World as family and friends, and they're out there among the "strangers," waiting for us to find each other. We also have kindreds who stayed in the Spirit World, and there are kindreds who were once with us but have since passed on.

On Earth, we will have a sense of familiarity, "destiny" or purpose when we meet one of our kindreds. But that doesn't mean the love which exists between our Souls will be manifested to the same degree here in the Physical World. We all have to cope with the challenges of being human, and even kindreds have to work on their earthly bond.

Every Incarnation Is a "Reality Play"

The Souls that are closest to us usually play the most important roles in our life.

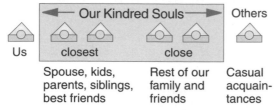

Each time we incarnate and experience a new "production" of life some of our Kindred Souls join us and fill major roles in our "cast." Likewise, we serve as a supporting actor in their lives. In some instances, they fill their parts without an earthly "audition"—as is the case with those who are born into our family. For most other roles —such as spouse, friend or business associate—we have to go out and look for our Kindred Souls.

We can get in trouble selecting people for key roles in our life who are not kindreds. That is not to say non-kindreds are out to hurt us or that we can't learn and grow by being with them. However, we are usually better off bonding with someone with whom we have that extra-special spiritual connection.

Actions Can Be Misleading

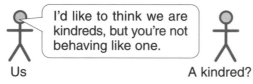

It is clear who is a Kindred Soul in the Spirit World, but on Earth it can be far less obvious. When people close to us are being hurtful it is hard to see them as kindreds—but they might be. If they are, we can be sure their Souls are feeling awful about how we're being treated. For some reason, or set of reasons, their Earthly Selves have gotten off track—perhaps because one of their kindreds hurt them. Basically, if we can sense deep down that a person really cares for us, or he or she is helping us (in a well-intended way) to face our issues and to grow, then he or she is most likely a Kindred Soul.

The distinction between kindreds is one of degrees. Our Soul loves and cherishes them all, but some are closer to us than others. Also, our spiritual relationships can grow stronger (or weaker) as we spend more lifetimes together. We can make new connections, and we can expand the size of our group. There is no limit on how many Kindred Souls one can have. Ideally, we would see *everyone* in that light—which is how we all began our existence.

We Have a Match Made In Heaven

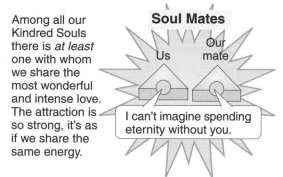

Among all our Kindred Souls there is *at least* one with whom we share the most wonderful and intense love. The attraction is so strong, it's as if we share the same energy.

Soul Mates are as close as two Souls can possibly be—and we *all* have a companion like that and maybe even more than one. (That's okay, because jealousy is not a factor in the Spirit World.)

Soul Mates often incarnate together so they can be each other's spouse or life partner, but that is not always the case. In some lives, they will play different roles—such as parent and child, or as very best friends (who are not romantically linked). It is also possible our Soul Mate did not incarnate with us and is instead helping us from the Spirit World. Even if our Soul Mate is here, there is no guarantee we will find each other or if we do, that we will *stay* together. From a spiritual perspective, however, Soul Mates are forever one in love.

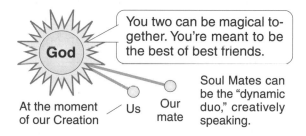

We all have had a Soul Mate since "day one." God made it so each of us would have someone who knew us better than any other Soul and who would be our eternal traveling companion. We complement each other so well that together our creative, "Let there be ..." power can be far "greater than the sum of our parts." On a spiritual level, we also know how to best bring out the love and joy that is within our Soul Mate. We have each other's best interests in mind, and we are meant to work in union on our personal growth. Of course, it doesn't always work out that way on Earth. Although our time together in the Physical World will most likely not be easy or totally harmonious, our *Souls* can always count on each other.

Please remember that in the Spirit World you and your Soul Mate are deeply in love. If you find each other on Earth, do your best to honor the bond that exists between your Souls.

The best way to find Kindred Souls is to do what you love. You'll be with like-minded people, and you will be at your joyful best.

Our Soul

Isn't it wonderful? There are people here who are predisposed to love us. But beyond those that might be in our family, we have to go out in the world and find them. Pursuing activities which use our talents or which make us happy is a great way to meet kindreds. We might also bump into them by sheer coincidence. Some kindreds will stay with us for the rest of our life; others will appear for just awhile to help us through a crisis or to advance a creative project. We might not even see them as a kindred at first.

Some people find a lot of kindreds, including their Soul Mate, early in life. Others spend years mostly alone and without their special companion. Being alone does *not* mean we're unlovable or there is anything wrong with our Soul. Perhaps this particular life was meant to be a more solitary journey, so we could really focus on our personal or creative growth. Or maybe we will find more of our kindreds, including our Soul Mate, later on in life.

We are not in a contest to see who can assemble the largest group of kindreds on Earth. One can have a fulfilled life without having a big family or a multitude of friends. If we can find even a few of our Kindred Souls, and learn to treat each other well as human beings, then our time in the Physical World will be enriched indeed.

We Made A Deal With Our Kindreds

Let's do our best not to hurt each other when we "get physical."

Before beginning this lifetime, we were hanging out with our kindreds in the Spirit World. We all agreed that should we ever meet on Earth, we would help each other to have a pleasurable life experience. Because of the challenges inherent in being human, we knew this would not be easy. We also agreed that when conflicts did arise between us in the Physical World, we would remember where we came from and how much we really loved each other. All of us are interconnected spiritual siblings, and we shouldn't harm anyone. But there is an extra measure of love and trust between Kindred Souls. Because we often build our lives around each other, it is important that our earthly bond reflect the strength of our spiritual love.

They're Hoping That We Will Make Wise Choices

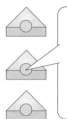

We're kindreds who will incarnate after you. We're counting on you to be ready as parents and to give us a world that is in good shape.

We expect our kindreds to be kind and thoughtful, and we are very disappointed when they're not. Imagine how the Souls who are coming to this planet must feel about our current state of affairs. Kindred Souls are like teammates in a relay race, and we are not giving our successors a good start.

Finally, there is no kindred relationship more sacred than that between a parent and child. The Souls who will be brought into this world know there are no guarantees and that life is hard. They only hope their earthly parents will be as ready as possible before conceiving so they can come into a safe and loving home.

There Is Love All Around Us
Including some very "special" Souls

Dearly departed

Animals

Other Souls *

Our Soul

Angels

Guides

I feel un-loved and alone.

But you're not. We are all near you.

Us

* Kindreds who didn't incarnate this time

Among the many Souls who are by our side and sending us love are *Angels* and *Spirit Guides*—and of course, God is too.

As mentioned before, Angels were created with expanded energy so they could focus on helping us. Among their powers is the ability to protect us from harm, which they can do by encircling our body with their energy or by appearing for a brief time in human form to intervene in some way. Since we do get hurt in life, it is clear they don't always step in to save us. It is not because God is insensitive but because pain and death are part of the Physical World. Also, God wants us to realize that *we're responsible* for a lot of the misfortune that exists in the world and that *we have the power* to make it better.

God

The Angels may not intervene all the time, but they are always sending you love and comfort for your Soul.

Angels are always near us, sending us their love and giving us strength to cope with the harsh realities of life. When we ask for their help, through meditation and prayer, we enhance our connection with these heavenly Souls.

One last point about the Angels—they also have the ability to orchestrate certain events. For example, they can send "leading thoughts" to our Unconscious Mind, which will prompt us to do something or to go somewhere to help us find one of our Kindred Souls. Again, it will seem like just a "coincidence."

One of our Spirit Guides

I can't intervene in your life. But I can send you answers and ideas, plus love.

Each of us has one or more wise, old Souls helping us out. They're known as *Spirit Guides*, and basically they are Souls like us —but with more life experience. Or they may possess expertise in a given area we need help with or in which we are creatively involved. The point is these Souls are in a position to share their wisdom and to counsel us. Through the use of our telepathic and intuitive abilities, they can send us insights and inspiration. But unlike the Angels, they cannot directly intervene in our life. They are constrained by a cosmic law that is similar to the "Prime Directive" from the science fiction series, *Star Trek*—which prohibits a crew from interfering in a planet's evolution.

Spirit Guides are helping us even if we don't believe in them or ask them for assistance. Like the Angels, they can be more effective if we acknowledge their existence and connect through our thoughts and prayers. Finally, the Angels and Spirit Guides are most anxious to help when we're facing serious problems in life and when we're pursuing an activity that will contribute to the fulfillment of our personal or collective mission.

If you were to remember nothing else, remember this ...

God

No matter where you are, or how you feel, you are never truly alone. You are always in the company of Souls who think you're great and who love you dearly.

Karma and Other Cosmic Laws

Each of us is on a "mission from God" to become a better and more energetic Soul. We work on that mission from life to life and when we're back in the Spirit World. We also work on it in the company of other Souls, especially our kindreds. We learned early on (during our Soul's orientation period) that we could fulfill our mission only if we honored God's Values and Beliefs. We also learned there were other fundamental principles that would govern the nature of our Soul's journey. One of the most important of these cosmic laws is called "karma."

What We Put Out, We Get Back

"Instant" Karma – we feel it right away

"Delayed" Karma – later in this lifetime, or in a subsequent one

In my youth, I didn't know what karma was. I thought it might be a Middle Eastern food. ("I'll have a falafel and a side order of *karma beans,* please.") But karma is really a simple idea which, like reincarnation, has been around for thousands of years. It too is in the Bible. The basic concept is this—*what we put out there will come back to us in one form or another.* So, we should do unto others as we would want done unto us.

When we say or do something to others (negative *or* positive in nature), we create the likelihood of a "karmic reaction" which can happen at any time and in different ways. We *might* experience the same fate as the person we affected did. Or something else will occur which will cause us to regret our action (if it was harmful) or to appreciate what we did (if it was good).

> ... for whatsoever a man soweth, that shall he also reap.
>
> Paul (Galatians 6:7)
>
> With what measure ye give to others, it shall be measured to you again.
>
> Jesus (Matthew 7:2)

God created the law of karma as a way to raise our awareness and to help us become better "choosers." If we could experience how it felt to be treated the way we treated others, then perhaps our future choices would come from a place of greater sensitivity and empathy. Karma is meant to be a learning aid for our Soul. However, here on Earth we tend to deny any connection between our actions towards others and what subsequently happens to us. We would rather see our problems as being caused by fate or someone else. If we want to really benefit from the law of karma, we need to accept its existence—and be more mindful of how we would react to what we're about to say or do to others.

We shouldn't use "it's their karma" to explain everything that occurs in a person's life.

It is tempting to use karma as the full explanation for the unfairness of life and to give meaning to our suffering. In one, neat little concept, we can place the blame or credit for the state of someone's life entirely in his or her hands. We could say life is solely a matter of personal responsibility. There are no accidents. If someone is in pain and suffering, it is because he or she has lessons to learn. We could also believe, as many people do, that the total effect of our actions or conduct in this life will solely determine the nature of our next life. We could look at a homeless person and believe he or she "screwed-up" in a prior life and is now working off "bad karma." But this view is too simplistic.

Karma is a powerful force. It can even be the primary factor behind the state of this lifetime or of the next one. But the nature of the Physical World is more complex than that. Accidents do happen and our reality is affected by forces beyond our control. So, as useful as karma is to understanding why good or bad things happen, it is only part of the story. (We will examine this subject in Part II, especially in the chapter *What Else Affects Our Reality.*)

Karma follows me from one life to the next.

Still, we don't want to underestimate the impact of karma. Within the context of a single life, karma will cause events to occur that will teach us a lesson so we can learn to make better choices. If we die before we have a chance to experience all of the karmic events that "we had coming," then we will have to face them in a subsequent life. The key point is our current life is but an episode in our Soul's grand adventure. And we carry over our unlearned lessons and unresolved karma from one life to the next.

Negative karma is **not** a given. It is preventable.

We have the power to shape the future. Specifically, we can head off bad karma before it happens by asking forgiveness and making amends with the people we hurt, by doing a good deed to offset our harmful act, and by taking a new, more loving path in life. We might not forestall every event meant for us, but we can lighten our karmic load a lot by changing our ways. Of course, the best way to prevent negative karma from happening is to be good in the first place.

The "Bottom Line" Is That Choices Have Consequences

If you lie, people won't believe you.
If you cheat, people won't trust you.
If you're cruel, people won't love you.

From *How Do You Spell God?* by Rabbi Marc Gellman and Monsignor Thomas Hartman

Karma is the law of *action and reaction.* It may not always seem to be working because people who act badly often get away with it and lead pleasurable lives, at least from a material perspective. But sooner or later, in this life or the next, all harmful behavior receives its negative karmic reaction—unless it is prevented, as described above. And ultimately, all good deeds will receive their karmic reward.

Now we will take a quick look at some of the other universal truths that govern our lives.

Nothing is stationary. There is nothing permanent except change.

Heraclitus – Greek philosopher c540–470 BCE

Everyone and all things are in the process of transformation. What once was will never be exactly that way again. Generally, change occurs slowly—which is why patience is a virtue. Change can happen in an instant too. Sometimes we're the victim of change, but mostly we are "agents of change"—responsible for how we grow, how we react to the change that is beyond our control, and how we change the lives of those around us.

God

Some change is inevitable, and you will just have to accept it. But you also have the power to say "Let there be ... a change for the better." It then takes courage and determination to make it so.

Take Nothing For Granted

unseen asteroid headed for Earth

Anything can happen, at any time, and without warning.

And it doesn't matter if I've been a good planet, or you've been a good person. Bad stuff can still happen.

We should expect the unexpected. While there is a high degree of order in the Physical World, there is also *chaos*. Everyone and all things are moving through space and time together so we're going to "bump" into each other on occasion. Also, the forces of nature are going to act when they see fit, not when it's convenient for us. This could mean our bodies might take a turn for the worse prematurely and without warning. There is a random or unpredictable nature to life. As the dinosaurs learned, we can't count on unexpected events to always be in our favor.

Suitable Conditions Are Required

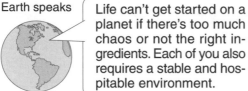

Earth speaks

Life can't get started on a planet if there's too much chaos or not the right ingredients. Each of you also requires a stable and hospitable environment.

It wasn't until objects from space stopped bombarding the Earth that life could evolve. And while all of us need change (for the stimulation and the chance to face new challenges), we can't create a satisfying life if there is *too much* instability and uncertainty. We need relative harmony in and around our home and within our relationships. We need food and shelter, good health care, the chance to use our gifts, and to be self-sufficient. Life cannot flourish without these conditions.

Nothing Physical Lasts Forever

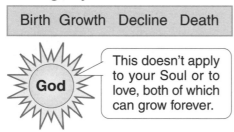

Birth　Growth　Decline　Death

God

This doesn't apply to your Soul or to love, both of which can grow forever.

We all know we're going to die. That is reality for *everything* in the universe. This natural cycle of life is not entirely beyond our control, however. The quality of our choices can affect the timing and nature of our decline and death. We can even *temporarily* reverse the process. Also, the cycle applies differently to each of our "parts." We can keep growing mentally, emotionally and spiritually even while our body is in decline. When this incarnation is over, our Soul will live on.

Left Alone, Things Will Fall Apart

The input of energy is needed to counteract the natural tendency for things to move toward disorder and decay.

In order for anything to grow, or to withstand the "elements" and the passage of time, energy in some form must be applied. To keep our body in shape, we need to exercise. To keep a nation strong, it is necessary to educate its citizens and to maintain its infrastructure, among other things. This law also applies to businesses, which need ongoing research and development; and most importantly, to *relationships* (even kindred ones), which require our love and personal attention.

We Live With "Dualities"

Love	Fear
Good	Bad
Birth	Death
Pleasure	Pain
Hot	Cold
Light	Dark
Order	Chaos

The two sides go together, but not all of the stuff in the right-hand column has to be as widespread as it is now.

We live in a universe in which there is suffering—not because God is mean, but because that's the way it is. We don't have to like the dual nature of our reality, but it does help us to learn and grow. The bad things help us to appreciate all the *good* parts of life. The most important point to remember is we have it within our power to *shift the balance,* so that the good far outweighs the bad and there is much less suffering in the Physical World.

All forms of life coexist in a delicate balance, and when we mess with the natural order we stand to lose in ways we may forever regret. Of course, death is inevitable, and it's natural for species to disappear. But God must truly be alarmed at the way we are escalating the process and allowing death to be so prevalent.

Everything Is Interdependent

Can we afford to lose them?

That person or that tree, or even an insect in the rain forest, might provide a cure for cancer. There is no telling what you're going to miss if you let people and other living things die needlessly.

There Are "Windows of Opportunity"

When you see a chance to be loving, joyful or creative, take it. Seize the moment while you can.

Knowing anything can happen and our life could end at anytime adds a sense of urgency to each incarnation. Our Souls want to savor the simple pleasures of life, but they're also eager to express their creative side and to see and do as much as possible. All aspects of the Physical World —including one's health, career, and financial situation—are subject to periodic setbacks. So, when conditions are favorable we need to take advantage of that reality. At the end of each incarnation, when our Soul conducts a *Life Review*, there are always regrets—over what we did that we wish we hadn't and over what we wish we had done but didn't. The goal is to minimize our mistakes and lost opportunities.

> The above law applies to problem resolution too. In many situations, we can reach the point where it is too late to take any remedial action— such as when we're being harmful to ourself or to someone we love, or when a species is headed for "premature extinction." We must find the Will to change our ways when we see the first "warning signs."

It Only Takes One To Make All The Difference In the World

One star out of trillions produced the matter you are made of, and another solitary star is now keeping you alive.

You can have a major impact too—if you use your gifts and help even one other Soul to reach his or her potential.

The history of the universe and of humankind shows that both stars and people can make a major contribution even if they are quite "ordinary" and live relatively short lives.

We came into this world as children of God, blessed with special talents and the power to create new realities. It is up to each of us to make the choice to be an agent for *positive* change and to make a difference in the lives of others—especially for the children and the Souls who will incarnate after them.

Don't forget that everything you say and do will not only affect the people around you, but it will ultimately affect you too – if not in this life, then the next. Now, let's wrap-up the "Big Picture"; and then we'll come "down to Earth."

A Summary of the "Big Picture"

This chapter recaps the key points from the previous eight chapters. If you have read this far in one sitting, you may want to skip this summary for now, because it might seem too repetitive. You could come back to it later, when you want to refresh your memory. But if you want to see how all the pieces fit together, then by all means keep reading. Otherwise, proceed to Part II, which takes a close look at the Soul's earthly adventure.

Our Creator

There is a supernatural force responsible for our existence. Though beyond our comprehension, I envision this force as a Divine Being, called "God." And while God is undoubtedly without gender or form, I like to see Her feminine side and to picture Her as the Spiritual Sun—radiating unconditional love here, there and everywhere. God is at home in the Spirit World, but She is also a part of all we see. God is infinite energy and all powerful, yet kind and forgiving. She is a loving parent with whom we can have a personal relationship. God looks over us and intervenes now and then, but She has chosen not to fix all our problems, so we can make it better for ourselves.

Why I Believe In God (in spite of our pain and suffering)

1. Life itself is so astounding. It couldn't be just an "accident."
2. Our vast universe had a beginning and is perfectly suited for us.
3. The emergence of the first living cells seems miraculous.
4. So much of what we cannot see is or appears to be real.
5. Lots of people have "experienced" God or the Spirit World.
6. The holy books contain many divinely inspired words.
7. Belief in God puts my life in a broader, spiritual context.
   — Plus, I know in my heart God is real. I have "faith."

I almost forgot to say that God wants us to be respectful of each other's spiritual views, and that She doesn't like it when people say they alone know the truth about Her.

Our Souls

you — me

God

We were made from God's energy so we could share the wonders of both worlds and bring life to the planets.

Spirit

Will

Unconscious Mind

Our Soul

The essence of every Soul is **Love, Joy** and **Creativity**.

Because we are all children of God, you and I are spiritual siblings. Before there was a universe, our Souls were created as an expression of God's love and *"Let there be ..."* power. We will exist forever and live mostly in the Spirit World. God created a variety of "Soul types" because She knew each of them would have a special role to play in the Physical World She planned to make.

Each Soul has three elements. The *Spirit* is the "receptacle" for God's energy and is the source of our consciousness. Our *Will* is free to make choices. The *Unconscious Mind* remembers everything, talks to God and other Souls and is full of knowledge and great ideas.

Our Souls were made in God's image, and we inherited Her basic traits. That's why it is in our nature to be *loving, joyful* and *creative*. Like God, but on a much smaller scale, we can say "Let there be ..." and make new realities. Each of us can do that in our own special way because God gave *every* Soul some one-of-a-kind talents.

The Universe

The Big Bang!

12 to 18 billion years ago God created the Physical World.

The Spirit World is a glorious place, but it is missing a few things that God felt would be both pleasurable for our Souls and important for our growth. We needed a place where we could create tangible realities, experience physical sensations and face challenges that would develop a Soul's *Will* and inner strength. So, God made the universe. This new world came out of nowhere and was designed so in due time lots of habitable planets and forms of physical life would exist.

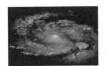 Our Souls can travel throughout the universe. We can be anywhere in an instant. God wants us to "illuminate" each planet that we live on with the love that is inside each of us. We're like the photons of light emitted by the Sun.

It's As Easy To Remember As "1-2-3"

1. God and the Spirit World always were and always will be.
2. God said "Let there be ..." and created our immortal Souls out of Her own divine energy. It was the Big Kaboom.
3. Then with a Big Bang, God created the universe. Everything that we see as physically real came from a single point.

Evolution

The divine creation of the universe and evolution are both true. But it took a lot longer than the few days described in the Bible before we could walk the Earth. The *stardust* we are all made of had to be produced first; God had to place the *seeds of life* on various planets; and then our spiritual cousins, the animals, had to arrive. Finally, one of the many species had to become "human."

God and nature are both responsible for what exists today.

Stars, planets and life forms all had to evolve before we could "get physical." God set everything in motion and then She let nature take its course.

Out Of the Unity of God Came Worlds of Diversity
Everything came from the same source, but we are all unique.

All of God's creations are made of the same essential ingredients —energy and matter. These basic elements have been manifested in a countless variety of objects and species, all of which come in different sizes, shapes and colors. As we proceed on our journey, it is God's hope that we will come to realize that there is some of Her in *all* that we see. She wants us to honor and respect our differences— and to act together as members of the same spiritual family. God wants Her children to live in harmony.

> I believe in the absolute oneness of God and, therefore, of humanity. The rays of the sun are many ... but they have the same source.
>
> Mohandes Gandhi; 1869–1948
>
> Trees ... flowers (and animals) ... all are our brothers and they enjoy life as we do, share heaven's blessings with us, die and are buried in hallowed ground, come with us out of eternity and return into eternity.
>
> John Muir – American naturalist; 1838–1914

Of course, we can't live in harmony with all things. There is a "food chain" and we need to protect ourselves from some creatures. Still, we can be more respectful of life.

The "Mission"

We're Supposed to Grow and Expand Our Soul's Energy

You, at first

You, now

Acts of **love**, **joy** and **creativity** make this happen.

I'm becoming more godlike.

Our Souls began their journey as spiritual "infants" and with a tremendous amount of potential—after all, we are *God's* children. Now, it is up to each of us to develop our inherent godliness and to become a more radiant and energetic Soul. We enhance our Soul's energy whenever we express love for ourself and others, bring joy into our life or use our "Let there be ..." power to create positive realties. All Souls and Soul types can grow, and we need each other's help to attain our goal. God isn't expecting us to be perfect Souls, but She does want us to do our best.

Earth speaks ...

You come to live on me not because it is easy but because it is a challenge. And so you can see my beauty and feel what it's like to be "human."

Your "collective mission" is to make it so all Souls who come here have the chance to be loving, joyful and creative.

Each planet is a unique "school" for our Souls. Wherever we go we are expected to join with the other Souls there to make the planet as close to "paradise" as we can. Together, we're to complete what God started. In fact, making a meaningful contribution to the collective goal (and helping other Souls to grow, or at least helping to relieve their suffering) is something we each need to do in order to fulfill our own mission.

Values/Beliefs

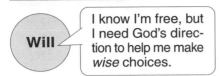

Will — I know I'm free, but I need God's direction to help me make *wise* choices.

Some people say there are no "shoulds"—that Souls are not required to behave in any prescribed way. That is true to the extent we are free to choose as we will. But the path that will take us to a higher state of godliness has certain rules and guidelines. *God's Values and Beliefs* are based primarily on *love*—for one's self, for others, and for all She created. Early on, our Souls had to make the Big Choice—would we do our best to be good Souls? Most, but not all of us, said "yes." On Earth, we struggle everyday to honor our pledge to God. So, before we make a choice to say or do something, we need to ask, "Is this in accordance with God's Values and Beliefs?" If it is, we can proceed with a clear conscience.

Multiple Lives

This isn't our only time here.

last life   next life

I couldn't possibly reach my full potential in one life. So I will keep "getting physical" until I do.

Each life is another episode in our Soul's learning process. We carry over our lessons and develop our talents from life to life. We play different roles each time so we can become a well-rounded Soul. God wants us to make the most of this life, but the eternal destiny of our Soul is not determined by this one trip to the Physical World.

Most of us are near the *beginning* of the reincarnation cycle, and collectively, we have had relatively little time to create "Heaven on Earth." So, it is no wonder this and preceding lifetimes have been so difficult. Eventually, we will make it so our Souls are eager to return to Earth because the pleasures will outweigh the pain.

Buddha speaks

I'm a wise, old Soul – and you can be one too.

Surely, God Wouldn't Limit Us to Just One Life

(We) will come back, come back again, as long as
   the red Earth rolls.
(God) never wasted a leaf or a tree. Do you think He
   would squander souls?
Rudyard Kipling – British poet; 1865–1936

Kindred Souls

No One Is Truly Alone

A lot of Souls love you.

Each of us is part of a circle of Souls who enjoy being together. These are our *kindreds*. We are drawn to them because they help us to grow, or we like their energy (at least on a spiritual level). We tend to incarnate together and play key roles in each other's lives. If we're lacking family and friends on Earth, we are *always* in the company of loving and supportive Souls, including Angels and Guides. They are sending us love from the Spirit World. The best way to find our kindreds on Earth is by doing what we love. Still, the focus is not on the quantity of kindreds we can find but on the *quality* of our relationships. The goal is to make the earthly bond as strong as the spiritual one—but that is never easy to do.

Our Soul Mate

If you haven't found me yet, don't give up. But don't expect me to be perfect. I will have human weaknesses like everyone else. If we're already together, let's take our love to new heights. And if I'm not on Earth, I will send you my love from the Spirit World.

Cosmic Laws

Karma

Be careful of what you say and do for it just might happen to you. That is the law of *karma*—the "force" that follows us from life to life. Karma is not the sole cause behind the state of our life, and we can always take actions to prevent bad karma.

Change is the one sure thing. • Take nothing for granted. Bad stuff can happen to good people at any time. • Suitable conditions are required for our lives to flourish. • Nothing physical lasts forever, but our Souls do and love can. • If we don't supply energy, things will fall apart, even relationships with Kindred Souls. • We live in a universe of "dualities." Some of the suffering comes with the territory, but a lot of it is self-inflicted and within our control to reduce or eliminate—which is one of the lessons we're all here to learn. • Everyone and everything is interdependent. • There are "windows of opportunity." We must live fully while we can. • It only takes one body (celestial or human) to make all the difference in the world!

God Has Sent Us On Our Way, But We're Always Connected

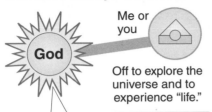

Me or you

Off to explore the universe and to experience "life."

Bon voyage, My child. I know life won't be easy, but do your best to be a good Soul. Stay in touch with Me. I love you.

Here on this beautiful but overcrowded planet, where most of us are struggling to lead satisfying lives (and too many people can only try to survive), it is hard to imagine we are spiritual beings made in the image of God. But we are.

Also, the notion of expanding our Soul's energy and becoming even more godlike may seem implausible or, at best, a distant dream. But it is doable.

Indeed, God knows we can make progress towards that goal, even in this challenging environment. If, by the end of our journey, we feel we have learned some valuable lessons and, *on balance,* we were more loving than hurtful, then we will have grown. Our Soul will have become more radiant, and we will move closer to God.

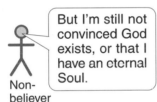

But I'm still not convinced God exists, or that I have an eternal Soul.

Non-believer

Even if I'm not real, it is a miracle that you're all here—and it matters a great deal what you do with your lives and what happens to the Earth.

Only good can come from living by My Values and Beliefs and believing you are on a mission of personal growth.

I have told a story in this part of the book that, for the most part, cannot be proven. Still, I hope you will agree with me that even though one can lead a good life without believing in God, it would sure make it more meaningful if this story were true. Finally, there is nothing to be lost in acting as if God is real and that we are here to learn how to be *loving, joyful and creative.*

Now, it's time to get "down to Earth" and to see out how we can make the most of this life.

Part II – Down to Earth

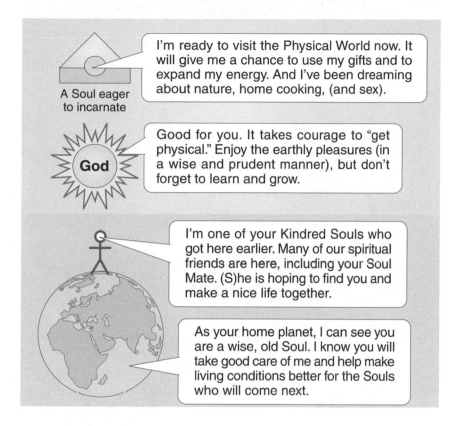

Our Souls like coming to the Earth because it is such a beautiful planet, and there is so much to see and do. They long for the chance to experience the sensations of the physical body, to use the powers of the intellect and to feel human emotions. Of course, they also come to learn how to make wise choices.

Part II looks at how we got here, why we got the kind of life we did and who we are on Earth. It examines other broad subjects too, including—love and forgiveness, being creative and making choices, what else affects our reality, the elements of life that we need to be fulfilled, and the pursuit of happiness. We will also cover these topics: family and friends, children, work, life partners, sex, and aging. Part II is meant to help us understand what we are trying to do here and how we might do it better. We will conclude this part by considering what happens when the journey is over and we die and return to the Spirit World.

This picture of the "Earth-rise" was taken from the Apollo 8 spacecraft as it orbited the moon in 1968. Maybe our Souls have a similar perspective of Earth when they're arriving to be born.

(NASA photo)

What It Means to "Get Physical"

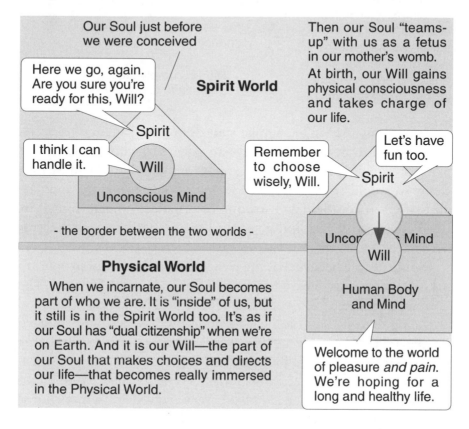

Incarnating, or "getting physical," is a union of cosmic proportions. Miraculously, a Soul is able to join forces with a newly conceived human being so it can experience *physical* life. It is like two parts of a spaceship, both of which are required to make the journey and accomplish the mission, coming together and "docking." For as long as the two elements are coupled we have the ability in this realm to manifest our love and joy and to create new realities. This union is also like a marriage between two people. Together, they can do wonders—indeed, things they could not do on their own. But they also have to cope with the many challenges that inevitably come up during their time together.

We are spiritual beings living as humans in the Physical World.

Our **"life situation"** defines the overall condition in which our Soul will experience its earthly adventure. It includes the mental and bodily traits we receive, as well as the economic, family and physical environment into which we are born.

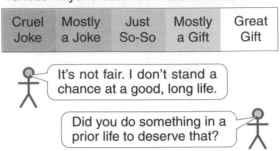

Some Get a Nicer Life Than Others
Various ways to describe one's life situation:

Cruel Joke	Mostly a Joke	Just So-So	Mostly a Gift	Great Gift

It's not fair. I don't stand a chance at a good, long life.

Did you do something in a prior life to deserve that?

We are not all born in a similar state or into similar circumstances. Why is that? As Souls, did we have any say as to who would be our parents? Could we choose the state of our mind or body? Did we pick where we would be born or which socioeconomic group we would be part of? Were all the details of our incarnation predetermined by God? Or are we each simply given the life situation our Soul deserves because of past karma?

Some people believe that the rich, smart or beautiful people are the Souls who must have been good choosers in prior lifetimes. The notion is that these people accrued a lot of positive karma points and are being rewarded in this life. The poor, disabled or disadvantaged people are the less evolved Souls who are being punished for being bad in the past, or they're in their current state because they have lessons to learn. Such explanations might be true in *some* cases, but in general, they are much too simplistic. Very evolved Souls may choose to incarnate into difficult situations to help those in a similar state. Not so evolved Souls may be born rich so they can learn how to live with humility and to help others by sharing their wealth.

Growing up as a Catholic I was taught that my Soul did not exist before this lifetime and that I had no choice in my incarnation. The situation I got was, in effect, the luck of the draw. A Soul was needed for the baby my parents conceived, and I was it. This means the Souls of everyone in my family were virtual strangers, meeting for the first time and with no prior history together. As I see it now, the act of getting physical is more involved than just karma or some spiritual lottery. Our *preexistent* Souls are very involved in the process. In fact, before each life we are asked to prepare a plan describing the conditions we would like to experience. There is no guarantee we will get what we want, but it's important we state our preferences.

A Summary of a LIFE PLAN Prepared By An "Incoming" Soul

Destination – Earth; number of prior lifetimes on this planet: 7

The Big Mission – to expand my energy by bringing as much love, joy and creativity as I can into all I say, think and do.

My incarnation preferences – to be a woman (race is unimportant, but black would be nice); born in the United States (ideally in a warm climate); to come of age during the 1960's; and to be part of a close-knit family. I don't need to be born into wealth, but I would rather not be poor. I've been there and done that.

What I really need to do – overcome the influence of fear; learn to treat other humans and the rest of God's creations with respect and kindness; and learn to love myself.

I also have some special issues I need to resolve, including learning how to be more forgiving. In my last lifetime I was too bitter toward my parents. Plus, I must deal with the karma of having been so greedy and hurtful in my fifth lifetime. I can do that by being of service to others this time around.

My electives (what I really want to do) –

My higher vision – to use my gifts and "Let there be" power to help create more peace and beauty on Earth. I want to inspire others and reduce the amount of suffering.

More specifically, I would like to build upon my prior lifetimes and further develop my talents as an artist and musician. And this time I would like to try being a writer.

I want to find some of my Kindred Souls, and I would like to find a life partner and create a loving family; I want intimate friendships and to be part of a community of like-minded Souls.

Of course, I want to see the world and enjoy nature, especially the mountains and old growth forests (if there are any left).

Typically, a lot of thought goes into these plans. We do a Life Review after each incarnation to see what lessons we still need to learn, and we consult with our Spirit Guides. Some Souls choose not to make a plan. They go through life without direction or purpose.

There are Souls who ask for life situations that are especially challenging. They want to face many of their biggest fears all in one lifetime so they can accelerate their growth. When we look at someone who has suffered greatly we shouldn't think, "What did he or she do wrong?" Instead, we can imagine they have a courageous Soul, which could be true even if they didn't specifically ask for a difficult life.

Our Life Plan reflects our Soul's state of spiritual development prior to this lifetime. It includes what we hope to learn and how we hope to express our gifts. Our preferences represent the life attributes our Soul "resonates" with. For example, it may be our goal to make a contribution to a specific place or group of people. Or we feel that being of a particular race or sex would provide the best opportunity to apply our special talents. Or maybe our Soul just likes the food and music of a given culture.

We're Planning To Be a "Family"

Before we (or our parents) incarnated, we had a telepathic chat to discuss our desire to be their child in our upcoming "reality play." We covered a wide range of issues, including how we could help each other to grow and whether we would be their first child if they had more than one. The interesting point is we had this type of meeting with several sets of Kindred Souls because there is no guarantee our "preferred couple" will actually meet and conceive a child.

A Soul's telepathic connection with its prospective parents remains in place after the parents have incarnated. So, if a woman or man gets a recurring and powerful urge to have a child, it *might be* a Kindred Soul-in waiting giving him or her a gentle nudge. Of course, that isn't reason enough to actually "do it." We need to be sure we're ready before we bring a kindred into this world.

It's a School With Great Playgrounds

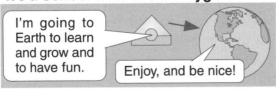

Life is not meant to be something we must "get through" so we can be happy after death. God wants us to enjoy the journey itself—and to help the people who can't create a joyful life on their own.

Life is a very special occasion for our Soul. Experiencing the wonders of the Physical World and the pleasures of being human are an important part of our mission—which is why every Soul includes lots of fun time in its Life Plan.

Now Meet the "Casting Director"
(This is the most fanciful part of the story.)

Every planet has special Angels assigned to it. We don't have wings or halos, but we've got lots of energy.

It's my job to help you find a life situation that will meet your needs for spiritual growth.

Sadly, I also find Souls to volunteer to be the children destined for real pain and suffering.

The Angels are responsible for coordinating the incarnation process. They review our Life Plan, monitor what's actually happening on Earth and place us in a specific life situation which may or may *not* be what we had desired.

It's possible a Soul will be told it "must" experience a certain kind of situation because of its harmful actions in a prior life. The Soul might complain at first, but then it will realize that it can't get around the law of karma. If it is to progress spiritually it will need to accept its earthly assignment, just like a student must take certain required classes to graduate.

A Summary of the Four Possible Incarnation Scenarios

1. We got the life situation we wanted, or close to it. It might be great, *or* it could be the major challenge we requested.

2. It is a karmic situation. We got a bad life (or a good one) because of what we did in one or more prior incarnations.

3. We took what was available—because it met some of our criteria, or it was the only way to be with our Kindred Souls.

4. We volunteered for hazardous duty. (See the text below.)

It's time to play "Let's choose a life." Which scenario will it be?

It's the spiritual version of a "game show." Any choice involves risk.

| Life #1 | Life #2 | Life #3 | Life #4 |

Until we make this world a less painful place to live, the Earth Angels must look for volunteers to incarnate. They need to find Souls who are willing to inhabit the bodies of children born into very bad or hopeless situations—such as an AIDS or crack baby, a child born in a famine or war area or a child born with a fatal disease or severe impairment. Sadly, the Angels have to ask for a lot of volunteers.

The Souls who volunteer to become these unfortunate children are the real heroes of the Spirit World. They won't have the opportunity to fully enjoy life or to grow up and make adult choices. Instead, by coming to Earth they're teaching the rest of us lessons about love and compassion, about the need for good people to intervene against harmful behavior and for persons in science and medicine to find cures for diseases. Because of their selfless service to humankind, volunteer Souls receive a large increase in their spiritual energy and thus move closer to God.

> In every child who is born, under no matter what circumstances, and of no matter what parents, the potentiality of the human race is born again; and in him, too, once more, and of each of us, our terrific responsibility toward human life ...
>
> James Agee – American writer; 1909–55

Now remember what we told Forrest Gump's mom: "Life is like a box of chocolates. You never know what you're gonna get."

There is no guarantee that a chosen life situation will work out as our Soul might have hoped it would. Just before our birth, an Earth Angel said to our Soul— "Here's a situation that is *likely* to provide you with the conditions and events you desire. But how your life will actually unfold is not predetermined. I can only send you off in a direction that appears to be right for the lessons you want to learn. You should *expect the unexpected,* and be aware that what other people, especially your parents, choose to do will have a profound effect on your life. Of course, the choices you make, including how you respond to what others do to you, usually matter the most."

Every unborn baby is susceptible to the effects of fate which may be for the better or the worse. He or she might receive an extra allotment of intelligence or be born with a serious challenge. Our Soul probably had a good idea of what kind of mind and body it was going to get, but the unexpected might have happened *even while we were in our mother's womb.* Indeed, some of us received our biggest obstacle, or gift, in life before we were even born.

One of the Biggest Unknowns: Do We Have Time to Spare?

I wish you'd tell me how much time I've got to carry out my mission.

I can't say. It depends a lot on the choices you make.

Time is nothing in the Spirit World. On Earth, we need to treat every minute as a gift.

When Souls begin their journey they know it is a "round trip," but most don't know how long it will take. (Some of the "volunteers" do.) As a rule, the length of our lifetime is not predestined. There are several factors that determine how long we will live. I will cover them in the chapter *What Else Affects Our Reality*.

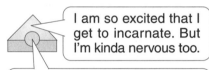

I am so excited that I get to incarnate. But I'm kinda nervous too.

No human mind or body is perfect. And all those earthly temptations. But I'm hoping to have a great time being alive.

Souls tend to approach life hopeful and enthusiastic. Yet, they know it won't be easy, and the nature of their journey depends a lot on the choices made by Kindred Souls already on Earth. Again, life is like a "relay race." We want our parents to create a good environment for us, and the Souls who might be *our* children have similar hopes.

We Begin "Predisposed" to a Path

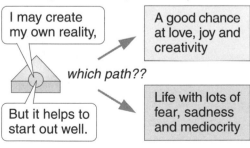

I may create my own reality,

A good chance at love, joy and creativity

which path??

But it helps to start out well.

Life with lots of fear, sadness and mediocrity

Of course, we don't all end up on a promising path, which isn't necessarily just our parent's fault. Collectively and historically, we have let a lot of incoming Souls down by allowing poor life conditions to persist.

Still, for many of us it isn't where we "land" when we incarnate that is most important but rather what we land with—namely, the amount of spiritual energy we possess, the strength of our Will, and our intentions for what we will do on Earth. If our life situation is different from what we would like it to be, our Soul is hoping we will find the strength and courage to change what we can and to put ourself on a more fulfilling path.

I'm fortunate. I am basically able to choose my path "at will." Others are stuck on the path of sadness, for reasons beyond their control.

Life is what we make it—always has been, always will be.

Grandma Moses
American painter; 1860–1961

God

If you're on a good path, I hope you will help those who aren't and who want a better life. But don't assume that everyone who has less "stuff" than you isn't happy. Freedom to choose and the ability to create one's reality is the Soul's measure of happiness.

You must remember this — you are all interconnected and your mission is not just to tend to your own needs. Be good to yourself, but also be of service to others. Doing so is the best way to expand your Soul's energy.

Incarnating Is a Major Shock to Our Soul

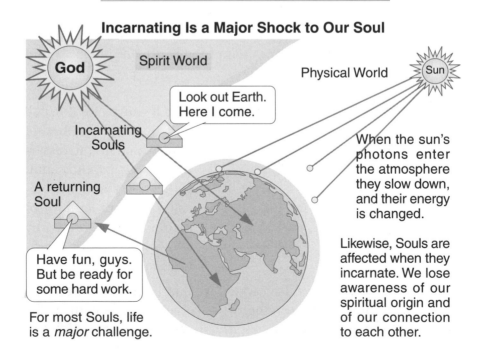

God

Spirit World

Physical World

Sun

Look out Earth. Here I come.

Incarnating Souls

A returning Soul

When the sun's photons enter the atmosphere they slow down, and their energy is changed.

Have fun, guys. But be ready for some hard work.

Likewise, Souls are affected when they incarnate. We lose awareness of our spiritual origin and of our connection to each other.

For most Souls, life is a *major* challenge.

When we incarnate and enter the denser reality of the Physical World, our Soul's vibrational rate slows down quite a bit. (Like everything that exists, our Soul vibrates at a frequency appropriate for its natural state, which for spiritual beings happens to be very fast.) This step-down in frequency doesn't affect our Soul's ability to travel among the stars, but it can give our Will a bad case of *spiritual amnesia.*

We forget where we came from and why we are here. We also forget God's Values and Beliefs, forcing us to learn them all over again here on Earth. We lose sight of our spiritual nature and of our immortality. Our Will is exposed to the passage of time and to the effects of aging on our human mind and body. Frankly, the whole process of getting physical is quite a shock to our system. We choose to do it because it helps us grow.

Actually, the amnesia doesn't happen completely at the time of our birth. As infants, we still have some sense of our spiritual origins and of our mission. But after just a few years in this very material world most of us lose that awareness entirely.

And so the journey of life begins—our quest to rediscover why we incarnated and to reestablish our awareness of and connection with the Spirit World.

You need to create a reality that reflects your Soul's Life Plan. But first, it's essential that you understand who you are in the Physical World. That is the subject of the next chapter.

PS. It's not a given that you must suffer "spiritual amnesia." Children brought up in an "enlightened" and less materialistic environment will retain much of their spiritual awareness.

Who We Are On Earth

When We Incarnate, We Become a "Reality Maker"
The union of body, mind and Soul

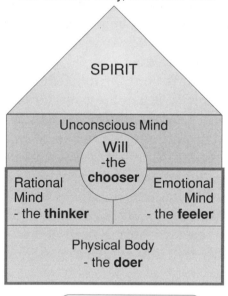

SPIRIT

Unconscious Mind

Will
-the **chooser**

Rational Mind
- the **thinker**

Emotional Mind
- the **feeler**

Physical Body
- the **doer**

As a Reality Maker, I can implement my Soul's Life Plan.

We are wondrous beings, capable of incredible things. We can think, feel emotions, sense the pleasures of the physical world—and make our dreams come true.

Each of us is a *Reality Maker,* with six amazing elements—three parts from our Soul (Spirit, Unconscious Mind and Will) and three earthly components (a Rational Mind, an Emotional Mind and our Physical Body). It is the union of these elements that gives us the power to be loving, joyful and creative here on Earth. If we're a Reality Maker who's in a positive and harmonious state, there is virtually no limit on what we can do.

Carl, he's making it too simple.

Sigmund Freud   Carl Jung

Don't worry. This is not meant to replace your theories of psychology.

(Photos: CORBIS/Bettmann)

In explaining "who we are," I can only scratch the surface of a complex subject. Still, the "model" and concepts put forth in this chapter do, in their simplicity, work well for me. They help me to better understand myself and to appreciate the potential we all have to create better realities. Besides, it's best if I leave the details of psychology to the experts.

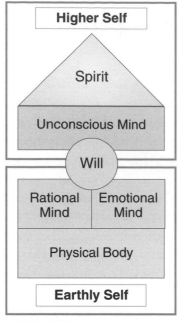

The Will spends most of its time with our Earthly Self, but it is connected with our Higher Self too.

Every Reality Maker can be viewed as having two "Selves." The Spirit and Unconscious Mind (two of our soulful parts) are called the *Higher Self.* Our three human elements are called the *Earthly Self.* The distinction is made because the Soul exists at a higher or more vibrant level than the human mind and body. Think of the Will as the "go between," holding our two Selves together.

We can't be really fulfilled in life unless *both* Selves are engaged and working jointly. But most of us are not tapping into the power of our Higher Self. We're living as if we were "only human" and not creating at our full potential. Reconnecting with our Higher Self is a key goal, which I will come back to later. Now, let's take a look at each of the six elements.

1. The Spirit ... the *energetic* part of a Soul, which is always connected with God.

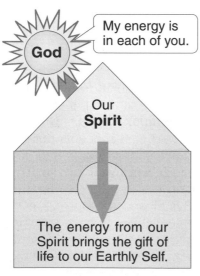

The energy from our Spirit brings the gift of life to our Earthly Self.

Our Spirit vitalizes every cell in our body with its divine energy. As we live in accordance with God's Values and Beliefs, we receive more spiritual power. And that allows us to be even more loving, joyful and creative!

The Spirit element of our Soul exists within *and* apart from our Earthly Self. It fills our body, but it is not solely in the Physical World. When we are sleeping, our Soul can visit with kindreds in the Spirit World or see the wonders of the universe. Our Soul can be "here (within our body), there and everywhere."

> The word **spirit** is defined as "the vital and essential force within living beings." It is from the Latin word *spiritus,* which means "breath"—as in the breath of God. The Spirit within each of us hopes we will use our divine energy in ways that honor God.

2. The Unconscious Mind ... the Soul's multipurpose element

Records everything from this lifetime – all we say, think, feel and do, and all that happens to us – (for use in our Life Review)		
Stores memories from our past lives; retains "collective" human memories		Keeps the essence of our special, God-given talents
Accesses knowledge from the Spirit World	Talks with other Souls telepathically	Generates ideas and helps solve problems
Sends us insights and messages from our Higher Self and other Souls via intuition – and by creating our nightly dreams		

The Unconscious Mind is a powerful and *positive* influence in our life—not some dark and mysterious force responsible for us acting or thinking badly. For example, it plays a critical role in our creative process. Whenever we develop a vision or image in our head of something we want to do or have, the Unconscious Mind marshals the appropriate resources in the Spirit World to help make it real. This is especially true if what we desire is aligned with our Soul's Life Plan. If we need information or an idea, our "unconscious" might send it to us directly through our intuition, or it might get in touch with other Unconscious Minds (belonging to Souls who are also incarnated and who could help us). Together, they would coordinate some sort of encounter between our respective Earthly Selves. To us, it will seem like just a coincidence. But such events are really the handiwork of our dynamic Unconscious Mind.

> The unconscious is ... the source of the highest good ... (it is) superhuman, spiritual, and ... divine.
>
>   Carl Jung – Swiss psychiatrist; 1875–1961

> ## *... the "Chooser" and "Agent of the Soul"*
>
> ### 3. The WILL
>
> Takes input from all of the elements, but it's in charge and responsible for our life
>
> Is at its best when guided by God's Values and Beliefs
>
> Has to rediscover our Soul's Life Plan and create "visions" and goals to motivate us
>
> Requires good role models and "trial and error" in order to become a wise chooser
>
> Acts as the organizing force for the Reality Maker
>
> Provides determination, discipline and judgment
>
> Maintains a close relationship with our Higher Self
>
> At times, has to deny our Earthly Self what it wants

We come to Earth to have fun but also to show God we can learn and grow—and that we can make choices that reflect the essence of our Soul (love, joy and creativity). Therefore, it is our Will, as the "chooser," who has the most to prove on this earthly adventure. It is, of course, no easy task given the trials and tribulations it must face. It is not uncommon for a Will to feel at times that life is too hard, and that it wishes to "throw in the towel." But most find the strength to carry on. The Will is also responsible for remembering our Soul's Life Plan and discovering our special talents so we can pursue our calling. For most of us this too is a difficult task, and so I will return to it several times in the book.

4. The Rational Mind ... the "thinker"
5. The Emotional Mind ... the "feeler"

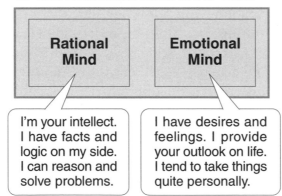

Rational + Emotional = Our Conscious Mind

Close your eyes and try to sit quietly. It's not easy because of all the activity going on in your head. One or both sides of your conscious mind is talking to you.

The intellectual part of our brain is called the *Rational Mind*. It is curious by nature and wants to find answers to the problems and mysteries of life. To help the Will make choices, it provides objectivity and common sense. It also likes to keep us busy, thinking about new ideas and things to do. To be totally effective, a Rational Mind requires a good education and a lifelong commitment to learning.

The *Emotional Mind* is a truly wonderful part of who we are. Without it, we could not experience on Earth the feelings that come naturally to our Soul. Indeed, our Emotional Mind loves to be in love, to have fun and be passionate, to feel good about the Reality Maker that it is part of, and to be kind and compassionate toward others. But it can also be temperamental and move quickly into a state marked by fear or anger or even hate. Of course, it can feel sorrow too. As the source of our earthly feelings, the Emotional Mind puts a smile on our face and makes us cry.

One of the major challenges of having an Emotional Mind is that it acts as an "inner critic" and judge. It can be very harsh with its opinions. When we are in this state it is virtually impossible to create a positive reality or to enjoy the pleasures of life.

We're Separate *and* Connected

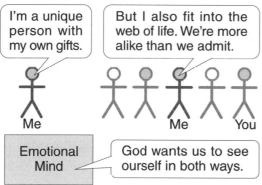

We want to feel we are unique in the world, which we are. But our Emotional Mind also tends to exaggerate the differences between us, instead of seeing our similarities and that we are all from God. When our need to feel different makes us believe we are *better* than others the results are usually not good. Feelings of superiority have led many a Reality Maker to acts of discrimination and violence. So, the Emotional Mind is key to creating peace on Earth. It is okay (and necessary) to feel unique, but we also need to appreciate our common heritage and connection to each other.

Don't emotions come from me?

It may seem inappropriate to describe the part of us that feels as the Emotional *Mind*—still, our feelings do originate in our brain. However, they don't stay there. We experience and express them through different parts of our body. For example, love, joy and grief are "heartfelt" emotions while anger and fear are usually felt in the "gut."

Furthermore, our thoughts and feelings are not contained within our body. They're forms of energy like television signals that move through space and can have a far-reaching effect. Negative thoughts and feelings, such as intolerance and hate, can actually pollute the "energetic atmosphere" of our home, neighborhood and the whole planet. So, we need to be careful as to what we put "out there."

I thought I had just one mind.

Yes, that's right. The "Rational" and "Emotional" are two aspects of our conscious mind. But since they play such different roles in our reality making, it is useful to give them their own identities. Just as we say the brain has two sides (left and right), we can say our mind has two elements.

6. The Body ... the "temple" for our Soul and home of our conscious mind. It's to be treated with respect.

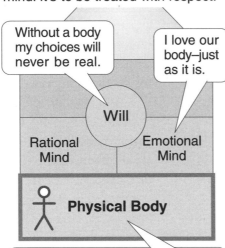

Without a body my choices will never be real.

I love our body—just as it is.

Will

Rational Mind

Emotional Mind

Physical Body

Please take good care of me, and don't make choices that will shorten my life. I have my hands full dealing with aging and fate.

Our body contains the matter of life, including the stardust that came from that ancient supernova. As the *doer* part of our Reality Maker, it is responsible for taking the action that is necessary to make our dreams come true. Of course, it also can experience the sensual pleasures of life (e.g. eating, drinking, holding hands etc., not to mention the joy of sex—which I will cover in a later chapter). And sadly, it must also endure pain—some of which is beyond our control and too much of which is caused by us.

We Tend To Be Self-Destructive

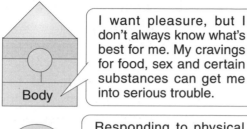

Body

I want pleasure, but I don't always know what's best for me. My cravings for food, sex and certain substances can get me into serious trouble.

Will

Responding to physical desires and taking care of the body are two of my most difficult challenges.

Higher Self

I hope my Will does its best to keep our body strong and vital – for as many years as possible – so I can achieve my mission and Life Plan.

Our body isn't perfect, and bad things will happen to it even if we make wise choices. Our Soul accepts that, but it also feels very sad when we deliberately cause our body to be harmed. We have things to do, places to see and people to meet and love. Our Soul wants and needs all the time it can get.

The good news is our body is doing its best to keep us going. It is regenerating itself by continuously making new cells. That doesn't mean we can live forever or overcome every disease. Rather, it is a sign that God gives us multiple chances to change our ways and to heal ourselves.

> If anything is sacred, the human body is sacred.
> Walt Whitman – American poet; 1819–92

Our Elements Are "Linked" To Each Other

Soul

Mind

Body

Breathing is the activity that unites us and that circulates our life energy. Slow, deep breathing is most beneficial.

A Reality Maker exists in a delicate balance. For example, an ailing or distressed body will impair the state of our conscious mind. Emotional anxiety will at best physically exhaust us, and it might even result in actual illness. And negativity of any kind will restrict the flow of energy and wisdom coming from our Soul.

Of course, it works the other way too. Enhancing the state of any element can have a positive and empowering effect on the others. For example, emotional healing is good for our immune system, and it is good for our Soul.

Every Reality Maker Needs a Strong Foundation

As Souls, we chose whether to honor God's Values and Beliefs. On Earth, we must also decide whether we will abide by them.

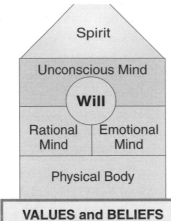

Our **character** is defined by the strength and goodness of our Will, and whether we're making wise and moral choices.

> Let all thy plans and behavior have a sound foundation.
>
> Amen-em-apt – magistrate of Egypt; c5300 BCE

"I value my freedom, as well as honesty and loyalty in my relationships. I believe we are all children of God and that it is wrong to hurt each other." These are examples of the principles and spiritual truths that underlie a wise and moral Reality Maker.

Whether or not we will choose to live by God's Values and Beliefs while we're on Earth is a complicated issue. We begin our journey in a vulnerable and impressionable state. As children, we're exposed to a lot of influences—parents, teachers, friends, clergypersons, and of course the media. Given the mixed messages we receive, it is a challenge for any Will to develop a positive and moral foundation.

The quality of our life is greatly affected by the nature of our Values and Beliefs. For example, if we don't see ourself as a spiritual being here on a mission, or if we don't believe other people should be treated with kindness and respect, then we're bound to make harmful choices.

It is also possible (indeed, it is very common) for people to have positive Values and Beliefs but then not to act in accordance with them. For example, some parents have "family values" and believe the children should come first but are neglectful or even abusive. Such a parent probably knows better, but there is something wrong with their Will or Emotional Mind (such as a lack of self-love) that is causing them to be disconnected from their moral foundation.

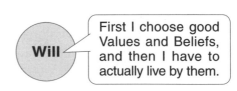

A Quick Look At Some Reality Maker Dynamics

In the next few pages, I present some of the inner workings of the Reality Maker I find most interesting. As I said before, this chapter is not meant to replace traditional views of human psychology. Nevertheless, these concepts have helped me understand why I am like I am and why I might want to change.

Traveling Through Time With Our Emotional Mind
The mind likes to wander and exist outside the "here and now."

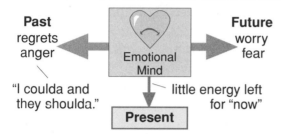

Past
regrets
anger

"I coulda and
they shoulda."

Emotional Mind

little energy left
for "now"

Present

Future
worry
fear

It's all about energy.
"Mind travels" divert our energy away from the present. By not "living in the moment," our reality becomes more like what we're worried about.

Thoughts of the past and future don't go away easily, nor should they. For they make us aware of the areas of our life that need attention. Regrets and anger remind us of what has not gone well so we can either (a) take responsibility for what we did and learn how to make better choices (so the past won't repeat itself), or (b) see the need to forgive others or ourself (so we can release those feelings and move on with our life). And while most fears and worries are unfounded, some may be warning us about an area of our life that is headed for real trouble.

Mental time traveling is a call to action. If we don't respond, our thoughts will become a permanent drain on our energy. Ironically, this will create more regrets and worries—because we will either repeat the past or experience the future we fear.

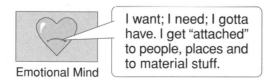

Emotional Mind

I want; I need; I gotta have. I get "attached" to people, places and to material stuff.

It is both natural and healthy for us to have desires and to form emotional ties in life. But when we get *too* attached to physical things we set ourselves up for future sadness and suffering—either because we sacrificed too much to get them or because things wear out or can be taken from us in various ways.

There Is a Battle Going On

Who's in charge of our choosing?

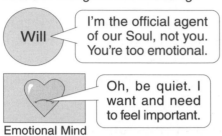

Will — I'm the official agent of our Soul, not you. You're too emotional.

Emotional Mind — Oh, be quiet. I want and need to feel important.

One of the most powerful statements we can make is: *"I Will."* This declaration focuses our time, energy, and mental and physical resources so we can achieve a goal that is important to our Soul. But, we're not always so dedicated or "willful." That's because the Emotional Mind likes to be in charge too. If we're doing things because we're feeling overly needy, or seeking the unnecessary approval of others, or responding to a fear that is uncalled-for, then our Emotional Mind is in control of our actions. Chances are high we are doing things that are not in our best interest and that may be harmful to others.

Don't Disparage Our Emotional Side

Emotional Mind — Sure, I have my shortcomings, but I can be positive and loving as well. I like to have fun and to be happy.

So far, I have described some of the unappealing aspects of the Emotional Mind (and I will be presenting even more), but it's not right to think of it as only a troublemaker. It has great qualities too and is doing its best under very difficult circumstances. Besides, it is not the only part of us that might be having a hard time.

No Will Is Perfect; We All Have Flaws

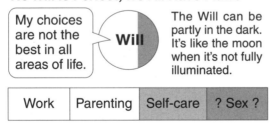

My choices are not the best in all areas of life.

Will

The Will can be partly in the dark. It's like the moon when it's not fully illuminated.

Work	Parenting	Self-care	? Sex ?

We might be successful in one area of our life (such as our career) because we're making wise choices and acting with determination, but we're ineffective or harmful elsewhere. If this is the case, our Will is "compartmentalizing" or being strong in one or more areas and weak in others. Eventually, however, our weaknesses will spill over and hurt the good areas too. So, why do we make poor choices? Partly because we don't receive adequate training in the most important areas of life such as parenting and self-care. We will consider other reasons later in the book.

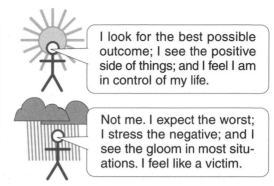

It's more probable your **attitude**, rather than your aptitude, will determine your altitude in life.

(Unattributed)

I look for the best possible outcome; I see the positive side of things; and I feel I am in control of my life.

Not me. I expect the worst; I stress the negative; and I see the gloom in most situations. I feel like a victim.

What Explains Our Attitude?

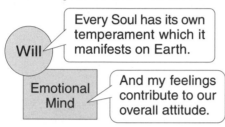

Will

Every Soul has its own temperament which it manifests on Earth.

Emotional Mind

And my feelings contribute to our overall attitude.

Our Will and earthly elements were influenced by our home environment, the experiences of childhood and by our role models. We also inherited part of our outlook from our parents. And if our brain chemistry is off, that can affect our attitude too.

Our current emotional state (including the way we look at ourself and life in general) is not solely the result of conscious choices. It has been shaped by many forces including heredity and our upbringing. Whatever the causes are, we know that our emotional outlook has a profound effect on the quality of our life and that we are better off when we're in a "positive" state.

I may have a negative attitude, but that doesn't mean I can't change it.

A Positive Mind Attracts Good and Repels Bad

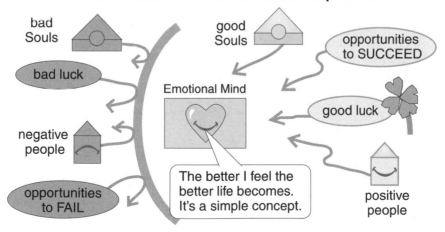

bad Souls

bad luck

negative people

opportunities to FAIL

good Souls

opportunities to SUCCEED

Emotional Mind

good luck

The better I feel the better life becomes. It's a simple concept.

positive people

We won't keep out all the bad stuff, but we will have a lot less of it.

If our Emotional Mind is in a positive state, we will have a much easier and more enjoyable time in life. Not only will we attract positive people and opportunities, but we will also be a lot more creative. The flow of spiritual energy throughout our body will be greatly enhanced, and just being with other positive people fortifies the Will and our passion for life. Of course, we need to appreciate that no one can stay positive all the time.

Sometimes We're "Up" and Sometimes We're "Down"

One aspect of our human mind can be active and in the forefront of our consciousness while the other is in the background waiting to be heard.

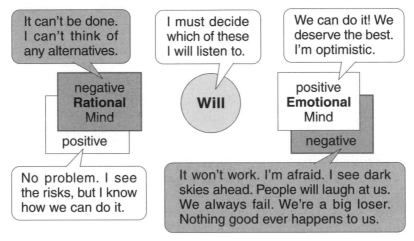

We all have our moments when one or both of our "negative minds" is directing our internal dialogue. If either one of them becomes our *predominant* voice, hold on to your hat, because ...

An Impaired Mind Is a Prescription For Trouble

Our negativity opens the "doors" to other negativity. Like attracts like.

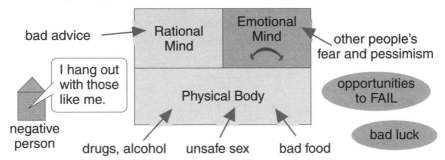

Making choices (especially ones that affect other people) when we are in a negative state usually leads to harmful results and regrets.

> The mind is its own place and in itself can make a hell of heaven or a heaven of hell.
>
> John Milton – English poet; 1608–74

Are They Talking To Me?
Each element has its own "voice"

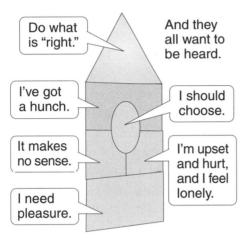

Do what is "right."

And they all want to be heard.

I've got a hunch.

I should choose.

It makes no sense.

I'm upset and hurt, and I feel lonely.

I need pleasure.

It is not as if we actually hear six different voices in our head. Most of us "hear" what appears to be one continuous train of thought. But each part is unique in *what* it is saying and often in *how* it says it. For instance, our body will chime in with a thought of what it is craving and also trigger various biological feelings to get us to listen to it.

The key point is we can learn to make better choices by becoming more aware of "who" is saying what (and *why* they might be saying it). We can also do ourself a great service by listening to the voices coming from the Spirit World.

Making a Connection With Our Higher Self

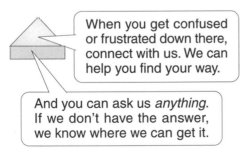

When you get confused or frustrated down there, connect with us. We can help you find your way.

And you can ask us *anything*. If we don't have the answer, we know where we can get it.

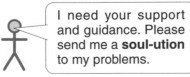

I need your support and guidance. Please send me a **soul-ution** to my problems.

Let's finish this chapter on a positive note by looking at how the Higher Self can become a more active part of who we are. First, think of your Higher Self as your best friend and most trusted advisor. Go ahead and give it a name. I call my Higher Self, "Harvey." Of course, I can't see "him," but I know he is there.

We're sending answers, ideas and warnings – *plus lots of love.*

No one walks alone in life. We have our wise Soul as a companion.

Our Soul wants more than anything for us to lead a happy and fulfilled life. And it knows the Earthly Self can't do it on its own. We need to be "whole" with our Higher Self fully engaged in our reality making.

Intuition is the "tool" of choice for the Higher Self. It is a form of inter-dimensional communication either Self can use. For example, we can ask for our Higher Self's opinion on key life decisions—"Should I take the job? Is she the right person for me? Does buying this house make sense?" Or, we can be more mundane—"Where did I put my glasses?"

Sometimes the Higher Self will take the initiative by sending us messages without having been asked anything. Messages may be sent when there is an impending danger for us to be aware of, or when our Higher Self has an idea it wants us to act on. That idea might come from others in the Spirit World, perhaps even God. Whatever the source, it will be an important message.

The Higher Self can use a variety of ways to communicate with us. It may produce an emotional feeling or a physical sensation (like in the "gut"). We might develop a sense of clarity or calmness, or maybe we will have a helpful dream or even hear voices. Or perhaps we'll just "know" what to do or what the answer is to our question. It will be like a realization or a flash of insight. Finally, we need to be on the watch for those coincidences, or acts of *synchronicity,* when things just sort of happen—like getting a phone call or meeting someone who can help us.

We have to be "listening" to benefit from any intuitive effort, which means being aware and mindful of how our Higher Self expresses itself. Not all Higher Selves do it the same way. And not all answers come promptly. We have to be patient. Finally, if the question we're asking is not in our best interest, or if the timing is not right, we might not get any response. Or it may not be the answer we were hoping to hear. That's alright, because our Higher Self knows what is best for us.

> Each of us has all the wisdom and knowledge we ever need right within us.
> Shakti Gawain; author of *Creative Visualization*

Not only do we need to be a good listener, but we also need to be responsive and take action when we're being "guided" by our Higher Self. It is a sign of respect and will help enhance our intuitive abilities. Besides, I have found that I really regret it when I don't heed the guidance of my Higher Self.

While We Were Sleeping,
our Will took a rest in the Spirit World, and our Unconscious Mind was busy creating our dreams.

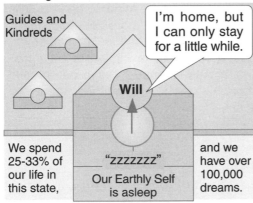

Guides and Kindreds

I'm home, but I can only stay for a little while.

Will

We spend 25-33% of our life in this state,

"zzzzzzz"

Our Earthly Self is asleep

and we have over 100,000 dreams.

Dreams are produced by the brain, but their content is scripted by the unconscious. They're another way for our Higher Self to send us messages. It may be responding to questions we posed during the day, or we might be hearing from one of our spiritual friends. Or perhaps we are being given a vision of what may, or will, happen to us or a loved one. The unconscious talks with images, which our *conscious* mind has a hard time interpreting.

The information that is "out there" in the spiritual dimension can be of unlimited value to our lives, if we tap into it. It can help us to make better choices and to avoid costly mistakes. Examining all the ways we can access that wisdom is beyond the scope of this book. So, I will just list some useful methods to consider, and I will make a brief comment about one of these methods on the next page.

Ways to Connect With Our Higher-Self (and Recharge Our Will)

Develop our intuitive skills	Be in nature and with animals
Record/analyze our dreams	Listen to uplifting or calming music
Ask empowering questions	Be artistically expressive
Practice conscious breathing	Do yoga, tai chi (holistic exercises)
Meditate and pray	Keep a daily journal

Other Benefits: adds a spiritual perspective to life; enhances the flow of self-love and creative ideas; brings strength and inner peace.

By the way, asking "How can I solve my problems?" is an empowering question. "When will my problems end?" is not.

Meditation is a way to put your Reality Maker in "neutral" for a brief moment and to open the communications channel with your Soul. It is not a "New Age" idea or something created in the 1960s. It's been around for thousands of years.

In fact, early Christians were taught how to meditate (and to visualize) as a way of making a personal connection with the life and wisdom of Jesus. Still, many Westerners view people who meditate as weird. (Maybe we're just envious of anyone who can sit still and be at peace.)

Sitting with crossed legs and chanting "Om" is not the only way to meditate. The goal is to quiet the conscious mind, to get the Will above the fray of everyday life and to become more contemplative. I prefer to do T'ai Chi, the Chinese exercise that is "meditation in motion." I also find serenity and harmony by taking walks in nature or by sitting quietly in a hot bath. And whenever I take one of my "meditative moments," I almost always hear something from my Higher Self that can help me in my life.

A Summary of Our Six Elements

1. Spirit
2. Unconscious Mind
3. Will
4. Rational Mind
5. Emotional Mind
6. Physical Body

God: You all have the same elements, but like snowflakes, no two of you are alike.

Each of us is a combination of the spiritual, mental and physical. We weren't all equally "equipped" or equally situated in life. Still, most of us have the capacity to create wonderful realities and to enjoy the pleasures of being alive on this amazing planet.

As Reality Makers we possess great potential, but we face many challenges as well. Our earthly parts are strong and resilient, but they're not perfect—and that makes it hard for us to always make wise and loving choices. And so God is hoping we can find the Will to overcome our weaknesses, to connect with our Higher Self and to rediscover why we came here and what gifts we brought with us. For that is how we will create positive realities for ourself and for others.

Now we'll look at *love*—something every Reality Maker needs.

All We Need Is Love

God Sent Us Off With Love In Our Souls — She Expects Us to Use It

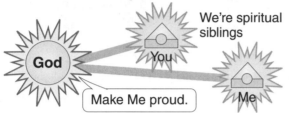

Each of us is on a "mission from God"—to bring the energy of our Soul into the reality of the Physical World. Naturally, it is a very difficult mission. In the Spirit World, we see ourselves as part of God's family. But on Earth, where we are joined with human minds and bodies, we have lost sight of our interconnectedness. Still, it is God's wish that we regain that vision and manifest the love that is within us all.

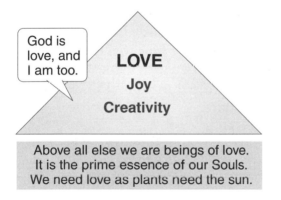

Love is the highest form of energy in the universe. It can heal our troubled world and provide the peace and harmony we all desire. It is the best remedy for fear, which is responsible for so many of our negative realities.

Love is much more than just a feeling of affection or of passion. Love is making choices and acting in ways that can help others (and ourself) to have a more joyful and creative journey. Love is a way of life. It is the path of compassion, respect and kindness for all people and living things. Love is honoring our connection to each other.

The Oneness of Spirit – Everyone and everything, here and everywhere, came from God's divine energy. Love is respecting our common heritage and acting with reverence for all of life.

God Does Not Discriminate

She loves all people, regardless of ... class, religion, race, age, nationality or sexuality.

And She loves all Soul types ... the animals, trees and plants, and Earth.

God loves everyone and everything—and She is asking us to recognize the divinity in all She created and to see past our earthly differences. To believe in our mutual connection with God and to act accordingly is the very essence of love.

> God bless us, everyone.
> Tiny Tim —*A Christmas Carol*

The journey of life can be wondrous and joyful, but it can also be lonely and frustrating. When life is a real struggle we may feel as if no one loves us, not even God. But that is not the case. God *always* loves us, and Her love is *unconditional*. She loves us just as we are, regardless of our faults or how well we have lived. But that doesn't mean She is always pleased with us, or we shouldn't change. Still, God knows we are involved in a physical experience that is not easy for any Soul to endure.

The Many Facets of God's Love

It's nice to hear that "God loves us," but how do we know it's true? And what does it mean? That we exist at all and can experience life is testament to Her love. Granted, life includes much pain and at times can be very difficult, but it also provides many pleasures. Plus, God gave us the freedom and the power to create a better reality for ourselves.

God expresses Her love in many other ways. To help ease our pain, God sends energy to support the compassionate people who minister to the suffering. God responds to our prayers too—usually by giving us a sense of peace and empowerment and occasionally by performing a real miracle. And of course God comforts us when our journey is over, and we return to the Spirit World.

If God didn't love us, then our pains would be permanent (but they're not); our losses would never be restored (but they are—we get to be with our loved ones again); and She would not forgive us for our poor choices (but She does—we can try again, in this life or the next). The best proof that God exists and that She loves us is the creation of children. With the birth of every baby, God is saying "Let there be ... another expression of My love." More than anything, God wants us to be happy and to feel the joy that comes from being creative. But God is sad. She knows many of Her children are really suffering.

> God sends us Her love unconditionally, but we must choose whether we will receive that love.

Opening our heart to receive God's love will enhance our life—for when we accept God's love we acknowledge Her existence. And that allows us to embrace our own spirituality. By sending Her love, God is reminding us that we are very special and it is our divine right to be joyful and fulfilled.

God's love flows freely to our Soul, but it is the state of our Earthly Self that determines whether it touches our everyday life. If we are consumed with fear and other negative feelings, the flow of love is blocked. We open the channel to God's love by staying as positive as we can and by asking Her for help and guidance.

Our Spiritual Sources of Love

Angels and Spirit Guides

God

All of our Kindred Souls

Our Spirit

How do we bring this love into our life?

Prayer and Meditation
Memories of loved ones

All of us are receiving unconditional love from the Spirit World. It is coming from Souls who want only the best for us. Among them are kindreds who once loved us on Earth but have since passed on. Love is eternal; it survives death. For us to feel the peace and comfort this spiritual love provides, we need to believe it exists.

Love Flows From The Soul

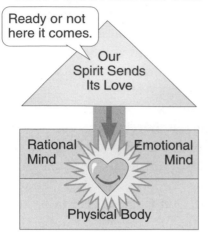

Love is felt and expressed through the heart. Our human "parts" need to be in a positive state if we're to receive our Soul's love.

Acting with love should come naturally to us. Nothing has a more profound effect on our emotional and physical well-being. When we give love we feel good for bringing joy or comfort to others. When we receive love we feel special or consoled in our moments of grief and pain. Just thinking about love can actually make us healthier. It fortifies our body's immune system.

We were all created with an abundance of love in our Souls, and it is the nature of love to flow from our Soul into our heart and then out to the world. But the flow of love can be blocked. Like a dam holding back a river's current, an impaired mind or body can stop our love in its tracks. When love is blocked we think and act selfishly—and bad things happen.

As human beings, we have some strong and persistent negative tendencies, but we also have a great capacity for love. So the challenge is to bring our "good nature" to the forefront of our consciousness. To do that, we need to teach our Emotional Mind some "new tricks" and to break our old patterns. If each day we perform an act of love—no matter how small—we will *eventually* transform ourself, just as the steady flow of water can wear down the hardest stone. Each of us has our own set of issues that block love. We have to make a real effort to overcome them and to open our hearts. God does not expect perfection but only that we do our best to grow.

Love is the most potent force in the universe, but it needs to be called forth. And that is the job of our Will. In each moment of our life, we need to choose whether we will act from a place of love or of fear. When we choose love, we strengthen our connection with God.

SELF-LOVE

Does love flow to our family and friends, but not enough to ourself?

For Others	For Us
	Little or No Love

When we unblock the self-love, we can love others even more.

Self-love is our own unconditional acceptance of who we are, exactly as we are, at this moment in time. To love ourself no matter how we look, regardless of what we have done so far with our life, and in spite of what other people have said or done to us, is one of life's greatest challenges.

There is nothing more important to our happiness and well-being than enhancing the flow of self-love. The way we feel about ourself has a profound effect on every aspect of our life—from how we treat others, to the choices we make about our work and personal relationships. When we love and value ourself, we make choices based on the belief that we deserve the best in life—which, of course, we do.

The most compelling reason why self-love is so important is that it affects our ability to be a good parent. Our self-love, or lack thereof, will impact how our children feel about themselves—which will affect the rest of their lives, the lives of their children, and so on.

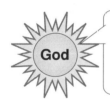

God

Self-love is the greatest love of all. It will transform the quality of your life, and it can have a positive and lasting impact on other people. Self-love is not about ego or selfishness. It is seeing the beauty that is inside of you and being self-accepting.

We Were Born With Lots of Self-Love In Our Soul

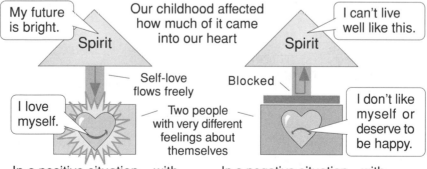

My future is bright.

Spirit

Our childhood affected how much of it came into our heart

Spirit

I can't live well like this.

I love myself.

Self-love flows freely

Blocked

Two people with very different feelings about themselves

I don't like myself or deserve to be happy.

In a positive situation – with parents who love their child, each other and themselves

In a negative situation – with hurtful parents who have self-love problems of their own

As Reality Makers, we begin life ready to feel great about who we are. In fact, Souls are eager to share their love with their Earthly Selves. But this "love transfer" can occur only if one's Emotional Mind is in a positive and receptive state. And one's emotional state is, to a great degree, affected by the experiences of childhood.

If we're raised in a good environment, the self-love can flow freely into our heart, giving us the confidence, self-acceptance and optimism we need to succeed in life. If we're raised in an atmosphere of fear or abuse, the flow of self-love is restricted, or blocked completely. We then become pessimistic and self-doubting, and our life is likely to be a major struggle.

Typical result from childhood

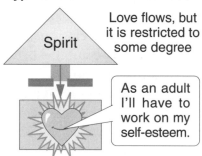

Most of us grow up without the full measure of our Soul's love. Usually it isn't just because of "bad parenting." There are other factors that impede the love. Fortunately, the love is still there, waiting for us to heal our Emotional Mind. When we restore the flow of self-love, our life will be greatly enhanced.

Other Reasons Why Self-Love Gets Blocked (any time in our life)

- Real (or perceived) physical or mental shortcomings
- Thoughtless criticism from others – parents, siblings, peers, etc.
- Society's emphasis on looks, winning, materialism and youth
- Racial and sexual prejudice, poverty, and personal setbacks

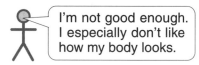

We all have things we don't like about ourselves, generally of a physical nature. We know no one is perfect, but we compare ourselves to the "beautiful" people in the media and judge ourselves as inadequate. Many of us also have the bad habit of frequently saying how flawed we are. We can be very unkind, especially when we universalize our weaknesses with criticisms like: "I *always* screw up," or "I'm *completely* stupid."

Words have incredible power over our Emotional Minds. They can leave an indelible mark on our psyche—for better or worse. So we need to be more aware of what we are saying to ourself *and* to others. This is especially true when it comes to what parents say to their children.

"But I was only joking. I didn't mean to be hurtful."

Acting with love means we choose not to harm others, either physically or emotionally. It isn't loving to make fun of people, or to criticize them, just to satisfy or to amuse ourselves (or to release our anger)—especially if the comments are about physical or mental traits that can't be changed.

We need to be more aware of situations when a joke might produce a very brief laugh and a prolonged hurt. Belittling other people damages their self-esteem. It is immature and a harmful way of compensating for our own insecurities and self-love issues.

Before you say an unkind word, imagine how you would feel if it were said about *you*.

Can I Ever Forgive Myself?

I screwed up my life. I hurt people; I didn't fulfill all of my dreams; and I missed some great opportunities.

Another sign that our love is blocked is an unwillingness to be self-forgiving. If we have intentionally hurt others, we shouldn't let ourself off the hook too easily. But most of us are punishing ourselves for offenses we didn't mean or that happened when we were young and didn't know better. Or, we are beating ourselves up for what we wish we *would have* done.

"Let There Be ... More Self-Love"

Will

Unblocking the love isn't easy, but it can be done. It's up to our Will to find the strength, determination and discipline to change our life and to put us on a path of emotional healing. It begins with a simple, yet powerful statement that we say to ourself.

I love and accept myself exactly as I am. **And** I will do all I can to improve my mind and body.

What We Can Do To Restore the Flow of Self-Love

- ☐ Recognize our divinity
- ☐ Open our heart to God's love and to the love from others
- ☐ Give love and help others without wanting anything in return
- ☐ Accept ourself as we are
- ☐ Forgive ourself for the bad choices we made in the past; promise to do better
- ☐ Make improvements in the state of our Reality Maker, and practice better self-care
- ☐ Change our self-beliefs; say and think nice things about our mind and body
- ☐ Nurture ourself; do what we love and what is joyful; periodically reward ourself for making progress
- ☐ Improve the quality of our "space," especially at home
- ☐ Find a job that uses our gifts
- ☐ Remove or protect ourself from negative people
- ☐ Get professional help?

It Is A Sign of Self-Love and Self-Respect to Just Say "No" ...

and to choose what's in our best interest

Take drugs. Light a smoke. Get drunk. Have unsafe sex. Eat lousy food. etc.

What good will it do me, other than getting your approval? And I can live without that.

"Friends," peers, and advertisers

We may feel alone, but we'll feel better about ourself.

Maybe we need to hang out with more positive people who will raise our energy.

What we choose *not* to do, or whom *not* to be with, is very important too. We need to select only those activities and companions that contribute to our well-being and help us feel good about ourself.

I love my Earthly Self so much.

Spirit

I never knew self-love could feel so good.

Once we start taking steps on the path of self-love, even if they're only little ones at first, the barrier between us and our Spirit will begin to dissolve. The love will flow into our heart and touch all areas of our life.

"I See the Light"

When we look in the mirror and see that we're really a spiritual being that is very special and full of self-love.

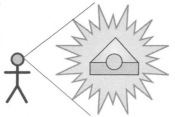

We can enhance the flow of love by reminding ourself that we were created by God and that She made us with Her own divine energy. This means we are not only entitled to a life of love, joy and creativity but we have the inherent power to achieve that goal. When we really believe this, we can begin to change our reality.

God: When you choose to live a better life and realize that you deserve it, that is an act of self-love.

God would also tell us that we are each beautiful in our own unique way. Perhaps we were blessed with an extra special talent, or a very loving heart or a friendly smile. We need to uncover our "gifts" and allow ourself to use them. It is our self-loving path to happiness. We may not think we possess any unique qualities but we do. If we look with loving eyes, we will find them.

Giving Our Love To Others

Remember the "Golden Rule"

What is hateful to thyself do not do to another. This is the whole Law; the rest is commentary.

Hillel–rabbi; 30 BCE–9 AD

Do unto others as you would have them do unto you.

Jesus

God: Great Souls like Jesus and Buddha have shown you how to be loving.

God wants us to be more loving toward ourself and with others, but that doesn't mean we need to love everyone in the same way. For example, the love we feel for our family, especially our life partner or children, is clearly far more intense than what we feel for a casual friend or let alone a stranger. God understands that we all have "special" people in our lives and so there are different levels of love.

– The Three Levels of Love –

Basic Love

I see the divinity in you.
I won't cause needless harm.
I will treat you with respect
  and kindness.
I wish you happiness in life.
I will extend a helping hand.

Higher Love

I think you're very special.
I like to share moments with you.
I will help you achieve happiness,
  and I will try to ease your pain.
I would do almost anything for you.

Highest Love

I can't imagine being without you.
I would give my life for you.

Your love keeps lifting
me higher and higher.

Causing no harm
and treating others
with kindness is the
least I expect. That
alone will begin to
transform the world.

Basic Love is an elaboration of the *Golden Rule*. When we look at another human being, God wants us to see that we both came from Her. She expects us to treat each other with respect and kindness.

The *upper levels* of love are usually reserved for family and close friends. When we love someone at these levels we try to help them feel good about themselves by focusing on their positive traits. Instead of judging them for how they look, or for their "mistakes," we see the beauty and light that exists inside. We support them on their path and encourage them to do whatever brings the most joy into their life. We listen with an open and understanding mind and heart. And we help relieve their pain and suffering.

The extent to which we are willing to give of ourself to another person is what really distinguishes one level of love from the next. Another measure of our love is the degree to which we would miss the other person if they were no longer a part of our life.

To love someone, even at the highest level, doesn't mean that we always have to like them. Sometimes other emotions, such as anger and disappointment, can be involved too. That's okay as long as love is the predominant feeling, and we don't harm the other person. The intensity of our love can change over time too. We may move one person out of the highest level while the love we feel for another soars to new heights. And when a person is no longer active in our life, our love may diminish, perhaps to be rekindled later.

But It's Not Easy To Love

> I love humanity, but I hate people.
> Edna St. Vincent Millay
> American poet; 1892–1950

To treat everyone with respect and kindness (Basic Love) is a wonderful thought, but it can seem unattainable. Spending a few minutes in heavy traffic is all it takes to make you feel it's a lost cause. But it isn't. If we were "only human," the pessimism might be warranted, but we're not. We have Souls, with an unlimited capacity to love. Still, it is not easy to love other people. They look and think differently than we do. They may have different religious beliefs or speak a different language. And we see them as competition for many of the things we want like jobs and homes or just "personal space."

Our Paths In Life Are Different ... but we're all spiritual beings who face similar fears and problems and are in pursuit of common goals.

If you treat each other with love and kindness, you'll both get to where you want to be—in less time and with more joy.

- Love and happiness
- Good health
- Long life
- Creative expression
- Freedom from worry

Let's open our hearts and be loving to each other.

Me   You

Most people are like you and me. They have flaws and they're trying to lead good and decent lives.

We also need to respect our diversity and what is unique about us.

An important first step on the path of love is to stop thinking that other people must believe or behave as we do before they're worthy of our love or of God's love. The next step would be to wish no harm to anyone who is trying to lead a "good life." People living with good intentions deserve a chance to find happiness. That's a loving thought we can all have. We need to remind ourself that love is not something that just happens. Love is a conscious choice we need to make *everyday* and with each person we meet. We can try to remember that how we treat someone can have a "ripple effect," bringing love *or* harm to many others. It also helps to realize we are all part of the "web of life," interconnected and dependent upon each other.

> Let there be ... peace on Earth, and let it begin with me.

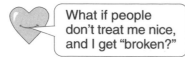
What if people don't treat me nice, and I get "broken?"

Acting with love makes us vulnerable to being hurt. Often, we are opening our hearts without always knowing how the other person will react to our expression of love. To give love requires faith and trust in the goodness of others, which can sometimes be misplaced. But the benefits of love are so great it is worth taking that risk. That is not to say we should rush out and give Higher Love to every person we know or meet. We need to have some sense of the goodness of a person's intentions before opening our hearts that much. Even if we are the most compassionate of Souls, the thought of loving everybody is overwhelming. So we could learn a lesson from Mother Teresa, who said she loved just one person at a time—the one right in front of her at any given moment.

But I also get fearful and angry.

Dealing With Fear and Anger

We need to recognize these emotions when they arise and realize we have a choice as to how we respond to them.

Responding with NO love

> We react with open hostility, or we repress our feelings.
> We stay bitter and resentful.

Responding with love

> We express our true feelings in a calm and direct manner.
> We wish others no harm.

Responding with *more* love

> We find a creative way to make the situation better.
> We wish the other person well.

Fear and anger are normal feelings to have, but it is how we process them that affects the quality of life for us and for the people around us. The goal is to deal with these feelings when they arise so they can pass through us quickly, instead of repressing them or letting them get stuck in our Emotional Mind. Unexpressed fear and anger can become *hate*, which is the most destructive of emotions. If we have love in our hearts, these potentially harmful feelings will come up less often, and when they do, we'll be able to express ourself in a more constructive manner.

Every encounter with other people is a chance for us to act with love. Our actions can transform their emotional state and behavior. Love changes negative energy (fear, anger, hate, etc.) into positive energy (peace, understanding, etc.). Of course, this doesn't always work. Sometimes we have to protect ourself from harm by getting away from the other person or by acting in self-defense. However, we generally make matters worse by responding to negativity with more negativity. As a rule, the best way to bring harmony into a difficult situation is to treat other people as if they were us.

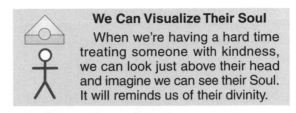

We Can Visualize Their Soul

When we're having a hard time treating someone with kindness, we can look just above their head and imagine we can see their Soul. It will reminds us of their divinity.

The Transformative and Protective Power of LOVE

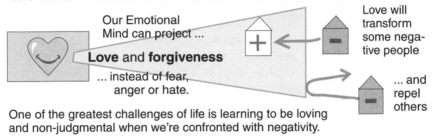

Our Emotional Mind can project ...

Love and **forgiveness**

... instead of fear, anger or hate.

Love will transform some negative people

... and repel others

One of the greatest challenges of life is learning to be loving and non-judgmental when we're confronted with negativity.

EMPATHY is "Walking a Mile in Their Shoes"

We have empathy when we understand and identify with another person's situation, feelings or motives. We "feel their pain."

We need to give most people the benefit of the doubt. Maybe they're being unfriendly because something bad has happened in their life which we don't know about.

It is easier to act kindly, especially toward people who have hurt us or who are behaving badly, if we can *empathize.* This means we imagine what their reality might be like and how we would probably act under similar circumstances. Empathy can also help us deal with the issue of forgiveness. We can try to understand why the other person did what they did, appreciate how difficult it might be for them to say they're sorry, and "sense" the guilt they are probably feeling. Empathy gives us a perspective that can make it easier for us to restore love and to heal damaged relationships. It is an essential part of peacemaking. For when we put ourself in our "adversary's" shoes, we can understand what motivates and concerns them, what scares them, how they view us, and what *we* might have done or said to provoke their anger.

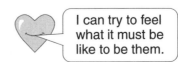

I can try to feel what it must be like to be them.

Most of Us Have a Tendency To Be Way Too Judgmental

We could all become more tolerant and accepting of others. We could listen more, be more supportive, focus on the positives, and give others the benefit of the doubt. Instead, we tend to be judgmental and to criticize others, often for trivial reasons.

We judge people for how they look or where they came from. If they don't believe or behave like us, we think we are better or know more. If someone hurts us (even by mistake), we often assume they had the worst possible motives. We will even "trash" a person for the way he or she is driving or because they did something creatively that we don't like. We can be merciless. Obviously, such judging is not coming from a place of love.

We should want everyone, especially family and friends, to love themselves as they are and to take personal and creative risks. And so, It would be helpful—and an act of love—if we learned to be far less judgmental than many of us are today.

COMPASSION is One of God's Favorite Values

We are being compassionate when we have an awareness of the suffering or special needs of other people (or other living things), and we do something to give relief or to improve the quality of their lives. Compassion is also seeing the divinity in other people and all of creation and doing our very best not to cause harm.

When you help those in need and give your love unconditionally, it expands your energy more than anything.

The upper levels of love are not just for family or close friends. When we choose to help people who are not part of that group but who are in need—because we feel everyone is special and no one should suffer—then we are truly expressing our divinity. Nothing could please God or our Soul more.

Acts of compassion are wonderful not only because they help relieve suffering but also because they highlight the depth of love and goodness that exists within us. I can believe in the possibility of a better future for the world whenever I see someone act selflessly. In the midst of all the negativity, the people who act with compassion are beacons of hope. We should honor them for showing us how to open our hearts.

There are many ways for each of us to be compassionate, from simple acts of kindness to devoting our life to helping others. We each can bring love to the world.

We can be compassionate by tending to the needs of one person, or we can use our creativity to mitigate or eliminate a cause of pain and suffering for lots of people. For example, the scientist working to finding a cure for cancer is acting with compassion. A family planner trying to prevent the suffering of more children in the poor and overpopulated regions of the world is compassionate too. Of course, people trying to save the environment or reduce the needless killing of animals are also compassionate. And so are many others who give of themselves.

One's life has value so long as one attributes value to the life of others, by means of love, friendship, (and) compassion.
Simone De Beauvoir – French writer; 1908–86

God

What we need ... is not division; but love and wisdom, and compassion toward one another, and a feeling of justice toward those who still suffer ...
Robert F. Kennedy; 1925–68

There is a special place in My heart for people who use their "Let there be" power to help others.

Man is here for the sake of other men.
Albert Einstein (a very smart man); 1879–1955

Your act may be very small, it may seem insignificant, but it is very important that you do it.
Mohandes Gandhi; 1869–1948

God expects us to treat other people and living things with kindness and respect. She has asked that we not cause needless harm and that we extend a helping hand to others. Of course, this is a difficult challenge, but it is not beyond our reach. As children of God, we were made to be loving.

God does not ask the impossible.
Canon Law; Decree vi (1564)

There Is No Limit On Our Love
God will send as much as we need

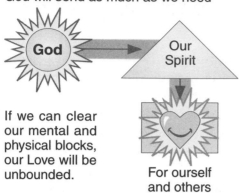

If we can clear our mental and physical blocks, our Love will be unbounded.

For ourself and others

If we decide to open our heart, we don't have to worry about running out of love— even though there will be times when we feel drained and unable to give anymore. If we make love our way of life we will be more creative and passionate. This is the result of our Soul's energy expanding, and it is God's way of saying, "thank you."

The Choice Is Ours To Make

I want more joy and pleasure in my life and less pain and suffering—just like you. If we could treat each other with more kindness and also love ourselves (even just a little more), we would transform our lives and change the world. If we made all of our choices based on love, especially regarding our relationships and work, we would be on a path of greater happiness. Of course, there will be bad moments, but with love in our hearts, we can find the strength to deal with them. *Love* is the answer to our prayers.

And So, Which Shall It Be?

Fear	**Love**
Pessimism	Hope
Disrespect	Optimism
Intolerance	Passion
Hate, etc.	Joy, etc.

Three simple, but powerful statements:

1. **I love God**.
2. **I love myself**.
3. **I love you**.

Have fun; create positive realities; and most of all, LOVE—yourself, others and all you can see.

No One Is Perfect (and some are far from it)

Even if we choose to walk the path of love and do our best each day to honor that choice, we will stray now and then and cause harm. We probably won't do it on purpose, but we will still be responsible for bringing sadness into someone's life. That doesn't mean we're a bad person. Rather, it reminds us that we are *partly* human and even our divine Soul is a "work-in-progress." We're on a journey to learn how to make wise and loving choices. We face many challenges on Earth, and at times we stumble and lose our way. The key question is—will we learn from our mistakes and evolve into a better person and Soul?

Our Two "Selves" Are Like Travel Companions With Different Natures

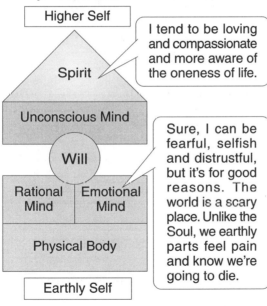

I tend to be loving and compassionate and more aware of the oneness of life.

Sure, I can be fearful, selfish and distrustful, but it's for good reasons. The world is a scary place. Unlike the Soul, we earthly parts feel pain and know we're going to die.

Our spiritual and earthly selves both have an unlimited capacity for love, but it comes more naturally to our Soul. Our human side is exposed to the harsh realities of the Physical World and has a lot more to worry about. So even though there is love within all of us, it can get blocked.

As a Reality Maker, we exist in a delicate balance. When any of our "elements" is in an impaired state, it can cause us to act from a place of fear or selfishness. Unfortunately, it doesn't take much for this to happen. The Emotional Mind is easily hurt; the Will must work hard to stay positive and determined; the Rational Mind is of limited value if not educated; and the Physical Body is extremely sensitive to pain and to chemical or energy imbalances. So, with all of these factors working against us, it is virtually impossible for us to be perfect and totally loving. We need to keep this in mind as we judge our own behavior or that of family and friends or of strangers. It can help us to be more understanding and forgiving.

Caution! We All Have a Dark-Side

We are the union of the spiritual and the physical, and each half can be in a troubled state. A Soul's "free Will" can make good or bad choices. And the human mind can harbor negative thoughts and feelings that may lead to harmful actions. We are all born with certain tendencies which we acquired from our earliest ancestors. For example, the instinct for self-survival exists in each of us. Of course, that is not bad by itself. But we also have a predilection for other states of mind which, in conjunction with the impulse to look out for ourselves, can easily block the flow of love.

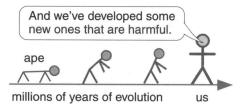

We Still Possess Some of Our Ancestor's "Animalistic" Traits

And we've developed some new ones that are harmful.

ape

millions of years of evolution   us

Some of the Forces At Work In Our Human Minds

FEAR	GREED	IGNORANCE	ANGER
HATE	ENVY	INTOLERANCE	EGOTISM

When we're living under the influence of these forces, we tend to make harmful choices for ourself and for others.

The line dividing good and evil cuts through the heart of every human being.

Alexander Solzhenitsyn – Russian writer

Each of us is capable of succumbing to our dark-side and of doing dreadful things. History is full of examples of good people acting very badly under certain circumstances or while under the spell of a forceful leader. But it's important for us to realize that negative behavior by humans is *not* inevitable, or at least it doesn't have to be as prevalent as it has been to date.

The dark forces that can take hold of our mind appear in our Reality Maker at birth as mere *seeds*—with the potential to become real troublemakers. But this doesn't happen all by itself. As children, we're taught to hate or to be greedy (or to be harmful in any other way) by the words and examples of the people around us. In fact, the seeds of negativity grow in the absence of positive alternatives. For example, if there is no love shown for another race, religion, or species, then hate, or at least disrespect, can blossom.

> The chief cause of human error is to be found in prejudices picked up in childhood.
> Rene Descartes – French philosopher; 1596–1650

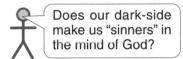

Does our dark-side make us "sinners" in the mind of God?

God *does not* see us as a wretched species that is incapable of change or self-redemption. First of all, we are not just human. We are glorious spiritual beings made in God's image and therefore are inherently *good*. But now we're teamed with Earthly Selves that have some harmful tendencies—which was part of God's plan. She knew humans and other beings in the universe would have "built-in" obstacles. We are here to learn how to be wise and loving in spite of those negative impulses. In fact, God wants our Souls to outgrow the dark side of human nature, so it no longer plays a predominant role in our lives. While this won't happen anytime soon, it is possible. And we need to believe we can do it.

Our Goal — To Evolve to the Point Where We Are "Living Spiritually"

We've come a long way, but we're not there yet.

now   future

We *can* "overcome" our negative traits and behave like children of God.

God gave our Souls the mission of creating "Heaven on Earth." That goal will be achieved not by eliminating all of our bad attributes, which can't be done, but by making our spiritual side a more "visible" partner here on Earth—and by consciously choosing to live by the *good*-natured side of our heart. We will never be perfect, but we can live with respect, kindness and compassion for all that God created.

There Are Three Broad Categories of People On Earth

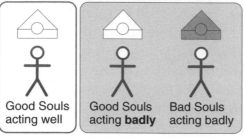

Good Souls acting well

Good Souls acting **badly**

Bad Souls acting badly

99.9% of us have basically good Souls. We came here to express our love, joy and creativity. And although Earth is not an easy place to live, a lot of us have managed to actually be good *most of the time.* Occasionally, we are hurtful, perhaps even seriously so, but it's not done deliberately or with malice. Youthful indiscretion is a common cause. Or like everyone else, we're dealing with personal issues which at times can get the best of us. That doesn't excuse our actions, but it puts them in a sympathetic light. In the end, most of us will be able to say, *"Taken as a whole,* my life reflected the efforts of a well-intentioned Soul, and I was good more often than not."

Unfortunately, not all good Souls will be able to make that claim. For some set of reasons, which usually includes the absence of love and good role models in childhood, their Earthly Selves got severely impaired. So they became stuck in a cycle of harmful behavior—even though their *Higher Selves* knew better. When the Emotional Mind is badly damaged or the foundation of Values and Beliefs is shaky, the Will can lose its spiritual bearings and become immersed in negativity. It is unable to make good choices.

Love isn't the only thing that can get blocked. If our mind or body are in a negative state, then the moral guidance our Spirit sends to our Will can be blocked too.

If I can't hear my Spirit, then I'm living without my conscience.

There aren't very many of them, but bad Souls do come to Earth. They like the fact humans have a dark side.

On Earth, We Can't Tell Which Is Which

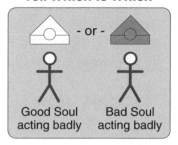

Good Soul acting badly   Bad Soul acting badly

If Souls say "no" to God's Values and Beliefs and have no compunction about causing harm (because it helps them satisfy their lust for power or to meet their material desires), then they deserve to be called "bad." But on Earth, where we can assess only a person's physical or mental state, we can't know for sure what kind of Soul someone has. We can think of dictators and other nefarious characters, past and present, who probably had bad or indeed "evil" Souls, but we won't see them for who they really are until we return to the Spirit World. Even then, only God will see the complete picture.

How God Knows the True Nature of a Soul

The four key questions –	Good Soul	Bad Soul
Did they decide before incarnating to be harmful?	No	Yes
On Earth, did they know they were hurting others?	Maybe	Yes
On Earth, did they show regret and remorse?	Maybe	Maybe
Will they be remorseful back in the Spirit World?	Yes	No

The main distinction between good and bad is INTENT and REMORSE. A good Soul does not intend for its Earthly Self to cause harm and is sorry when it does.

When a person is truly bad, there is more at work than an impaired Earthly Self. His or her Soul is a full accomplice in the hurtful deeds. And while we can't tell if a bad person also has a bad Soul, that is not an excuse for us to ignore or to accept harmful behavior when we see it.

Judge Not, Lest Ye Be Judged?

God

Some people say it's inappropriate to judge the harmful behavior of others because you don't know what "lessons" they were learning or what "karma" existed between them and their victims. I don't subscribe to this point of view.

If a person is intentionally harming or killing other people (for no morally good reason), then not only do you have the right to judge their behavior (but not their Soul), I also expect you to stop them.

Not All Harmful Behavior Can Be Put In the Same Category

1.	They acted selfishly or foolishly, but they didn't mean to cause harm. Perhaps they were "impaired" in some way.
2.	Their actions were motivated by greed or personal gain. They knew others would be hurt as a result, but they did it anyway.
3.	Their primary intent was to cause serious harm or even death without any moral justification. This is "evil" behavior.

We all will do things that fall into category #1. And we'll often face the temptation to act in the way described in category #2.

We can't make it through life without being hurt or causing harm. Even our Kindred Souls, in their roles as family and friends, will hurt us. In most cases, they'll be guilty of a "category 1" offense. Still, it won't always be easy to forgive them. But before we discard a kindred relationship on Earth, it would serve us well to remember our spiritual connection, and to realize the other person has a *good* Soul. Deep down he or she didn't mean to hurt us. In some cases though, we will need to break the earthly bond for self-protection, especially if the other person shows no signs of change. But often it is possible to heal the relationship, which would be welcomed by our Soul and theirs.

Indifference

"Maybe I care for you or maybe I don't. I will not 'consciously' cause you harm. Basically, I'm oblivious or insensitive."

Disrespect

"I don't hate you, but I am going to deliberately cause you harm. It's nothing personal."

HATE

"It is personal. I feel hostile, perhaps for no good reason. I want you to suffer or to even die."

Most of us are *unintentionally* hurtful. We're unaware of the consequences of our actions, or we are so self-absorbed we don't notice how we are affecting others. It is this mental state of "indifference" that plays a big role in the "category 1" behavior. If that were the only kind of harmful conduct any of us had to worry about, life would be a whole lot easier. But unfortunately, that is not the case. There are people out there who know exactly what they are doing. They're acting with *disrespect* or worse—with *hate*.

Some people are good in certain areas of their life (maybe they are a good spouse, parent, friend, or churchgoer), but they are harmful in their work.

In a previous chapter, we looked at how a person's Will could be wise in some areas, but be "in the dark" in others, especially with respect to sex and self-care. In other words, our goodness can be compartmentalized. And work is another area where we see otherwise good people acting badly. Take, for example, the chemical company executive who allows his firm to pollute the ground water, which results in innocent people dying. Or the tobacco executive who promotes policies that will get children addicted to cigarettes. The goal of these people is not to cause harm. Greed has led them to be *disrespectful* of life. It is safe to say that some of their values and beliefs are not in accordance with God's.

 I'm a good Soul who is about to incarnate. I want to be loving, joyful and creative, just like you. But what chance do I have if my life conditions are awful?

A worried Soul

Even if we were brought up in a great environment, it is still not easy to resist the dark-side. So imagine how difficult it must be for those who don't receive a good life situation.

It's Hard To Be Good If Our Childhood Was Bad

Without the proper "inputs," a Soul's Earthly Self is more likely to become impaired. As an adult, they will struggle in life and tend to make harmful choices.

| Abuse   Fear   Violence   Lack of hope Bad role models   Negative Values and Beliefs   Inadequate food, shelter, or education   Limited work opportunities |

I deserve better. It's not fair.

—— **childhood conditions / inputs** —————— **adulthood**

| Love   Nurturance   Good role models Positive Values and Beliefs   Education Proper food and medical care   Fun Appropriate discipline   Encouragement |

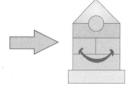

As Reality Makers, you are very resilient. Indeed, some of you overcome really bad childhoods and go on to lead great lives. But many people never get over a bad beginning. So I am asking you to focus more on the well-being of children.

It is said no one leaves childhood unscathed. Although that is true, there are too many children for whom the growing-up experience is a major trauma. They enter adulthood impaired emotionally, physically and/or intellectually. And they are ill-equipped to make wise life choices. This isn't just a matter of economics either because poor people can be good in every sense of the word, and the "rich and powerful" have caused much more than their fair share of pain and suffering. Poverty is a prime contributor to our earthly woes, but even a child brought up in a well-to-do home can become bad. It happens when any child lacks good role models or isn't taught positive values and beliefs. The point is the odds favor the child who is brought up in an overall positive environment.

They Need Our Help To Be Good

| Souls waiting for conception | Souls in utero | The children |

By improving the conditions into which Souls are born and those in which children grow up, we make it less likely that good Souls will become bad-acting people.

Children (and the Souls who will become children) are depending on us to clear their path of as many obstacles as we can. We can do this as individuals by being sure we are ready to be a parent, and we can do it collectively by changing our priorities. For example, we expend more money and mental energy on military matters than we do on the well-being of children.

All children should have the opportunity to grow into healthy and positive adults who have the ability and freedom to express their love, joy and creativity. We are doing "God's work" here on Earth when we help make that reality come true—whether it be in our own home, in our neighborhood or around the world.

Use your collective "Let there be ..." power and more of your earthly resources to eliminate poverty and hunger, to help people be better parents, to raise the quality of education and to give hope to those who have none.

The earlier we can improve the conditions of a child's life the better. There is a "window of opportunity" to consider. If we delay, it can become too late to fix the damage that is done.

Even The Worst Souls Were Once Good

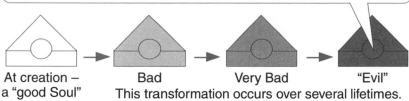 I started my existence just like you, but I was beaten down by the temptations and difficulties of physical life. I lost faith in God.

At creation –   Bad   Very Bad   "Evil"
a "good Soul"   This transformation occurs over several lifetimes.

Just because a Soul's Earthly Self has a bad childhood and goes through life as a harmful person doesn't mean that Soul will become evil. In fact, there are relatively few Souls that are that nasty and acting with malice. Still, we don't need to expose any more Souls to negative conditions that might lead to their metamorphosis. Some Souls chose not to be good early on in their existence, but most evil Souls get that way gradually. In many cases, they don't choose to forsake God. Instead, it just sort of happens as they get worn down by the trials and tribulations of physical life.

One of the things that really upsets God is the way that good Souls "aid and abet" people, companies and governments that are causing great harm. Financial investments, the sale of weapons, covert assistance, and appeasement all serve to encourage Souls that are probably bad or worse. Then when those malicious people go too far and wreak havoc, *good* Souls, embodied in young (and usually poor) Earthly Selves, are sent to stop the bad behavior. Many die in a war that was probably preventable.

If we're to create "Heaven on Earth," we need the courage and moral strength to stand against harmful conduct. If we don't stop injustice when we can, the word will spread in the Spirit World that Earth is a good planet for bad Souls to live on.

The only thing necessary for the triumph of evil is for good (people) to do nothing (or to help them, which is even worse).

Edmund Burke – British statesman, writer; 1729–97

Should Everyone Receive Love?

People who love us; people in need; and those minding their own business and causing no harm.	y e s
People acting badly, but who seem to be a good Soul, even if they're not sorry. Love might turn them around.	y e s
People who caused real harm, are not sorry, seem not to be a good Soul, and who might abuse our love.	?

I love all people, even the worst ones. That is too much to ask of you, but don't let anger or hate for someone ruin your life.

It is hard enough to love the people who generally behave well. Does God also expect us to love those who mostly cause harm? I believe God would say "It depends on the answers to these questions: How bad was their behavior? What was their intent? Are they sorry? Was their judgment impaired? What are the underlying causes for their behavior? Are they family? Were you the one hurt?" It would also help if we knew the nature of their Soul (which unfortunately we can't) because someone with a troubled Soul may be so far gone that only God's love will have an impact, and even that may not make a difference.

God loves all of us, including good Souls who are acting badly and evil Souls too. Of course, this doesn't mean She approves of their harmful behavior. She loves them because She knows they have the potential to be good. She is hopeful these wayward children will return to the path of light and love. As the eternal optimist, God never gives up on any Soul.

If it's not possible to love someone who was hurtful, you could pray for that Soul's redemption so others won't be hurt in this life or in the next one.

Most of us are fully responsible for our choices. "I'm a good Soul with some earthly problems" does not excuse bad behavior—unless the problems are beyond our control. Still, when we look at a harmful person we might imagine how any of us, even with good Souls, could become dysfunctional if we were subjected to the same negative circumstances. If we can look at a troubled person through empathetic eyes, then perhaps we can find a loving way to respond. Of course, we need to stop harmful behavior, and people should receive an appropriate punishment for their actions. But somehow we need to bring love back into their lives because change won't occur without an infusion of love.

It is not necessary that we all hug an evil person or we focus on the offenders instead of their victims. However, in most cases it was the lack of love (and of opportunities to be joyful or creative) that led to their bad behavior. An expression of love—even if it is just someone saying *"God* loves them"—may help them to arrive at a state of remorse and to choose a new path for their life.

Why even bother with people who act real badly? I can think of two reasons. First, we might help them change in this lifetime. Some pretty bad people have had amazing conversions. Second, even if our acts of love have no impact now, we may help transform their *Souls,* which will affect all of us in future lifetimes. Love can help prevent a bad Soul from getting progressively worse or help to make it good again.

When We Get Better The World Will Get Better

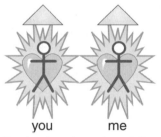

you   me

Each of us has the ability to live spiritually. We can tame our dark-side with the love that is in our Souls.

As good Souls who want to live in a better world, we can help children who are at risk or do our part to change the conditions into which children are born; or we could help adults who have lost their way. We can also make a profound contribution to the "collective mission" by taking a close look at the person we see in the mirror. Each of us needs to understand which "seeds" from the dark side have taken root in our heart. Is it anger or intolerance or one of the other forces causing us to be hurtful? With that self-awareness and a strong desire to change, we take the first step on the path of personal *and* planetary transformation.

It is better to light a candle than it is to curse the darkness.

Chinese proverb

The Stakes Are High

Earth is overcrowded.

With so many people here and on the way, it's becoming harder for us to be loving with each other. But it is more important than ever that we do just that.

Gaining control of our dark side has become a matter of great urgency because we're running out of space and there are fewer resources to go around to keep us all happy. We've taken "go forth and multiply" too far and have created conditions of scarcity and competition that could lead to catastrophic results. So it is essential we focus on our personal growth, and we work with others to bring love and compassion into the world. It would also make a big difference if we could stabilize the human population, but that's a subject for a later chapter.

You have your flaws, but I love you just as you are. Of course, it would please me greatly if you did your best to make yourselves "better." Also, don't lose sight of the fact that you are glorious spiritual beings.

Each day we face the question of whether we're going to stay as we are, or are we going to change? God does not expect us to be perfect because that is not possible. But She does want us to be better, even if it's just a little bit, than we were before. It is a matter of making progress from day-to-day. In the next chapter, we will take a brief look at how we can do that and more.

Let us dedicate ourselves to what the Greeks wrote so many years ago: to tame the savageness of man and to make gentle the life of this world.

Robert F. Kennedy; 1925–68

Letting Our Light Shine Through

> Our worst fear is not that we are inadequate; our deepest fear is that we are powerful beyond measure. It is our light, not our darkness that most frightens us. ... We were born to manifest the glory of God within us. It is not just in some of us; it is in everyone of us; and as we let our own light shine, we unconsciously give other people permission to do the same.
>
> Nelson Mandela – South African President

Love, joy and creativity are the "light" of our Soul. **Personal growth** is the process of removing the obstacles that block that light.

We are on Earth to love ourself and others, to create positive realities and to have fun. These activities come naturally to every Soul because that is how God made us. However, in the Physical World the expression of our innate abilities is diminished by our human weaknesses and by the misfortunes of life. The radiance of our Soul is blocked, and we're living at far less than our full potential.

We can function at a much higher level, mentally and physically, by reconnecting with our Soul and by addressing those earthly issues that are blocking our essential light. That will involve doing some *repair work* (to fix what was done to us by others and by ourself) and making *life-style changes* that will result in better self-care. By focusing on our personal growth we will bring forth our inherent power. When we're in a positive state we will radiate light and energy and affect the people around us. They will be moved by our vitality and passion for life, and perhaps they will be inspired to grow as well. That would please God.

You're capable of much more than you can imagine. Let the light that's inside each of you shine brightly.

The Purpose of Growth

To maximize our ability to be loving, joyful and creative.

Many Of Us Are Reluctant to Grow

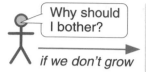

Why should I bother?	What could be – frustration, regret, pain and suffering, a shortened life

if we don't grow

If a better future isn't enough to make us grow, we can think of what not changing could mean to us and our loved ones.

We are changing whether we like it or not. But are we growing or declining? Are we making conscious choices to enhance the state of our mind, body and Soul? Or are we content with how we are, allowing the passage of time to wear us down? Or worse, are we bringing on or accelerating our decline by making harmful choices?

No one can force us to grow. We need to find our own motivation. Maybe it's to avoid the negative things that can happen to us if we don't grow. (They might happen anyhow, but why increase the odds?) Or maybe we want as much time and energy as possible to pursue our Life Plan. Or maybe there is a child watching us. As a role model, our actions will teach him or her how to live well and wisely and how to become a better person as *they* go through life.

The Ultimate Reward – a life of personal growth will expand our Soul's energy and move us closer to God

Us, before this lifetime   After this life

The Three Aspects of Personal Growth

1. **Progression** — seeking a higher level of mental, physical or spiritual existence than we have ever known.

2. **Healing** — recovering from a setback hopefully to regain a prior level of existence or so we can move even higher.

3. **Mindfulness** —

   a. **Acceptance** of our current state, with a determination to change what we can.

   b. **Appreciation** of all that we have accomplished and all that God has given us, including the ability to use our "free Will" to change our life.

   c. **Awareness** of each moment, each breath, of our feelings, of the beauty around us, and of our connection to each other and all living things.

Our Ultimate Goal – To Be In a Positive and Harmonious State

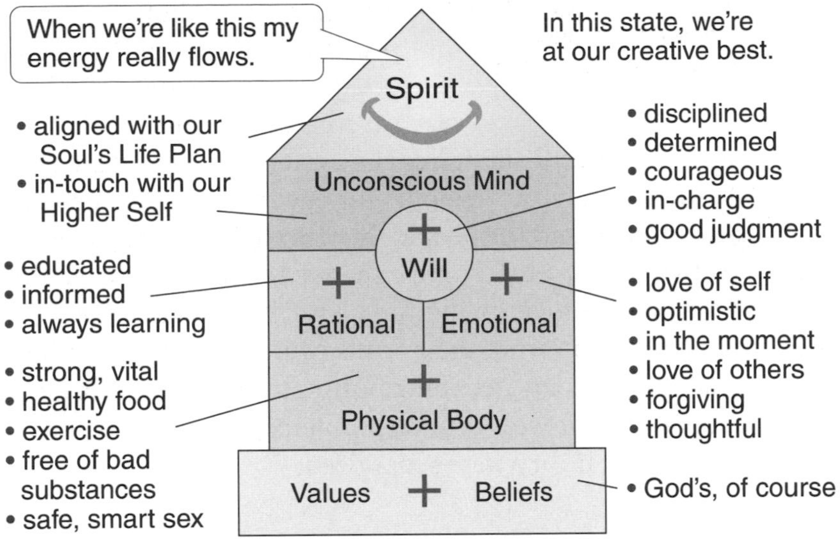

When we're like this my energy really flows.

In this state, we're at our creative best.

Spirit

• aligned with our Soul's Life Plan
• in-touch with our Higher Self

Unconscious Mind

+

• disciplined
• determined
• courageous
• in-charge
• good judgment

• educated
• informed
• always learning

+   Will   +

Rational   Emotional

• love of self
• optimistic
• in the moment

• strong, vital
• healthy food
• exercise
• free of bad substances
• safe, smart sex

+

Physical Body

• love of others
• forgiving
• thoughtful

Values   +   Beliefs

• God's, of course

We are not on a quest for perfection but rather for excellence and wholeness. It is the union of our spiritual, mental, emotional and physical elements that gives us our power on Earth. We want each part of our Reality Maker to be as strong and positive as it can be so we can live at our full potential. We also want to live in a manner consistent with our Soul's Life Plan. That means we are doing work that is our calling. We are making choices that honor our values and passions. We are facing the issues we came here to face. And we are living truthfully with the people in our life, which means we are expressing who we deeply are and treating them as loving kindreds. If we are in this state (as shown above) we are *"aligned* and *synergized,"* and we can make the most of our Soul's "Let there be ..." power. We are known throughout the Spirit World as a *"super-creator."*

ALIGNED	SYNERGIZED*
We're pursuing our Life Plan, using our gifts and doing what we love. We've got an intuitive connection with our Soul; we are living as we were meant to; and we're growing.	All the elements of our Reality Maker are in a generally positive state. They are working in harmony with each other and are guided by God's Values and Beliefs.

* From the Greek word *synergos,* which means "working together."

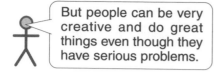 But people can be very creative and do great things even though they have serious problems.

If we are especially gifted and pursuing our calling, we can be prolific without being "synergized." History is full of accounts of creative geniuses who were emotionally or physically impaired. In some cases their distress was integral to their creativity. Generally though, these people ended up harming themselves and the people they loved. If they had been in a totally positive state it would have enhanced their creative faculties, as well as their ability to be loving and joyful. It also might have given them more time to do what their Souls came here for and allowed them to make an even greater contribution to the world. If a person can be a super-creator with serious problems, then they could be a *super-duper creator* if they were synergized.

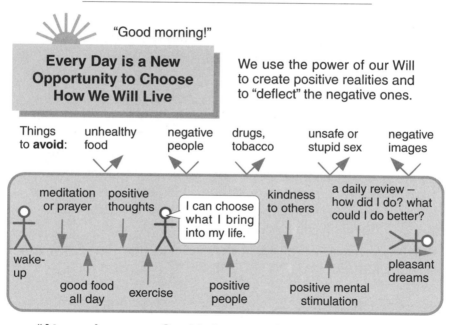

"Good morning!"

Every Day is a New Opportunity to Choose How We Will Live

We use the power of our Will to create positive realities and to "deflect" the negative ones.

Things to **avoid**: unhealthy food, negative people, drugs, tobacco, unsafe or stupid sex, negative images

meditation or prayer   positive thoughts   I can choose what I bring into my life.   kindness to others   a daily review — how did I do? what could I do better?

wake-up   good food all day   exercise   positive people   positive mental stimulation   pleasant dreams

"At sunrise every Soul is born again." — Napoleon Hill

Everything we do and expose ourself to affects our energy. Some of us are very sensitive in this regard. Indeed, there are more temptations and sources of negativity than any Soul can easily endure. So, if we want our light to shine brightly in this environment, we need to be very selective about what we watch, read and listen to, what we do for work and fun, how we treat our body, and with whom we associate. That takes a great deal of Willpower, but it is the only way we can improve the conditions of our life.

Will — It's up to me to rise above negative emotional and physical impulses so we can pursue our dreams. That is the essence of self-discipline.

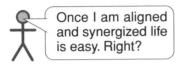

Once I am aligned and synergized life is easy. Right?

By following a regular practice of self-care that benefits us physically, emotionally, mentally *and* spiritually, we can move to a higher state of existence. Yet even when we're on the right path, we will continue to face challenges each day that will attempt to block our light. People will annoy us, setbacks will occur and the unexpected will happen. Still, that should not deter us from our goal. The more robust our energy is the better able we'll be to cope with our misfortunes, and we will be more effective during the good times. And when our energy is up, we won't be a "downer" for the people around us.

Do a "Reality Check" Of Our Reality Maker

We all have at least one element that could use some improvement.

A self-assesment:	A-OK	Needs work
Our Will		
Rational Mind		
Emotional Mind		
Physical Body		
Values and Beliefs		
Higher Self		

With the Higher Self, "needs work" means we could have a better connection with it.

Self-awareness or knowing which of our parts can and "should" be changed is the first step on the journey of personal growth. We need to be compassionate as we look at ourself, but it is also important we be honest—because amongst all our faults there may be some that require special attention. These are the ones that are causing us to be harmful or are seriously affecting our health and longevity. We also need to know what is keeping us from living the life we have imagined. A self-appraisal will identify those life issues our Soul wants us to overcome.

We All Have At Least One or Two Key Obstacles That We Need To Overcome

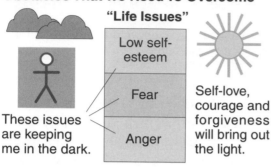

"Life Issues"

Low self-esteem

Fear

Anger

Self-love, courage and forgiveness will bring out the light.

These issues are keeping me in the dark.

Most of us are quite aware of "our issues." But if we're not, we only need to consider those areas of life that are a recurring struggle for us and then look a little deeper for the underlying cause(s). If, for example, we keep having bad relationships, it's not because we don't deserve a great partner but more likely because we haven't yet learned to love and respect ourself. One point of view is that our Higher Self keeps placing us in challenging situations until we outgrow whatever it is that is responsible for them.

We All Have Fears to Face

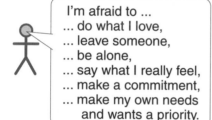

I'm afraid to ...
... do what I love,
... leave someone,
... be alone,
... say what I really feel,
... make a commitment,
... make my own needs and wants a priority.

We have common issues such as low self-esteem and anger which are manifested in similar ways in our lives. And the one big obstacle we all deal with is *fear*. Sometimes fear protects us, but most often it is standing in the way of what we want and is blocking our light.

> Take a risk a day—one small or bold stroke that will make you feel great once you have done it.
>
> Susan Jeffers, author of *Feel the Fear and Do It Anyway*

We Can Categorize Our Issues

Those that are causing us to be HARMFUL

Those that are HOLDING US BACK in life

Those that allow others to HURT US

We can't resolve every problem at once, so we need to prioritize. For example, drug abuse is the kind of issue that not only holds a person back, but it can also cause them to be very harmful. The fear of being alone is an issue that can keep us from leaving an abusive partner.

Both of these issues and others like them need to be addressed with a *sense of urgency*. A problem such as being afraid to speak in public may cause us emotional distress and hold us back in life, but it is not in the same league as the other ones. The point is this: we can have compassion and be self-accepting, but we can't always afford to be nonchalant when it comes to our personal growth.

Let's Take Another Look In the Mirror. What's Really Good?

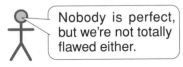

Nobody is perfect, but we're not totally flawed either.

We all have positive attributes. We need to see and appreciate them. Growth is not just about fixing problems. It is also about developing our strengths and using them in the pursuit of a fulfilled life. If we do what we love and what we are good at, we will feel better about ourself and thus be able to solve our problems more easily.

What's Inside Is Most Important

Higher Self

Beautiful bodies are nice, but you don't have to look like a god or goddess to be god-like in your life.

We live in a *Physical World*, so it's understandable that we idolize good looking bodies. But as a society we have taken it too far, and we don't give enough attention or respect to our mental, emotional and spiritual qualities. In the Spirit World, the favorite show is not *Baywatch* but *Soulwatch*, which looks at real-life stories of people who are beautiful on the *inside*. So, a person who acts with love is the real "star" to those viewing from the other side. Now let's consider the subject of "healing."

What If We Left Childhood Impaired In Some Way?
If our Reality-Maker is "broken," we need to fix it.

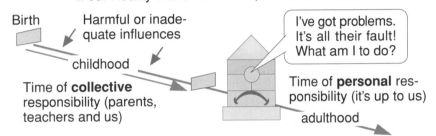

Performing "self-repair" is an unfortunate but necessary task for all of us. The longer we wait to do it, the more difficult it is.

There are many books available on the subject of emotional healing written by experts, which I am not. So I will just (barely) scratch the surface and offer a few ideas that I find helpful.

To Move Forward We May Need To Look Backwards First

When I remember my past, I see stuff that happened that I wish would not have happened, and I think of all that I wanted but didn't get.

We all have legitimate gripes regarding our childhood, with some people having a lot more to complain about. Our Reality Maker parts (especially our Emotional Mind and Will) were damaged or undeveloped in some way. The question now is what do we do about it? Can we lovingly give ourself what we didn't get from childhood? Can we find joyful ways to be self-nurturing? Can we be a good parent to the child still within us? By doing so we will reconnect with our Soul's light and love.

We Can't Always Do It Alone

Emotional Mind

I want to be healed, but some of my wounds are too deep and old to fix by myself. I need help.

Sigmund Freud   (Photo: CORBIS/Bettmann)

Find someone to talk with, such as a Kindred Soul. Or try a support group. Maybe you need "professional" help.

We could be so immersed in our emotional pain that we can't find our light on our own. We need to open up to those who love us or who've been through the same trauma. Or we may need to turn to people who have been trained to help.

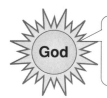

God

I'm no "shrink," but I know most of you can overcome your childhood issues.

People who had malicious parents or were born into an awful life situation can give God the "But I was a victim" explanation for the state of their life. Otherwise, She is less willing to accept that particular "defense." God is sympathetic of course to anyone who had problems as a child, but She still expects us to improve ourselves. She also wants us to have empathy for our parents. They probably left their childhood impaired in some way too, and they did the best job they could raising us. God is asking us to be forgiving (in most cases), to learn from our parents' mistakes and to transform our own behavior—especially if we have children of our own.

We Can Break Generational Patterns of Negativity

If we inherited certain weaknesses (or acquired them via osmosis), we don't have to keep them. We can create an "evolution" within our family by becoming more positive than the prior generation.

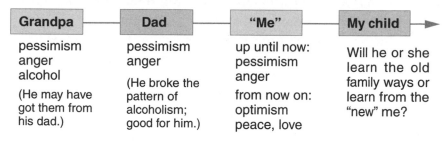

Grandpa	Dad	"Me"	My child
pessimism anger alcohol (He may have got them from his dad.)	pessimism anger (He broke the pattern of alcoholism; good for him.)	up until now: pessimism anger from now on: optimism peace, love	Will he or she learn the old family ways or learn from the "new" me?

But Don't Blame It All On Mom or Dad
Our nature is a combination of things.

Our Soul's own traits which we brought with us into this life.

What we got in this life from heredity and childhood.

Most of us are stuck in at least one pattern of harmful behavior such as overeating or smoking. Getting out of these ruts and developing new, constructive habits is at the core of personal growth. We might be struggling with a problem we were born with (such as alcoholism) or with behavior we picked up from role models. Or perhaps our pattern is an unconscious response to the lack of love and nurturance we experienced as a child. Of course, we also bring issues with us from the Spirit World that originated in our prior lifetimes. Regardless of who or what caused our harmful ways, we will not live with the fullness of our Soul's light until we break those patterns.

God

Heal yourself and you will create a "ripple effect." It will touch those around you and help chart a new course for the family of humankind.

As we each heal and progress to a higher level of existence we not only benefit ourself, we also make a contribution to the "collective mission." This is especially true if we're a parent—or thinking about being one.

Our Light Shines the Brightest When We're "In the Moment"

 Re-living the past and being anxious about the future diverts my energy away from the present.

We can't create a positive life if we're spending most of our time doing "mind travels." We need to be like a laser beam which is powerful because it is highly focused energy. If we're constantly upset about the bad events from our past or needlessly worrying about what *might* happen tomorrow, our light is scattered or blocked entirely.

So, the goal is to become a "here and now" kind of person. To achieve that requires our commitment to growth and honoring our Soul's desire to make the most of its earthly journey. Living in the moment is not easy, but there are things we can do to help us stay focused.

We Can Reduce the Energy Drain

For regrets and anger –

Forgive and learn

For worry and fear –

Have faith; take action

The Purpose of the PAST

To give us pleasant memories, wisdom and lessons to learn

Not for endless regrets

The Purpose of the FUTURE

To give us hope and motivation and a place for our dreams

To warn us of possible risks — Not for needless worry

The Purpose of the PRESENT

To help us **grow** by applying the lessons from our past

To **enjoy** and **appreciate** the gift and beauty of life

To **do** what is necessary to make our dreams come true

To **heed** the warnings coming from our future

The past is history, the future is a mystery, and today is the *present.* And that's why they call it a "gift."

Loretta LaRoche

God

When you live in the present and make the most of the gift of life that is your gift back to Me.

Becoming bigger, better and stronger is the *progressive* nature of growth. The *mindful* aspect focuses our attention on the here and now and seeks simplicity and stillness in our life. These two views of growth may seem in conflict, but both are essential to our well-being. One of the best things we can do to live in the moment is easy and enjoyable—and that is to concentrate our mind on the very essence of life: our **breathing**.

Breathing is the link between our body, mind, and Soul. When we're anxious or stressed, our breath tends to be quick and shallow. If we slow our breathing down and make it deeper, our mind will become more peaceful. As we practice "conscious breathing," it helps to silently recite an affirmation, like this one:

– Breathing in, I calm myself. Breathing out, I smile. –

By concentrating on our breathing, we can bring body and mind back together and become whole again.

Thich Nhat Hanh – Zen Buddhist monk

Don't Overdo It

Personal growth is hard work, but you need to have fun along the way.

If you feel joyful, that's a sign that you're aligned with your Life Plan.

We don't want to get worn out by trying to grow. So, we need to pace ourself and take time for "R and A" or *Rest and Appreciation*. We ought to stop now and then and admire our achievements, even if we've only

Some issues call for a sense of urgency. With others it's better if we take it easier and find joyful ways to learn and grow.

taken a few "baby steps." We can say to ourself: "I've done enough and I am good enough ... for now." If we can stop and "just be" for awhile, we will have learned one of the key lessons of growth, which is to be patient and kind to ourself.

Growth is not just about striving to be better. It is also about enjoying the moment and accepting yourself as you are (knowing that you are or will do your best to change what you can).

It's good to reward yourself now and then. Take a vacation. Buy some flowers. Walk in the woods. Pat yourself on the back.

It's Okay If Others Are Further Along Than Us

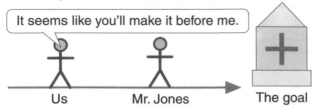

Our Life Situations are different. Our Souls have unique issues to work on. So, we shouldn't judge or compare.

We are not in a race to see who can become aligned and synergized first. Besides, often when it looks like someone is ahead of us they're not really. Outward appearances are usually deceiving.

> Those who insist they've got their "shit together" are usually standing in it at the time.
>
> Stephen Levine,
> author of *A Year To Live*

We Can Compensate For Our "Weaknesses"

I'm not a smart man, but my other parts all make up for it.

Forrest Gump

It takes more than paralysis to stop me. I have a strong Will.

A paraplegic

Some people have problems that can't be fixed. They were either born with those challenges or something happened later on to diminish the capacity of their Earthly Selves. Yet many of them rise to the occasion and are able to compensate for their loss. We all have within us the ability to transcend major limitations. Our body is very resilient of course, but when the going gets tough it is our Will and Emotional Mind that can really get going. If they're in a positive state, they will do whatever it takes for us to live with our light still shining through.

> Strength does not come from physical capacity. It comes from (an) indomitable **Will**.
>
> Mohandes Gandhi;
> 1869–1948

They Can Be The "Dynamic Duo"

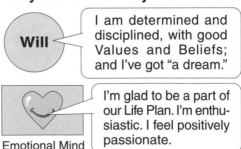

I am determined and disciplined, with good Values and Beliefs; and I've got "a dream."

I'm glad to be a part of our Life Plan. I'm enthusiastic. I feel positively passionate.

Emotional Mind

As we already know, no one is perfect, and we can't be positive 100% of the time. That's why our goal is really threefold:

   (1)   reach the level of excellence that we personally can attain,

   (2)   stay in that state for extended periods of time, and

   (3)   get out of a negative condition as quickly as possible.

To achieve these goals we need to focus on those things that we have some control over. The following list is a bit repetitive, but it doesn't hurt to review this material.

Growth Priorities For Our Will and Earthly Self

The Will — develop the following attributes:

1. The judgment to make wise, god-like choices.
2. The discipline to grow and to resist the temptations of life.
3. The determination to overcome the challenges of life.
4. The courage to take action when we're feeling afraid. (We can take "baby steps" at first, if necessary.)

The Emotional Mind:

1. Enhance our self-love and self-confidence.
2. Be more optimistic, grateful and enthusiastic about life.
3. Become more accepting of others and act with kindness. Appreciate our diversity and see our interconnectedness.

The Rational Mind:

1. Attend to the educational basics (reading, writing etc.).
2. Have a sense of wonder and discovery about all of life.
3. Maintain a lifelong commitment to learning and mental stimulation. (Avoid brain-numbing entertainment.)
4. Study other people's customs and beliefs. (It will help us to rid the world of intolerance.)

The Physical Body:

1. Do our best to be at a high level of vitality for as many years as possible so our Soul can fulfill its mission.
2. Avoid putting bad things in our body. Exercise and rest regularly and consume good food and drink.

We're Not On Our Own

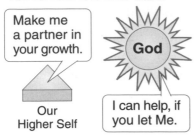

Make me a partner in your growth.

Our Higher Self

God

I can help, if you let Me.

If we want to increase the amount of "light" in our life, then it makes sense we should turn to the *source* of that light—our Spirit (which is a part of our Higher Self) and of course, God.

Attending religious services each week can be a good start, but there are many other ways we can bring the power of the Spirit World into our life. A list of things we can do to connect with our Higher Self is included near the end of the chapter *Who We Are On Earth*. Of course, we can also pray and talk with God at any time and ask Her for help and guidance.

> "God grant me the **serenity** to accept the things I cannot change, the **courage** to change the things I can, and the **wisdom** to know the difference. Grant me **patience** with the changes that take time, an **appreciation** of all that I have, **tolerance** of those with different struggles and the **strength** to get up and try again, one day at a time."
>
> A variation on the prayer of St. Francis

> Every day, in every way, I am getting better and better.
> Emile Coue – French psychotherapist; 1857–1926

Our ability to be loving, joyful and creative (which is the essence of our Soul's light) is affected by what we do, who we're with and where we live.
We all need a positive framework for our life, and that is the subject of the next chapter.

Just one last thing ...

We Can Grow Far More Than We Think We Can

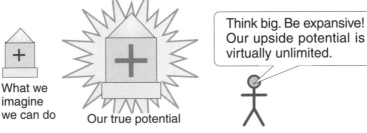

What we imagine we can do

Our true potential

Think big. Be expansive! Our upside potential is virtually unlimited.

Let There Be ... The Life We Have Imagined

I hope that my "light" will shine brightly while I am in the Physical World.

Our Soul

Before we incarnated, we made a Life Plan that described what we really wanted to learn and do on Earth. It was a vision of how we could best express the love, joy and creativity we have within us. Our Soul imagined a life that would make us feel passionate and good about ourself—a life that would make the most of who we are and result in an expansion of our energy. At the same time, we could see the life situation we were incarnating into, so we knew it wouldn't be easy to make our dreams come true. Still, we were full of hope and enthusiasm. We were determined to live the life we had imagined.

Typical Elements Of A Soul's Life Plan

- ☐ Pursue work that we love
- ☐ Express our creativity
- ☐ Make a contribution
- ☐ Face our life issues
- ☐ Find / love our kindreds
- ☐ Resolve our past karma
- ☐ Reside in a loving home

- ☐ Take good care of ourself
- ☐ Lead a balanced life
- ☐ Have fun; be joyful
- ☐ Become a better chooser

Optional items:
- ☐ Find / love our Soul Mate
- ☐ Create / raise children

Our **Will**

It's my job to rediscover our "gifts" and to create a reality that reflects the substance of our Life Plan.

Most of us when we are born lose sight of what we're good at and why we came here. So, we must spend a fair amount of our journey trying to reconnect with our Life Plan. We know that for us to feel joy and happiness on Earth, we need to create the kind of life that would satisfy our Soul.

> Go confidently in the direction of your dreams.
> Live the life you have imagined.
> Henry David Thoreau – American writer; 1817–62

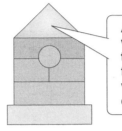

As Reality Makers, we can use our "**Let there be ...**" power to make our Soul's vision for this lifetime come true.

God made us in Her image, so we each possess the ability to transform our dreams and desires into reality. Our *"Let there be ..."* power is far more extensive than we realize. Almost anything we can conceive of we can manifest. And though we excel at creating material things out of the resources of the Physical World, we can do more. We can also use our divine energy to create new or better states of existence. For example, we can say "Let there be ... more happiness in my life," which is the essential first step in making that vision a reality.

Let there be ... what? That is the question.

God

We Can Use Our Power In Many Different Ways

"Let there be ..."

... a new work of art
... a child
... a new business
... an end to hunger
... a cure for a disease
... peace between me
    and my neighbor

Whenever we use our "Let there be ..." power we need to ask, "What reality am I trying to create?" More specifically, "Am I making choices and pursuing activities that I can imagine my Soul would support? Does it feel like I am aligned with my Life Plan? Am I creating in accordance with God's Values and Beliefs? Am I causing harm to other people or beings?" We need to be very selective in how we use our power. We're here to create realities that honor God and our Soul and that help others on their journey.

In the rest of this chapter, we will look at how we can use our "Let there be ..." power to create a framework for our life that will satisfy our Soul. We will examine some of the criteria that can guide us as we make our life-defining choices.

Each of us is the lead actor *and* chief writer of our own "reality play." Part of the script was written when we were conceived and became a member of our "parental" family. The first piece of our play's overall structure was then put in place. We may not have joined the ideal cast of characters, but our family set the stage for the story of our life. Then as we grow up and go out on our own, we make choices that define the rest of our play's form and basic "plot line." Each of us creates what is called *The Life Circle.*

A LIFE CIRCLE Provides a Framework For Our Journey

The six elements of the Life Circle are presented with a brief description of what each can provide us. Many factors can affect our ability to create, enjoy and sustain a good Life Circle, including how we care for our body, mind and Soul. That's why we're at the center of the Circle.

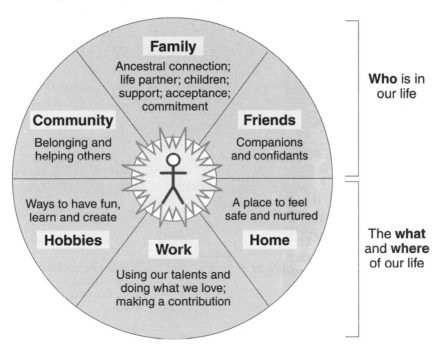

We need the **essence** of each element, but the specifics as to how we create a Life Circle varies from person to person.

A note about FAMILY: We begin with our "parental" family, which can include mom and dad (who might not be our birth parents), siblings, grandparents and so on. Many of us then choose a spouse or partner and create our own household, which might include children. In truth, we can get much of the essence of "family" from our very close friends and, of course, from our pets too.

"Let there be ...
a Life Circle that is
aligned with my Soul"

The First Choice:
What We Want In Life

Love Joy Creativity

- or -

Fear Sadness
and Mediocrity

A precious few choices (such as deciding what our vocation will be, whether we will have children and with whom, and where we will live) define the structure and character of our life. The Circle we create for ourself will determine how we use our time and energy each day and who will be "co-creators" of our reality. Indeed, a handful of choices will have a tremendous impact on how our life unfolds and on whether we will be able to manifest our Soul's light.

No one wishes to lead an unfulfilled life. One reason why many of us do is we don't have a clear vision of what we really want. We haven't placed the goal of being "fulfilled" firmly in our mind and heart. And we haven't asked ourself what our ideal life would be like.

When someone says "Get a life" they mean you need to create a good Circle.

But how do I know what "good" is for me?

Four Questions That Can
Help Us Make Our Choices

1. **What** do you love to do?
2. **Who** do you love to be with?
3. **Where** do you love to be?
4. **How** do you love to live?

To make the best Life Circle choices possible requires a great deal of *self-awareness*. We need to know what our gifts are and what kind of people, places and activities really nurture us. Our goal is to be aligned with our Soul, and that's why *love* is at the heart of each question. The best choices will reflect a genuine, deeply-felt affection or attraction, whether it be for a prospective partner or friend or for a job or career we are considering. If we don't create a Life Circle that allows us to feel good about ourself or to give and receive love, we will experience fear, sadness and mediocrity.

As we make our Life Circle choices, either for the first time or to change an element, it will serve us well if we make *joy* one of our key criteria. Too many of us ignore that part of our being that wants to have fun. We create tension and frustration and unnecessary burdens for ourself by choosing jobs and relationships that aren't good for us, by having children before we are ready or by taking on big mortgages.

When God made us She said "Let there be ... joy in every Soul." On Earth, our challenge is to create a Life Circle that will bring forth that joy. If we can do that for ourself, it can also bring joy to the people around us.

A Joyful Heart Enhances Our Life

It's easier to be loving.

- Better health
- More creativity
- Attracts "+" people
- Better relations

Joy radiates out from us and elevates everyone's energy. It is contagious.

The great person is he (or she) who does not lose their child's heart.
Mencius – Chinese philosopher; 372–289 BCE

A good Life Circle gives us the FREEDOM to live mostly as we wish.

We live from moment to moment, and there are two kinds of "moments."

Want to Moments	They make us feel happy or good about ourself, like when we're working at what we love, having fun, etc.
Have to Moments	Not how we'd prefer to spend our time. We can't escape them entirely, but we want to have as few as possible.

God gave each of us a Will that is "free" to choose. So, here on Earth we long for the kind of life that will allow us to spend time with our kindreds, to be joyful and to express our creative gifts. We don't want to be stuck in situations that restrict our ability to be who we really are.

Freedom doesn't mean we are without commitments or obligations. In fact, a Life Circle that satisfies our Soul will be built upon pledges of love and friendship between us and our kindreds. We will engage in creative alliances with people who will depend on us and we on them. But our life will be such that we will feel we are exactly where we want to be, doing what we really want to do, and with the people we truly want near us. That is a Soul's definition of "freedom."

Also, freedom doesn't mean we can avoid all the unpleasant tasks in life. Regardless of how we construct our Circle, we will have moments and even extended periods of time where we are doing things that we "have to." But that will happen less often if we create a framework for our life that honors our Soul. By creating such a life, we will be better able to cope with the inevitable "have to's."

I want a Life Circle that allows me to use my "Let there be ..." power to create positive realities for myself and others. I want to express myself and to pursue the goal of personal excellence.

It is essential we have our priorities straight and that we are driven by forces that satisfy our Soul. Life Circle choices that are motivated solely by the desire to have money and possessions or status and power—*and which cause needless harm to others*—will not be well received by our Soul. Choices made out of fear, such as selecting an inappropriate friend or Life Partner because we are afraid of being alone, are frowned upon as well.

When your Life Circle is aligned with your Soul you will "know" it.

If the life we are pursuing is off-target and full of "shoulds" and "have to's," we will experience anxiety, frustration and needless struggle. On the other hand, if our earthly reality is what our Soul hoped it would be, or if we are moving in that direction, we will feel energized and passionate. We will be at our creative best and become stronger emotionally and spiritually and probably physically as well. People will come into our life and events will occur that will help us on our journey. And even though we will still have our difficulties, we will have a deep inner sense that we made the right choices and all our efforts were worth it.

We Shouldn't Limit Ourself. Our Soul Says "Dream Big."

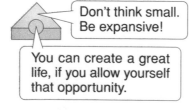

Don't think small. Be expansive!

You can create a great life, if you allow yourself that opportunity.

Our Circle can be as grand as we can possibly imagine.

We all want a joyful life that will make us feel passionate and truly grateful. If such a life is ever to be our reality, we must believe it is possible and within our power to make it so. Also, the life that provides us with all we want doesn't have to be "big" in the sense of fame or fortune. Our Soul's dream may be to live quite simply. That's not thinking "small"; it's being expansive in a very spiritual sense. Whatever our dream is, it is important to remember we are the chief writer of our reality play.

> Our future's not written yet. The future is whatever you make it, so make it a good one.
>
> Dr. Emmett L. Brown in the movie *Back to the Future III*

Our First Choices Are Key / A Life Circle Is a "Work-In-Progress"

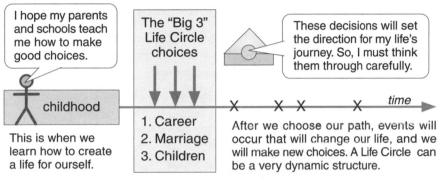

I hope my parents and schools teach me how to make good choices.

The "Big 3" Life Circle choices

These decisions will set the direction for my life's journey. So, I must think them through carefully.

childhood

time

1. Career
2. Marriage
3. Children

This is when we learn how to create a life for ourself.

After we choose our path, events will occur that will change our life, and we will make new choices. A Life Circle can be a very dynamic structure.

Many of us make the "Big 3" choices before we really know ourself (or the person we pick as our Life Partner) and without being fully aware of the potential consequences of our choices.

Each Life Circle choice we make expands or limits our other choices. For example, if we quit school or get married and have kids before we are ready, we will postpone *or give up* other paths in life we might wish to pursue. As a rule, putting a key part of our Circle in place prematurely is not the best thing to do.

On the other hand, one good choice can put us on the path to fulfillment. For example, if we pursue a career that uses our gifts and creates passion in our life, we will meet like-minded people who could become great friends. Not only will we be doing what we love, but we will probably be making a contribution to our community as well. We may even find our Soul Mate more easily.

Even when all the pieces of a Life Circle are in place it is never really complete. We will make new choices to correct previous ones or because we've grown and we want to change our life. Or we will have to rebuild our Circle when fate deals us a bad hand. We will lose friends and make new ones, and we will relocate, try new jobs or even new careers. Our family will expand through marriages and as children are born. And of course, people will pass on. The one constant in the universe is *change*. So, we shouldn't expect our Life Circle to remain intact for the duration of our journey.

All the pieces of your Circle don't need to be in place in order for you to be joyful. If you are on the right path or even moving in that direction, you can feel happy and satisfied during the journey as well.

It Matters A Lot How We Are Traveling Through Life

The **Explorer** — someone who is searching with the intent of self-discovery and in order to make wise Life Circle choices. (It doesn't mean every aspect of their life is planned out.)

The **Wanderer** — someone who meanders or moves about without a destination or purpose and who is basically aimless in life.

Creating a Life Circle that reflects what our Soul imagined is not easy—unless we knew as a child exactly what we wanted to be when we grew up, or we found our Soul Mate and all our friends in kindergarten. While some people do build their Circle early on, most of us need time to explore our options before we commit to a given path in life. As a rule, it is better to take as long as we need to make wise, long-lasting choices than it is to rush the process, especially when it comes to creating a family of our own.

Whether we are just starting out or still trying to "get a life," it's best if we proceed as an *explorer*. To be an explorer means we're doing our best, in a deliberate manner, to answer the four questions that were posed earlier (What do we love to do? etc.). The explorer does whatever it takes to connect with his or her Soul's Life Plan—including self-reflection, reading, schooling, heartfelt discussions with other people, and well-thought out "trial and error" (like when we choose a job or enter into a romantic relationship).

You don't have to create a "traditional" Circle with a spouse and kids, big house, corporate job and so on. Discover your own path and follow it.

Each of us is a unique being with our own Will. Therefore, no two Life Circles will be the same. And no one, not even our parents, has the right to tell us what our life should be like. As long as we aren't causing real harm, we ought to be free to create the Circle of *our* dreams. That is the only way we can satisfy our Soul and make the contributions we came here to make.

We live our life one moment at a time, and all our moments occur within the context of our Life Circle. Indeed, our Life Circle provides the structure and overall direction for our Soul's journey. Therefore, we want to make the choices that are right for us and that will allow us to be loving, joyful and creative. If that means we will make less money than our peers or it takes us longer than them to find our calling or Life Partner, that's okay. What is most important to God and our Soul is that we each discover and stay true to our own Life Plan.

If a man does not keep pace with his companions, perhaps it is because he hears a different drummer. Let him step to the music which he hears, however measured or far away.

Henry David Thoreau

A few words from our Higher Self —

If you are still creating the life I imagined, I can help. Listen to your intuition. That's me sending you guidance as you make your choices.

If your Life Circle is all in place, then cherish it and be grateful. Take good care of yourself, and enjoy what you have created.

In the next few chapters we will examine the elements of the Life Circle—namely, our family and friends, our work and hobbies, and our home and community. But first, let's take a quick look at the subject of "self-care."

How We Are Affects The Quality Of Our Life Circle and Vice Versa

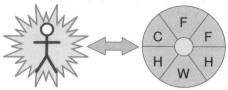

It is hard to create a good life if we are in a bad state. And if our Circle is negative, we will feel distressed.

The essence of *self-care* is treating our mind and body with respect and reverence so our Soul can make the most of its earthly journey. If we're not in a positive state, and especially if our self-love is blocked, we're more likely to make poor Life Circle choices. We might select an inappropriate partner or friend or pick a job we don't like or have a child for the wrong reasons. Of course, we could be in negative states and still create a good Circle. But we probably won't truly enjoy our life, and we may end up putting it all at risk.

We will not only make wiser choices when we're taking care of ourself, but we can also be a better spouse, friend and parent or whatever role we're playing in someone's life. These are compelling reasons for us to have a lifestyle and daily practice that will keep us in a healthy and positive state—physically, emotionally, intellectually and spiritually. When we are letting our "light shine through," as described in the previous chapter, we can more easily create a Circle that reflects the life our Soul imagined.

The Elements of a Good Life – Part A

We all need the essence of what a Life Circle provides. But we don't all find it in the same way or time or to the same degree. In this chapter we consider the first two elements of the Circle. There is a discussion of family and friends and also life partners, sex, and children. In the next chapter we will briefly look at how we can bring more love into our life. And then in the chapter after that we will cover the other elements of the Circle. My hope is these chapters will help us to create a good Life Circle or to enhance the elements we already have in place.

These Are The People Who Matter The Most to Me

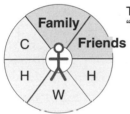

They provide the "essence" of –
Mutual love
Acceptance
Being there
Companions
Confidants

We need people in our life who will love, support and nurture us and for whom we can do the same. Not just because life is hard and we don't want to go through it alone, but also because we have a natural desire to be with our Kindred Souls. Deep down, we know that we are here to manifest the love that exists between our Souls and to help each other to learn and grow.

Parental Family

Mom and Dad, siblings, grandparents etc.

We first make contact with some of our kindreds when we are born, and we join our "parental" family. In theory, these should be among our best earthly connections, and indeed they are for many people. There are close-knit families where parents and their children and other relatives are mutually supportive and nurturing throughout their entire lives. They love each other and like being together. They have brought forth here on Earth the essence and special nature of their spiritual bond.

A good parental family (which, as noted before, might not include our birth parents), provides us with unconditional love, support, guidance and the spirit of kinship.

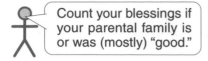

Count your blessings if your parental family is or was (mostly) "good."

No family is perfect, but many of us did not get what we really needed from our parents or siblings when we were growing up. We were part of a dysfunctional family. Our time together may not have been totally bad, but still our memories are mostly neutral or hurtful. So now, we're distant or even detached from some or all of those kindreds. Our shared history may keep us in each other's phone book and bring us together on occasion, but we can't sustain a meaningful or ongoing relationship. Such family situations are not uncommon, and they're a source of much sadness and regret.

God

Do what you can to improve your parental family relationships. And if it's possible, appreciate what you did have together. But don't lose sleep over what you didn't get. Instead, go create a group of kindreds who will give you what you need.

To be in a state of disharmony with a Kindred Soul is not good for us emotionally or spiritually. So if there is any hope of reconciling with or getting closer to a member of our parental family, we should make that effort. But we also have other options for bringing the essence of "family" into our life—such as finding a partner and having children.

Whether we are happy with our parental family or not, most of us want to create our own household. We're driven, in part, by the human instinct to extend our lineage and to live with others so we are not alone on our journey. Plus, we feel that if we choose our partner and maybe raise children of our own, we can create the kind of home we grew up in or wish we had.

But It's Not For Everyone

To create a family can be a wonderful choice, but it may not be right for us. Indeed, some of us are not equipped or at least not ready to be a good spouse or parent. Our Life Circle would be better off if we satisfied our need for love and acceptance in other ways. Other Souls *prefer* to be free of marital or parental commitments so they can devote more energy to the other elements of life, especially creative pursuits. Finally, some people choose not to make their own family so they can better help those in need.

There Is More Than One Way To Create a "Family"

We have alternatives other than getting married or producing children for giving and receiving love. We could adopt a child or be a foster parent, or be a mentor or a surrogate brother or sister. We could form several intimate friendships—or give a nice home to God's other children, the animals. We may be "alone" in the sense we have few if any blood or marital relatives, but there are many ways for us to realize the essence of "family."

We All Need A Group Of Loving Kindred Souls

Family, friends and pets who give meaning to our life.

Each of us is trying in our way and time to assemble a group of Kindred Souls who will love and accept us as we are and help us to be more loving, joyful and creative. These are the people (and pets) with whom we feel especially close and who nurture us. Our group doesn't have to be big or like anyone else's. And it can include people we don't see often but who are still important to us. Our group will change as kindreds come and go for a variety of reasons. And there will always be relationships that require healing or that could be made stronger. We all need to be in the company of loving kindreds, even though creating and maintaining such a group is not easy.

Love Is Thicker Than Blood

Ultimately, what matters the most is knowing that someone truly cares about our well-being and they want to be in our life. Genetic or birth family connections are powerful, but bonds that are based solely on love and mutual commitment can be just as strong. Indeed, some friendships can be even more satisfying than "normal" family ties because we have chosen to be with each other.

By the way, most of us have people in our families who are not Kindred Souls, such as some of our in-laws or step-relations. Still, we could become kindreds, and we can always learn something from those relationships.

Now, we will focus on a few of the many issues associated with creating our own household—namely Life Partners and children. And we'll take a brief look at the subject of sex too.

Life Partners

Co-Creators

We can be incredibly creative on our own, but there's an added power and magic that comes from combining our "Let there be ..." energy with that of a loving partner.

Most of us have a strong desire to share our journey with someone *extra* special. We want a partner who will see our happiness as part of their own and with whom we can be totally intimate—emotionally and physically. In the spirit of mutual love and respect, he or she will help us to become a better person and to realize our dreams. We will support each other and face life's challenges together.

A Life Partner is our companion and very best friend. We have common goals and values and are committed to each other. We are also "co-creators." We unite so we can make a good Life Circle together.

Making creative choices with a person we love is one of the great joys of life. Our combined "Let there be ..." ability can be wondrous. Whenever we are both focused on the same objective, whether it be building a home or writing a book, the results can be better and more satisfying than what we would create alone. We can be the "dynamic duo," if our Wills don't get in the way. And of all the areas in which we can be mutually creative, having and raising a child is the most profound. We will get to that subject shortly, but for now the point is partners need to be responsible in using their creative power.

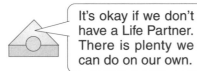

It's okay if we don't have a Life Partner. There is plenty we can do on our own.

A Life Partner is not easy to find or to keep. So, we might have "lovers" or temporary partners but no lifelong relationship. That doesn't mean we are flawed or our life has been a "failure." It could be our Soul wanted to make this journey pretty much alone so we could learn how to be self-loving or self-sufficient or to really develop our talents. Or maybe we just haven't found the right person yet.

God

If you're still looking for a Life Partner, don't give up. In the meantime, seek fulfillment as a single person. Pursue a creative or spiritual path and work on your growth. Much of the essence of a "partnership" can be found in the other areas of your Life Circle.

Who Is or Will Be Our Life Partner?

Each of us incarnates with at least one Kindred Soul who could be an excellent partner. We might find him or her early on and with little effort, or it could take us well into our senior years before our paths cross. The search for true love requires faith and patience. And if and when we do finally connect, we might be together for the rest of our lives or for just awhile.

Each of us would love to be with our Soul Mate because we were made for each other. But it may not happen in this lifetime; or if it does, it may not last. Still, we can be very happy with one of our "closer" Kindred Souls. We can create a good life together. We get into trouble when we choose a "distant" person who isn't compatible with us or with whom we have no spiritual bond.

Where Is Our Soul Mate? There are several possibilities:

1. We are already together as Life Partners or in other roles.
2. We will meet and fall in love sometime in the future.
3. He or she is on Earth, but we may not meet or "connect."
4. We were together, but are no longer. Maybe we split up, or they passed on.
5. He or she didn't incarnate this time; so, they're loving us from the Spirit World. We will be together in a future life and forever as Souls.

Life involves risk taking, but the choice of a Life Partner is so consequential that we need to be as sure as we can that we're selecting a person who is good for us. Although love is a matter of the heart and Soul, we need to engage our *Rational* Mind too and ask it if our choice makes sense. We don't want to overanalyze our decision or disregard the role of passion, but we're looking for a lifetime of love and companionship. Sexual desire alone will not sustain the relationship. In fact, it can result in a very tenuous bond. A partnership that generates a passion for all of life, including sex, will be much more satisfying and long-lasting.

What Makes For a *Poor* Life Partner Choice

☐ We are too young or impulsive; we're infatuated or just physically attracted.

☐ We are driven mostly by the need for companionship. We're lonely.

☐ We want children more than we want a fulfilling partnership.

☐ We are not really compatible; we will likely grow apart; there are warning signs of serious interpersonal conflict.

☐ We're choosing for selfish reasons such as wanting money or status.

☐ Our partner has weaknesses that will limit our bond or be harmful.

Make a choice that satisfies your body, mind, heart and Soul.

God

What are your heart and intuition telling you? If you have major doubts, then keep looking, especially if you want children.

Remember, no one is perfect. If you judge a potential partner by an arbitrary ideal such as physical beauty, you may be rejecting your Soul Mate.

We're here on a mission of personal growth. So we need a partner who can do more than keep us company, "wrinkle our sheets" or make babies. We need a person who can support and nurture us and who can help us expand our energy.

We can think of a partnership as *an intensive course in Life Lessons,* where two people each with weaknesses share a lot of time and space together. In such close contact, we can learn how to love and to bring forth the joy and creativity that is inside us. Or, if we choose a non-kindred or someone who is out-of-balance (or if we're in that state), then we will learn mostly about anger, distrust and so forth. The choice as to which lessons we will learn is ours. We are not predestined to have a bad partnership.

If a relationship doesn't work out, that doesn't necessarily mean it was a bad choice. Maybe it was the right person, but one or both of us made mistakes. Furthermore, difficult or short-lived partnerships can produce great results (such as children or a creative project), and they can help us grow. But some Life Partner choices are misguided, causing far more harm than good. Our Soul is praying that we will avoid these relationships.

How Do I Know If I Have Found a Good Life Partner?

- ☐ I love him/her with all my heart and Soul; I want us to spend the rest of our lives together.
- ☐ He/she loves me, believes in me, and treats me with respect, kindness and affection.
- ☐ IF we had children, he/she would be a good, loving parent.
- ☐ There is mutual support, acceptance and trust; we help each other to grow and to be fulfilled in life.
- ☐ We are best friends with common interests; we have fun together; we support and respect our individual interests.
- ☐ We're intimate; we talk about our feelings, hopes and fears.
- ☐ We would each do anything to protect the other from harm; (if he/she has been harmful in the past, they have truly changed.)
- ☐ If we have faced tough times, our relationship got stronger.
- ☐ I believe we will love each other as we age and "look older."
- ☐ I feel mostly joyful and passionate about life and good about myself because we're together; I miss him/her when we're apart.
- ☐ We're "compatible:"

Now	Future*		Now	Future*	
☐	☐	Physically	☐	☐	Spiritually
☐	☐	Intellectually	☐	☐	Values / Beliefs
☐	☐	Emotionally	☐	☐	Life Goals

* A "best guess" based on our closeness now and on our individual capacity and desire for growth.

The Soul of a potential Life Partner

You might find me at anytime or anywhere. But the best way is to do what you love and to be with like-minded people. Look for love in all the right places.

The quest for our Life Partner can be a challenge, but it is also an opportunity to prepare ourself for when we do finally find our mate. "Interim relationships" can help us to better understand who we are and what kind of partner we would like to have, and they can teach us how to be intimate and nurturing. If we keep choosing harmful partners, we are learning the importance of discretion and self-love. Every relationship can prepare us to be a better companion, if we're aware and willing to learn.

Good Partners Are In It Together

A partnership is a journey of mutual choices. You fall in love and create a Life Circle together. And when the going gets tough you work through it *together*.

Staying in love is a lot harder than falling in love. Even Soul Mates may find it difficult or impossible to live together harmoniously. The question is, will we use the obstacles on our path as a means of mutual growth or allow them to destroy our earthly bond? Will we do all that is necessary to honor our spiritual connection?

Typical Challenges Faced By Life Partners

Self-love issues cause us to be critical or hurtful of our partner.	The stresses of everyday life extinguish the romantic flame.
We argue about who is right, and we refuse to compromise.	We grow apart or get bored; we don't have enough fun together.
We stop talking; we blame our partner for all that is wrong.	We forget why we fell in love; we stop trying or give up too easily.

Just because there are problems in a relationship doesn't mean we are not with our Soul Mate. Nurturing an earthly bond is hard work. And we shouldn't assume we can solve all of our issues on our own. We may need a "professional" to help us.

What's Wrong With Our Bond?

Us   Our partner

???? Can we fix it?

☐ My choice was poor. He or she is not necessarily a bad person; they're just not right for me. I should leave.

☐ Good choice at the time, but now the bond is harmful, or the love is gone. It can't be repaired. I should leave.

☐ Good choice, but we are not relating well anymore. I want to make it better, and I believe that we can.

Both partners need to check the third box if the bond is to be repaired.

Every partnership will be "tested," but not every one can or should be fixed. If we chose wisely but are now in trouble because one or both of us screwed-up, it is God's hope we will stay together and try to fix what is broken —assuming of course there is still real love and the situation is not harmful.

When a relationship is headed for trouble, or if it already is broken, it helps to remind ourself why we were drawn to our partner in the first place. Thinking of what we once had together can dispel some of our negative feelings. Having a shared vision or a common goal that we can achieve together, such as fixing our bond, is also helpful. The union of "Let there be ..." power can be very healing.

Partnerships end, but the separation doesn't have to be awful or really hurtful. Be kind and honest with each other, and try to keep some love in your hearts.

Leaving our partner can be a painful and scary choice, even when we know it is the right thing to do. Charting a new course, especially at an older age, takes a lot of courage. Still, if we have given it our best shot and we feel our happiness lies elsewhere, we may have no choice. If the partnership must dissolve, God wants us to do our best to end it with love and understanding instead of anger or hate, especially if we have children. Now, let's finish this part of the chapter on a more positive note.

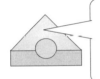

A good partner is a gift. If you have found yours, express your love often and be grateful for every moment you're together.

Communication is an essential element of a lasting relationship. The bond cannot grow or be sustained in bad times if we don't express our true feelings or listen in a loving way to theirs. In the Spirit World we can communicate telepathically, but on Earth we must learn how to *speak* what we are feeling in our heart.

Let's Talk About SEX

We live in a world obsessed with sex. Religious teachings make us feel guilty about our physical desires, and the distorted view of sexuality we see in the media makes us feel inadequate about ourselves and our relationships. In this environment, it is a major challenge for us and our partner to create a mutually satisfying sex life.

Sex is *not* by nature sinful, immoral or an uncontrollable urge. It is a glorious act *if done responsibly and thoughtfully and with joy.*

What Sex Can Mean ... if we have a real bond with our partner, we care as much about their needs as we do our own, and we focus on the process more than the end result.

- A celebration of mutual love.
- A sacred union of the body, mind and Soul.
- An opportunity for mutual pleasure and for physical or emotional healing.
- An occasion to enhance intimacy and harmony and to strengthen our bond.

The physical aspect of sex is very nice, but we would prefer to have "great sex." It happens when we also connect emotionally and spiritually with our partner.

Most Souls want to experience sensual pleasure in the context of a loving Life Partnership. They view sex as an exciting and sacred way to honor the bond that exists between two Kindred Souls. Also, they favor sex that is more than just physical. They like to feel the passion on all levels of their being. However, our Souls know we won't always have a Life Partner or be in a committed relationship. Still, it is the wish of most Souls that there be mutual caring, respect and honesty between us and our sexual partners. In that way, we can at least feel good about ourself and the choices we've made.

God Prefers That We Practice Higher-Level Sex

My partner and I are truly "making love."

We have a spiritual connection with our partner. We're in a committed relationship and the sex is an act of intimacy. It is safe and responsible, mutually satisfying and causing no harm. It's more than orgasmic.

Instead of Lower-Level Sex

I or my partner will regret this. It is not right.

We do it with someone we don't really care for or respect. We cause or risk harm to ourself or others. We're drunk or high. (Our Soul would rather we have a loving relationship with ourself than do this.)

What Is Proper and "Moral" Sexual Behavior?

RESPECT is the essence of morality. Are you acting with self-respect? Are you being respectful of your sexual partner and of others who may be affected? Are you being honest, or are you cheating on someone? And are you being respectful of the Soul that will incarnate if you have a child?

Are We "Ready" For Great Sex?

The State of Our Relationship

No affection or respect; lots of tension; or we have no partner	Affectionate and communicative; respectful; joyful and passionate

Our Personal State (and Theirs)

Emotionally impaired; low self-love; "negative"	Well-balanced; good self-love; "positive"

Our Everyday Circumstances

Lots of stress; little or no time with our partner	Relatively calm; plenty of time for romance

If we are living on the left-side of these categories, it is highly unlikely we will have a satisfying sex life. Many of us are somewhere in between the extremes.

The quality of our sex life is a "barometer." It reflects the strength of our relationship and of our emotional well-being and that of our partner. It also is a measure of how crazy our life is and whether we are satisfied with the other elements of our Circle. If we're not happy with our work, for example, or we are feeling anxious or inadequate in other ways, our sex life suffers.

 Sex and joy. They're meant to coexist in our life.

Sex is an expression of the "life-force" within us. If we want passion in the bedroom, then we need to make the other aspects of our life a "sensual" experience as well. When we can find joy and pleasure from simple activities—such as being in nature or with friends, cooking and eating food, watching a sunset or making each other laugh—we then become more amorous. *The "joy of sex" follows from being a joyful person.*

Sex Can Be Better If We're Better

 A healthy, balanced Reality Maker leads to a more satisfying relationship with our partner.

Men and women are different, but a lot of interpersonal issues are the result of "impaired" Reality Makers.

We often think of what our partner could do to make us happier. But the more helpful questions might be, "What can *I* do to enhance our relationship?" and "How do *I* need to change?"

Getting ourself into a positive state involves more than physical changes. Most of us need to develop *emotionally* too. It is this element of the Reality Maker that is typically out-of-balance, especially in men. Besides, having a kind and loving heart can be just as sexy as having a "hard body," if not more so.

Men and Women Seem To Be "Wired" Differently

In a woman's body, I usually need to be romanced and nurtured before sex.

Emotional Mind

But in a man's body, having sex helps me to open up and to be more loving.

In response to the question, "How often do you have sex?" The man says: "Hardly ever. Maybe three times a week." The woman says: "Constantly. I'd say three times a week."

From *Annie Hall* by Woody Allen

Clearly, there are differences between the sexes when it comes to sex. Some of those distinctions are due to biology and others to the way we are raised in our society. Whatever the causes are, these differences represent yet another challenge for partners who wish to create harmony in their relationship and to be mutually satisfied. Still, two Kindred Souls can, if they're coming from a place of love and cooperation, learn to be honest and revealing about their sexual needs and desires. They can create a sex life that embodies romance, spontaneity, regularity and variety.

We Are Really Alike

On a human level we seem like we are from different planets. But in a deeper, spiritual sense, we are actually the same.

Man's Soul   Woman's Soul

While we do have gender-based differences, it also helps to remind ourselves that we are foremost spiritual beings. We and our partner possess both feminine and masculine energy, and we want the same things in life (love, joy and so forth). Although the bodies we incarnate into are dissimilar and our Emotional Minds are wired a bit differently, we can still come together to form a passionate union. There is probably some form of "sex" in the spiritual realm, but we have this great opportunity to express our devotion to each other in the Physical World. We shouldn't let it slip away.

I think angels are envious of humans because we have bodies; they don't, and love-making makes the angels flap their wings in envy.

Matthew Fox in *Natural Grace: Dialogues on Science and Spirituality* by Rupert Sheldrake and Matthew Fox

Sex has its pleasures and perils.

Sex is a choice that can have far-reaching consequences. It can affect our emotional and physical well-being in positive *or* negative ways, such as causing an unwanted pregnancy or giving us a disease that has irreparable or even fatal effects. If we have a child before we are ready or with the wrong person, it will limit our other Life Circle choices. If we are not prepared to be a parent, we may severely damage our child's chance at a good life. If we're unfaithful or have sex with another person's mate, we can ruin one or more families. We need to treat the power of sex with great respect and be sure to use our better judgment.

Will

It's my job to control the sexual drive, especially when we're about to do something that we will probably regret later.

It's natural to be attracted to other people or to "lust in our heart." But if we love and respect our partner, we won't act upon those desires.

Our Will is tested every day, and few choices challenge our strength and moral character like sex does. At times, we must choose whether we will do something that *might* have immediate gratification but with negative or at least questionable consequences. When it comes to sex, our choices ought to leave us feeling physically and emotionally better and closer to our partner—and without any regrets. Ultimately, it's about who we allow to share our energy. We want partners who are "expansive" and good for us.

We Need To Teach Our Children Well

Raging hormones, peer pressure, self-esteem issues and natural inquisitiveness can all make the sex drive in teenagers overwhelming. Parents need to provide their children with knowledge and guidelines which will help them to make wise choices. Discussing the concept and benefits of "higher-level" sex, which involves mutual respect and commitment between partners, would help young adults begin their sex lives in a healthier and more satisfying way.

God

Deciding when and with whom to have sex are two of the most important choices you will ever make. So please choose wisely. There are lives at stake. Always remember that I meant sex to be an act that was good for your heart and Soul too.

Let there be ... Children

For Many, This Is "The Meaning of Life"

To Create a Family

We are here to learn how to be more loving, joyful and creative. Becoming a parent and raising children can be one of the best and most gratifying ways to do that. Indeed, there is no act more sacred than procreation. To conceive a child is to participate with God in the miracle of life, and to be a parent is to be a guardian and teacher for one of our dearest Kindred Souls.

Having a child is also one of the most consequential of acts. So, God wants us to make that choice with great care. We're to think it through completely before we engage in unprotected sex. We need to consider if creating a new life would be good for us, for the Soul who would be our child, for other members of our family, and for the Earth and people already here. Procreation is meant to be the most "conscious" of acts.

The Four Key Parenting Choices

God

1. Will you have children?
2. When and with whom will you have them?
3. How many children will you have?
4. How will you raise them?

What Having a Child Can Mean and Is Supposed to Mean

A manifestation of adult love; a sign of a strong, committed bond	Devoting one's self to a Kindred Soul and giving unconditional love	A chance to be a good parent and to prepare a child for their journey

Regrettably, this is not always reality. People have children before they're ready, with partners who aren't committed to them or when their relationships are in trouble.

It is God's strong preference that Her "co-creators" be two adults in a stable and loving Life Partnership and who are prepared to be good parents. But God knows not all relationships last and that a responsible and loving individual can provide a good home too. She has great respect for single parents who raise their children well. Of course, God is also eternally grateful to the people who care for and adopt the children who were conceived by others and who need a loving family.

Why do you want a child? Are you sure being a parent is what your Soul wanted to do in this life, or at least at this particular time? Maybe you should wait.

If we're thinking of becoming a parent because we believe having a child might help fix our relationship or make up for a lack of love or meaning in our life, or give us companionship on holidays or when we're in the nursing home—or because we feel it's what we're "supposed to do"—then we should rethink our choice. We need better reasons than these. The Kindred Soul who would be our child is very concerned when we're thinking mostly of our self-interests.

What Am I Giving Up?

Parenthood can bring us great love and joy, but it is also a path of hard work, total commitment and financial responsibility. It can limit or even preclude other activities that are important to us, such as our education or career or having time for ourself or to be with our partner. So, before we have a child we need to consider what the personal sacrifices will be. We may decide parenthood doesn't fit into our Life Plan or there are other things we want to do first. We should go into it with our eyes wide open.

What-If The Unexpected Happens?

Even if we're sure we would like being a parent, there is no guarantee our health, finances or relationship will remain in a positive state. And forces beyond our control can make life difficult for our child. So, we need to ask ourself if we have what it takes to cope with a disability or serious illness or any other challenge that might arise, including being a single parent. Of course, people "rise to the occasion" when bad things happen. But if we have real doubts about our ability to cope with the "what-if's," then it's best if we wait until we're more assured or conditions are more favorable.

It takes a lot of self-awareness to know if having a child is right for you. Are you willing to sign up for a lifelong adventure that will be full of surprises, not all of which will be good? Do you have an adequate reservoir of emotional and physical energy you can tap into? Is there already too much stress or uncertainty in your life? Parenting can be a glorious calling, but it's not for everyone. And that's okay.

I really want to have children. It is definitely part of my Life Plan. But now the question is ...

Am I Ready To Be a Parent?

- ☐ I love myself (for the most part).
- ☐ I am a mature, responsible adult.
- ☐ My partner (if I have one) is kind, loving and committed to me, and he or she will be a good parent.
- ☐ I have a safe and loving "home."
- ☐ I have the means to provide for a child's upbringing.
- ☐ I have the time and energy to love and raise a child, even if I must cope with big problems.
- ☐ I'm in a positive state; or at least I have no harmful weaknesses.
- ☐ I'm a good role model and teacher.

 If you're not ready, then please wait — and use "preventative measures" if you're having sex.

A child's Soul is not expecting a perfect life situation, but it does want a promising start to its earthly sojourn. Though our child's fate is not entirely up to us, we generally are the major factor in the "equation." So, if we are not ready enough, we put the quality of their life and ours at risk.

Each of us has a group of kindreds in the Spirit World who are "waiting" to be our children, and we (for the most part) decide if and when they will incarnate. If we bring them into the world before we're ready, they will accept that challenge and learn the lessons of their life. Most Souls, however, would prefer to be born into good conditions, especially if it is in our power to give them a better start. In fact, one of the lessons *we* are here to learn is how to make life less of a struggle for our children and ourselves.

It's All About "Preparation"

Phase 1: We prepare **ourself** and our **partnership** for parenthood.

Phase 2: We prepare our **child** for a meaningful and satisfying life.

If we don't do a good job in Phase 1, it is *much* harder to do Phase 2.

When we are happy with the state of our life and relationship and with who we are, we can better nurture and raise a child. That is why our Kindred Souls are hoping we will "get it together" *before* we become a parent.

What's the big deal? Most Souls are born into "less than ready" conditions, and many go on to make good lives for themselves.

Most of us probably wouldn't be here or be who we are had our parents waited until they met all of the "Am I Ready?" criteria. (Besides, we all turned out fine, didn't we?)

Of course, it's possible to emerge from a difficult childhood and to create a good or even great life for oneself. But for each person who accomplishes that feat, there are many others who don't. Their life conditions are too onerous to overcome. Moreover, we are now at a point in our planet's history where we need to be extra careful about *when* we bring a child into the world and about *how many* children we have.

The Souls coming to be children are hopeful but are very concerned too.

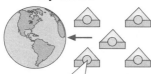

It's too crowded and they've made a mess of a great little planet.

A New Slogan For the New Millennium

I'm replacing "Go forth and multiply" with this: **Be more ready for parenthood and have fewer children.**

In many ways these are the best of times for a Soul to incarnate. Medicine and technology have made the journey longer and more exciting than ever before, and many aspects of life are far easier. But at the same time, a lot of us are "stressed out" by the pace, expense and demands of our existence.

In spite of our advances, there are still limits as to how many children two people (or a single parent) can properly care for. When we exceed those limits we create undue suffering for ourselves and our children. Of course, the Earth has its limits too. So, even if we can handle more kids in our own family, we now need to practice restraint. We will take a closer look at the population issue in the chapter *Creating Heaven On Earth*.

Every child comes with the message that God is not yet discouraged of man.

Rabindranath Tagore; Bengali philosopher; 1861–1941

But I am troubled. So many children are living in poor conditions. A child should be wanted and well cared for.

We Can Use Our "Let There Be ..." Power In Other Ways

Not having children (or having fewer) can be a very positive choice. It gives us more time for our own growth, which is not "selfish" but honoring our needs. Plus, we can use our gifts to help create a better world for everyone—including the children who are already here and the ones who are on their way.

Childbearing is not a necessity, it is a choice. Indeed, it is a vocation. Those who are called to have children should do so ... But those who are not called are equally important, for their creativity becomes available for the larger human family.

Barbara Marx Hubbard – futurist and author

If we do have children, how do we help them to become happy and fulfilled adults?

A child is a loving Soul placed into our care by God. So, naturally we want to do our best to be a good parent. But it's not easy. There are so many factors beyond our control that we must contend with, including the fact that every Soul comes with its own personality and issues to resolve. So, despite our best efforts, we cannot guarantee our child's happiness. Still, it is our role to do all we can to help our Kindred Soul make the most of his or her journey.

Giving your child **unconditional love** and helping them to be **self-loving** are at the top of the list of what parents do.

Whether we're four or ninety-four, we all need to know that someone loves us exactly as we are, "warts and all." As a child, our self-love can't flow if we feel mom or dad's love is contingent upon how we act or look. And we need to know that if we screw up, even badly, they will still see the goodness of our Soul and love us. That doesn't mean our parents should condone our negative behavior, but that they will always "be there" to help us become better. We need to start our journey in the care of people who love us unconditionally. Only then will we feel good about ourself and believe we deserve the very best in life. Finally, it makes a big difference if prospective parents deal with their own self-love issues before having children.

A full discussion of how to raise children is beyond the scope of this book (and my expertise). So instead, I will present just a few additional perspectives for your consideration.

The Essence Of What Our Children Need

Ideally, we would be able to describe every young adult in this way.

Spiritually – They see themselves as a child of God and are aware of their connection to all of life. They're connected with their Higher Self and God through intuition, meditation and prayer.

Will – They know how to make wise choices in the face of fear and temptation and uncertainty. They have good judgment. They are determined and self-disciplined. They have "Willpower."

Emotional Mind – They love and accept themselves as they are. They're able to express their feelings and to love others. They are kind, tolerant and compassionate. They have a passion for life.

Rational Mind – They're educated. They have "book smarts" and common sense. They understand the "facts of life."

Physically – They respect their bodies and have a regular routine of exercise, eating healthy food and preventative care.

Values and Beliefs – They're guided by moral principles. They believe in their right and ability to be loving, joyful and creative.

Their Calling – They have discovered and are developing their gifts. They're on the path that can bring them happiness and allow them to make a contribution to the world.

Every child is unique. So, tailor how you raise and nurture them.

All children have similar developmental needs, as listed above, but that doesn't mean they should all be raised the same. A child is a "gift from God," but each one arrives in its own "package," so to speak. Therefore, parenting calls for sensitivity. By really getting to know our child, we can adapt our methods to fit his or her needs. For example, some kids need gentleness; others need more firmness. We want to nurture and guide each child in a way that is best for his or her growth so they can become who they are meant to be. Ultimately, we want our child to leave the nest ready, willing and able to fulfill their own Soul's Life Plan.

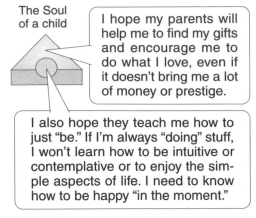

The Soul of a child

I hope my parents will help me to find my gifts and encourage me to do what I love, even if it doesn't bring me a lot of money or prestige.

I also hope they teach me how to just "be." If I'm always "doing" stuff, I won't learn how to be intuitive or contemplative or to enjoy the simple aspects of life. I need to know how to be happy "in the moment."

Every Soul arrives with God-given abilities that will provide joy and passion in their life and help others too. Parents are on a quest with their children to discover those gifts so each child can pursue his or her calling. It is the parents' role to be supportive and to instill in their children the belief that they can realize their dreams. Of course, parents can show a child what it's like to be fulfilled and "creatively satisfied" if *they* are doing what they love.

For children (or anyone) to find their "calling," it is important for them to be self-aware and in touch with their Soul. When we're quiet and reflective our inner wisdom is revealed to us, which can help us in all areas of life. Instead of teaching our children how to be "at peace" in the moment or to be "mindful," we often have them and ourselves on a treadmill of endless activity and stress. We can get so focused on consumerism and competitiveness that we ignore or forget our children's spiritual side (and ours too). This reality makes for sad Souls. While we came to Earth to achieve and do things, we were also hoping to learn how to just "be." Spending time in nature, learning how to be a good friend, becoming more intuitive and being playful are near the top of every Soul's Life Plan.

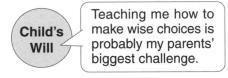

Child's Will

Teaching me how to make wise choices is probably my parents' biggest challenge.

We are here to learn how to be better choosers, and it is the parents' role to be their child's principal guide and teacher. The education of a child's Will is meant to be a deliberate and conscious process that occurs throughout the child's formative years. By establishing early on a practice of thoughtful dialogue with their child, parents can address the many aspects of making choices. They can discuss: the Life Circle and how to create a good one; how to best care for one's body, mind and Soul; proper values and beliefs; how to treat others; and how to consider potential consequences *before* one acts.

"I've Been There, Done That."
Sharing Wisdom With Our Child

I'd like to tell you about my life. What I've learned might make your journey easier.

Parents are "trailblazers" who experience the lessons of life before their children do. Yet in many families relatively little of the parents' wisdom is passed along. So, children proceed on their journey without the benefit of a good road map, and they end up making many of the same mistakes as their parents did. It doesn't have to be this way. Parents can help their children avoid at least some pain and heartbreak by sharing the story and lessons of their lives. Of course, the children must be respectful and willing to listen, which is more likely to be the case if they and their parents have been engaged in an ongoing dialogue. Finally, children need to realize that parents are *not* condoning negative behavior by being open about their own past.

Don't Just Tell Them, Show Them

We teach our children not just by what we say but also by what we do. They are watching to see if we're living as we're preaching or if we are hypocrites. They will be more apt to listen to us if we are "walking the walk." Since children tend to emulate our behavior, we need to ask ourself what sort of lasting impression our words and actions might leave. If we're setting a harmful example, we need to change our ways—and be a role model for personal growth!

Children learn what it's like to be a "whole person" when they see their parents leading full and satisfying lives.

Raising children requires a lot of self-sacrifice. As author Calvin Trillin put it, "Children are either at the center of your life or they're not. The rest is commentary." Of course, it is also important that we find a balance between the responsibilities of parenting and caring for our own needs. When we're feeling physically, emotionally and spiritually well, we can give more to our child.

Ideally, we would model how wonderful life can be by taking good care of ourself, using our creative gifts, having fun, helping those in need and spending meaningful time with our family and friends. Unfortunately, this is not possible for many parents who are facing economic pressures and other major challenges. Still, I am re-minded of how Alice Walker (author of *The Color Purple*) described her mother—who, in spite of financial hardship, regularly found the time to tend to her flowers. Gardening was a joyful activity that used one of her gifts and was important to her Soul. By honoring her own needs and valuing herself, she not only created beauty in the form of flowers, but she also inspired her children.

> She handed down respect for the possibilities — and the will to grasp them.
>
> Alice Walker writing about her mother; from *In Search of Our Mothers' Gardens*

Some Final Thoughts On Children ...

God

From a spiritual perspective, a parent and child are usually contemporaries. They're Kindred Souls who want to express their mutual love and respect. But on Earth the parent is "in charge" of the family.

A child's Soul may be "old and wise," but it still needs kind and loving care. I know that no one can be the perfect parent, but please do the best you can. And please know that both your child's Soul and I appreciate all your hard work and love.

We're All Trying To Bring More Love Into Our Lives

We want to be with our Kindred Souls so we can receive *and* give love.

Being with a Life Partner and having children can be wonderful ways to bring more love into our life. But as we have seen, those choices are not for everyone. And when they are right for us, it is important that we be ready and make thoughtful choices.

Regardless of what our group of kindreds looks like, most of us want to enhance the quality of our relationships. We want a more intimate, meaningful and satisfying connection with our parents, siblings, spouse, children or friends. So, before we consider the other elements of the Life Circle (our work, home etc.), let's take a brief look at how we might improve the bond between us and the people we love.

Bringing More Love Into Our Life

A Good Relationship Reflects The Specialness of Our Spiritual Bond

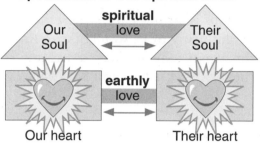

After we leave this planet and return to the Spirit World, we're going to run into the Souls of the people who were a part of our life as family members or friends. We will reminisce about our time on Earth, and we will reflect on how we treated each other. It is useful to ask ourself now, while we are still here, how those conversations might go and whether we will be pleased or saddened by them.

What Will Our Soul Be Saying To Each Of Our Kindreds?

> All in all, we honored our spiritual bond. It wasn't easy, but we stayed connected on Earth and even became closer. We were loving, and we helped each other to grow. Good for us.

> We could have done much better. Our earthly bond never was satisfying, or we let it get weak or broken. Maybe one or both of us was really hurtful. I wish we had been more loving. What a shame.

We're also going to be saying this to some of our kindreds:

> We never met on Earth because one or both of us didn't use our gifts, have enough fun, or follow our intuition. So, we missed the chance to find each other. We would have been great together.

To a certain extent, the nature of our Soul's "after-life conversations" will be a measure of how much love we experienced. Yet even if we think we're not going to like many of those dialogues, we shouldn't be too hard on ourself. Everyone returns to the Spirit World with regrets. But more importantly, there are things we can do from this point forward to bring more love into our life. We can set the stage for some better or even great Soul-to-Soul talks.

"Find, Enhance and Heal" – It's how we bring more love into our life.

FIND some of our kindreds out there in the world; make new friends; maybe find a Life Partner	ENHANCE the relationships we are in now; make them stronger and more intimate	HEAL some of the bonds that are in bad shape or broken; restore the love or let go of the past

The *quality* of our relationships is far more important than the quantity of people in our life. But many of us would like to find a few more kindreds. While this is not easy, we keep searching for people who will share our interests and values and who will love and accept us as we are.

It has been said before, but it's worth repeating: By doing what you love and what brings you joy, you will be among your kindreds. You'll be more "attractive" too, energetically speaking. Get involved in groups and community activities. And treat each person you meet with kindness. He or she might be a kindred.

Kindreds. You can't live without them. And sometimes you can't live *with* them.

Finding a kindred is just part of the challenge. We also need to create and sustain a meaningful relationship. Since we have something to learn or to resolve with each of our kindreds, we can think of these relationships as "test cases" or opportunities for our mutual growth. Indeed, we are here to learn how to be loving in spite of our human weaknesses.

Even though kindreds are predisposed to be loving towards each other, we are, *while embodied in our human forms,* also prone to be hurtful, although that is not our intent. So, we often find that our relationships with the people who matter the most to us can be our biggest source of stress and frustration. Some of our earthly bonds might be seriously impaired; others will be broken. To restore the connection (which may not be possible in all cases), we will need to heal our emotional wounds.

Healing is the act of releasing our feelings of anger and hurt through understanding and forgiveness. We can't heal every bond, but some relationships more than others really call for us to give it our best shot.

We all have certain relationships, like with a parent or sibling, which are problematic and about which our Soul is thinking: "Please try to heal the bond and make peace. The two of us have been kindreds since the Big Kaboom. We don't want to end this life full of sadness and regret." Forgiveness and healing are so important that I devote an entire chapter to them later in the book.

Now, let's focus on the *second* option for bringing more love into our life, which is to enhance the quality of our relationships. This is a big topic, and we will briefly consider just one aspect of it.

We Want To Be "Up Close and Personal" With Our Loved Ones

The **Intimacy** Zone -where we express our true feelings and a real connection is made

Superficiality Zone -where we keep to our- selves emotionally and we don't really "connect"

Have you ever finished a phone call with a friend or left a family gathering and asked yourself, "What was that all about?"— knowing that you and your kindred(s) didn't open your hearts to each other, even a little? Many of us spend a lot of time in the Superficiality Zone with the people we love, and that makes us sad and frustrated. We want to be "real" and share some of our innermost feelings, but instead we discuss trivial matters and remain mute on our personal affairs. We are talking with each other, but we're not really connecting in any meaningful or satisfying way.

> What we have here is a failure to communicate.
> From the movie *Cool Hand Luke*

Emotional Mind

> I am mostly responsible for relationship problems. I'm easily hurt and disappointed. I get defensive, judgmental and self-centered. I am very sensitive too. So, I don't usually say what I really feel, or I say something hurtful I don't really mean.

There are many reasons why we are not more intimate with the people in our lives. These days most of us are so busy and stressed and geographically separated that we don't usually have the time and energy or the opportunity to get "closer." Moreover, there is a part of us, namely our Emotional Mind, that can get in our way.

I am afraid.

Emotional Mind

Fear is blocking the road to intimacy. We're afraid of what others might say, do *or think* if we express our true feelings. We are concerned that we will be criticized or have our emotional secrets, once revealed, thrown back at us in some way. We are vulnerable when we're intimate. And being in such a position can be disconcerting, especially for men, who feel the need to be "manly" and in control of their emotions.

Most of us don't know how to be intimate. We didn't get that kind of training growing up.

We shouldn't be too hard on ourself or our kindreds for not being more intimate. We each have our Emotional Mind issues, and most of us didn't learn how to be close. So now we must develop new ways of relating if we are to leave the Superficiality Zone. We will look at some suggestions in a minute, but first we need to remember that "it takes two to be intimate."

We shouldn't try to make a relationship something that it isn't or won't be. Some family members and friends may not have much in common with us anymore beyond a shared history. Or they may be unwilling to make the effort. So, it's best if we focus on those relationships which are likely to grow and where the other person also wants to get closer to us. And we may want to take "baby steps" at first. If we can make each moment together just a little more meaningful than before, we will eventually create an earthly bond that reflects our spiritual connection.

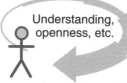

Just because a relationship can't be more intimate doesn't mean we should end it or disparage the other person. People express love in their own way, and we can be grateful for what they do give us. Besides, people change. Maybe we will get closer in the future.

We Must Give What We Wish To Receive

Understanding, openness, etc.

It's "relationship karma."

Perhaps the best way to enhance our relationships is to treat our kindreds as we want to be treated. Also, we need to take chances and overcome our fear of being ourself. There is no guarantee the other person will join us in the Intimacy Zone, but it won't happen at all if we don't try.

Twelve Guidelines For Relating In "The Intimacy Zone"

 This is how we treat each other in the Spirit World. It takes more effort on Earth, but we usually find that it gets easier with practice and that the results are well worth it.

1. Always honor the love that exists between our Souls; do our best to cause no harm; be loyal and trustworthy.

2. Be understanding, supportive and empathetic. How would we feel, or what would we need, if we were in their shoes?

3. Make it a **judgement-free** zone, except when someone is really harming themselves or others.

4. Be open and clear about our needs and feelings instead of holding them in; express them without blame or judgement.

5. Allow each other to be heard; really listen; respect each other's heartfelt feelings and vulnerabilities.

6. Offer suggestions and opinions in an informative, non-pushy way, and let others make their own choices.

7. Talk about meaningful topics; share joyful thoughts, hopes and dreams, as well as fears and worries.

8. Know and respect what we and the other person can and cannot give to each other; have realistic expectations.

9. "Be there" when we are needed; don't give up on the relationship when the going gets tough.

10. Deal with problems as they arise; accept responsibility for what we may have done; give each other the benefit of the doubt.

11. Let go of worn-out issues from the past; be forgiving; help each other to grow; be "in the moment."

12. Be affectionate. Share the initiative in making contact. Have fun together.

The key is to feel "safe" and free to be ourselves.

The "Three A's" of Mindfulness Are Important Too

Awareness – of how we are behaving and of each other's needs.
Acceptance – of the non-harmful weaknesses we each have.
Appreciation – of each other's love and good qualities.

Being intimate is hard at times. So, it's okay to go "off-line" now and then and to take a break from our bonding. We should also be allowed to say "ouch," which means we feel the other person has broken one of the guidelines and hurt us. And there should be, on balance, a fairly equal amount of give and take. Intimacy is meant to be a two-way street.

No two people, not even Soul Mates or the closest of kindreds, will be harmonious all the time. Disagreement and conflict are not inherently bad. We can learn and grow from such experiences. The key is to keep talking and be honest—and to have love in our hearts.

We Can Only Do So Much

Relatively speaking, our Souls are traveling in "first class," where it is far easier to be loving. As humans, we're crowded together in the "coach" section, where it is much harder to exist. So, we need to be realistic about what we can do. For example, we can't find all of our kindreds. If we meet and connect with several of them, we have done well. We are not going to heal every difficult or broken relationship either. If we can restore the love with just one person (and release the negativity we feel towards others), we have also done well. Finally, we are not going to be intimate with everyone or have perfect relationships. If we can get really close to a few kindreds and a little bit closer to the others, we deserve a round of applause.

Learning how to be more loving is the major lesson of life for all of us. So, when it comes to relationships, it is helpful to ask ourself this before we speak or act: "Am I honoring the bond that exists between our Souls? Will my behavior bring us closer or push us apart?"

Just one more thing: Do joyful things with your kindreds. Partaking in the simple pleasures of life together is a terrific way to enhance your relationships. We Souls like to have fun.

I almost forgot. If there is someone we want to get closer to, we could ask them if they also would like to enter The Intimacy Zone. And then we would agree to observe the "guidelines" and to be patient and understanding with each other.

Now, let's take a look at the rest of the Life Circle—or more specifically, at the elements of community, home, work and hobbies. We will also consider the subject of money.

The Elements of a Good Life – Part B

**A Sense Of Belonging
And Our Special Place**

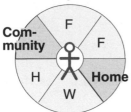

We need ways to feel connected with others; we want a sanctuary for our body, mind and Soul.

Given how difficult interpersonal relations can be, it is understandable that sometimes, or even often, we wish to be left alone. But within each of us there is a longing, which is coming from our Soul, to make a meaningful connection with other people.

We began our spiritual journey, way back when, as members of God's family. We were *and still are* part of a community of Souls. Here on Earth, we are looking for ways to recreate the sense of *oneness* and *interconnectedness* that we enjoy in the Spirit World. We feel the need and desire to be with other people, even though being with them is not always easy. Deep down we know that fellowship is essential for our personal and collective well-being.

"**Community**" means **with unity** or oneness—the essence of which is harmony, sharing and a concern for others.

We can get much of what we need in the way of community from our Kindred Souls —that is, from our family and friends. But our need for connection and belonging extends beyond our immediate kindreds. We want to join with members of our "larger family" to share joyous and deeply meaningful moments, to provide for our mutual needs, and to pursue common goals. We also want to express our Soul's love and compassion and help those who are suffering. We each need a Life Circle that includes personal or kindred relationships and that also provides a broader sense of community.

Life is far more satisfying when you approach it not as a solitary journey, but with the perspective of "we are all in this together." Join with others for support and companionship. Be of "service" and give back to your community. It will please your Soul and Me.

Communities Exist On Many Levels

Places, like neighborhoods, towns etc.

Civic, religious and school organizations

Intimacy / support / recovery groups

Shared interest groups of a personal or professional nature

Groups with a common mission, such as to create social change

There are different kinds of communities with different purposes. Some we belong to as a result of where we live or where our children go to school. Others we are drawn to because we want to be with people who are like-minded or who have similar problems or needs. Such groups can be independent of where we live, as demonstrated by the many electronic communities thriving on the internet.

The communities we are part of should give us a sense of belonging or the feeling of being "at home." From a spiritual perspective, it is important they be "higher-level communities" that will help bring forth our love, joy and creativity. They must also foster our personal growth or contribute to the well-being of others. The people, places and ideals that we associate with should respect and honor the sanctity of life and bring out the best in us. Choosing to become part of a group that promotes harmful thoughts or behavior can cause our Soul great distress.

Each Community Is A Collection Of Co-Creators

Will we use our collective "Let there be ..." powers in a positive way? Will we work harmoniously together, yet also respect our individuality?

People who coexist in a physical space, such as a neighborhood, or as a group with common interests, have the power to affect reality in a significant way. It is important for us to feel that we belong to communities that are doing *good* things. Also, we want to be able to participate in our own, unique way and in an atmosphere of mutual respect and congeniality. However, we must remember that although communities are organized around a shared purpose, they are also a "collection of diversity" made up of individuals with distinct gifts, needs and emotional issues. So, we can view joining a community as an opportunity for us to develop our relationship skills and to learn how to resolve conflict and work as part of a team. These are lessons all of us have come to Earth to learn.

Some Final Thoughts On Community—

Life is so busy that it is hard to participate in community activities. But doing so, even if it's only a little and especially if it involves giving to others, is good for our health. It is also a great way to find some of our kindreds.

Earth speaks

Telecommunications has plugged you into the global community. But don't let that isolate you from your local communities. Preserve those aspects of life that support face-to-face contact with other people.

Home, Sweet Home Every Soul, while it is here on Earth, needs a place to call "home." Even our ancestors of ancient times had caves to call "home." We don't have to own the place in which we live, although that has its benefits. But we do need a dwelling that is affordable and where we can feel safe and secure from the outside world. A "home" is much more than a physical structure, however. It is a place that meets our emotional and spiritual needs as well. It is where we can nurture ourself and our loved ones and feel comfortable and at peace. So, if the place we are living in is full of stress or negativity, we may call it a house or an apartment, but we're not really "at home."

> Home is a feeling. A state of mind. A sense of being where we truly belong ... home is a sacred place ... Like a supportive friend, ... a home embraces you from the moment you walk through the door.
>   Robin Lennon – from her book, *Home Design From the Inside Out*

A Home Shared With Others Is ...

a place where we can be loving and supportive and help each other to grow.

Living under the same roof with anyone, even with kindreds, is not easy. To make the space we share with others a "home," we need to honor our spiritual connection and create an environment of mutual respect. This is especially true if there are children involved. For them, a home is where they learn how to bring forth the light of their Souls. It should be a place that allows the love of a family to flourish and that is remembered fondly by the children after they "leave the nest."

Every Soul has at least one place in the world where it feels "at home." If you're drawn to a particular place, it may be for a "higher purpose."

Some people live "happily ever after" in or near their hometown. The community in which they were born and raised really resonates with their Soul. Others, like me, are more nomadic. There can be practical reasons for moving to new places, such as pursuing our education or career. But there can also be other, less obvious forces at work. For example, we might be drawn to a particular spot by our Higher Self so we can find some of our kindreds and be among like-minded people. Or maybe the "energy" of the place is exceptionally good for us, and it's where we can be most creative. As we search for the place where we feel we belong and want to sink our roots, it is important we listen carefully to our "inner voice"—because our Soul knows where "home" is.

 Regardless of where we live, our Soul is happiest when there is some form of beauty around us.

Our inner well-being is affected by the state of our outer world. We need both emotional harmony and physical beauty in our home. Even if we can't improve our surroundings as much as we'd like, we can still find simple and inexpensive ways to bring art, color and nature into our space. We can also reduce the clutter in our home. These external enhancements will lift our spirits and inspire us to make other meaningful changes in our life.

As we increase the spiritual energy in our home, the quality of our life improves. Many people use the Chinese practice of "feng shui" to help them achieve this. It deals with the shape and placement of buildings, of the rooms within them, and of the objects within the rooms.

Big and Expensive Is Not Necessarily Better

Just because someone lives in a spectacular house, doesn't mean he or she is happier (or better) than us. A house can never be a "home" if it is absent of love. And if we have to spend all our energy working at a job we don't like in order to pay the mortgage, then our house has become a burden. It is not a special place for our body, mind or Soul.

There are people who prefer to live in cabins or studio apartments or even travel the open roads in mobile homes who are more content than some of the people who live in big houses. I admire those who travel lightly through life with a sense of freedom and who realize that large edifices (and egos) often tax the Earth and take resources away from others. We can aspire to live in a magnificent home, but our Soul would rather we aim for a *loving* home— because prestige and square footage are no substitute for love.

 My "dream home" is full of love, brings out my Soul's light, and is "gentle" to the natural world.

No matter what, no matter where, it's always home, if love is there.
Unattributed, from a plaque in my kitchen

 I am very troubled by the fact that so many Souls do not have the essence of a good "home."

Everyone should have access to some form of adequate and affordable housing. When this element of a person's Life Circle is missing, uncertain or a financial burden, it is very hard to focus on or do well in the other areas of life. Of course, the stress and lack of stability is especially bad for children because it profoundly affects their intellectual and emotional development. Housing issues don't just affect the people and families involved, our society suffers in many ways as well.

 Making it possible for all people to have a decent place to live is part of our "collective mission"—a subject that we will return to in the chapter *Creating Heaven on Earth.*

The main essence of the community and home elements is the feeling of *belonging*—the realization or sense we are living in a place that is good for us (even if it's not perfect). We want to "fit in" with the people who live where we do and who are involved in the groups or activities in which we participate. Of course, it is possible to live without this sense of belonging. Many people do. But to live the life our Soul imagined, we need to find the place and people who are "right" for us.

Using Our Gifts; Doing What We Love

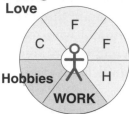

Our "work" could include:

a. A paying job
b. Parenting
c. Volunteering
d. All of the above

God gave each of us "gifts" or special talents. These abilities, which are an integral part of our Soul, help to make us unique and able to do things that no one else can do or in a manner that is unequaled. We all have multiple gifts, some of which are "bigger" than others. They can be specific in nature such as being adept at playing the piano, or they can be more general such as having a gift for communicating. Some gifts are obvious while others are latent and waiting to be discovered. The best sign of a God-given gift is that it brings forth the essence of our Soul (our love, joy and creativity), and it can be used to do something good in the world. We were given our gifts so we could feel fulfilled in using them and so we could make a contribution to our collective mission.

 We each need to determine what our gifts are and to find appropriate ways in which to express them.

There are many activities which will allow us to manifest and develop our talents. Some will pay us money, others won't. While many people seek fulfillment in "professional" or "regular" jobs, others find that raising children or being a volunteer is the best expression of their gifts and the ideal way to contribute. Some of us will pursue multiple paths at the same time and use different gifts in different ways. Others will use their gifts sequentially in life, such as choosing to be a full-time parent before or after having a career. Or a person might first be in business, then become a writer and later become a teacher. We could be on some paths for only a short time, while other paths will carry us through most or even all of our life. Some activities will be solitary, others will be collaborative. The range of possibilities as to how we can express our gifts is endless. The challenge is to find what is best for us.

 The activities that use your gifts need not be grandiose. If they satisfy you and are positive in nature that's all that matters. Also, work (especially parenting) can be invaluable even if it doesn't pay.

Hobbies Are Important Too: They are part of the Life Circle for these reasons: 1) most of us will express one or more of our gifts through our hobbies; 2) they provide a lot of joy; 3) they help keep our mind and body active; 4) what we do for fun and creative expression, for little or no money, can be a sign of what we might like to do for "work;" 5) if our job isn't satisfying, then our hobbies can be the primary way for us to express our gifts and "Let there be ..." power; and 6) they're an excellent way for us to meet and be with our kindreds. God made us good at and interested in many things. A full life includes the time and means to pursue as many of our interests as possible.

We Have Found A Great Way To Express Our Gifts If ...

- ☐ We generally love doing it and are eager to do more of it.
- ☐ It comes naturally to us, though we may have a lot to learn.
- ☐ We might've had an interest in or talent for this activity as a child.
- ☐ We have the ability to do it very well or even excel at it.
- ☐ Other people believe it is right for us and are supportive.
- ☐ Money is not the sole reason why we're doing it.
- ☐ We "fit in" with many of the people involved in our activity.
- ☐ Doing it makes us feel good about ourself and our life.
- ☐ We can make a positive contribution by doing it.
- ☐ We just "know" this is something our Soul wants us to do.

If a particular activity satisfies the items on this checklist, then we have found a "**calling**." Such an activity is not only a great way to express our gifts, but it is also something our Soul included in our Life Plan before we incarnated. A calling is, to paraphrase author Alice Walker, an activity "our Soul must have." Again, we can have multiple callings, some of which are work-related (which could be our paying job, parenting or volunteer work) and some of which are associated with our hobbies. Basically, "callings" are those activities we can't imagine *not* doing.

If family and friends don't support the way we've chosen to express our gifts, that doesn't mean we're wrong. They may be projecting their own preferences, prejudices or even jealousies onto to us. We have to listen to our "voice."

When it comes to work, having feelings of **joy** is another sign you have found your calling.

If we're taught as we grow up that work is just an obligatory part of life and unjoyful by nature, then we are far less likely to find the activity that will please our Soul. It is important for us to realize work is meant to be a blessing, not a burden, and that it can be fun. In fact, as author Barbara Sher put it, "Fun indicates the presence of a gift. It is the first beacon of talent."

The work that will most please our Soul won't be an "I should" activity, such as "I should be a doctor because that's what is expected of me." Or, "I should do this work because I'm afraid to pursue what really interests me." We need to be independent and expansive in our thinking and *follow our joy* wherever it leads. If we reluctantly pursue a career, we will be bothered by a nagging feeling that we are meant to be doing something else. Even if we are successful at our profession, we will know deep down we are not honoring our Soul's Life Plan. And that will make us sad.

Do what will make **you** happiest.

More than anything, we want to work at an activity that we love and is fun and that makes a contribution —for that will bring us the greatest reward. However, most of us do have practical concerns, such as making money. And while that shouldn't be the main criteria for choosing our path in life, we can't ignore the reality that we need to pay the bills. But what sort of job will we choose? Will it be good for us or be a source of regret and frustration?

Generally Speaking, There Are Four Kinds Of Jobs

1. **Stuck-in-a-rut**: it is mostly or totally unsatisfying, uses few if any of our gifts, and saps our energy and passion for life.

2. **Suitable support**: it uses some of our gifts and pays the bills, which lets us do what we really love; we like the work, for the most part; it might be our job for much of our life.

3. **Steppingstone**: it's using and developing our gifts, teaching us lessons and skills, and/or providing money—all in preparation for the job that our Soul came here especially to do; we might not see this job for what it is while we are in it.

4. A "**calling**:" as defined on the previous page; it really uses our gifts and brings forth the essence of our Soul.

Please be careful not to make other Life Circle choices, such as having children too early, that will push you into a job that you and your Soul will regret.

No one makes it through life without regrets, but it is very sad to look back and realize we could have pursued our calling—if only we had made a few wiser choices. That is *not* to say we are a failure if our job isn't our calling or that such a job is a prerequisite for happiness. We can be quite content in a job that provides suitable support. It may not use all of our gifts or generate a lot of passion, but if it allows us to live comfortably and to pursue other interests, we should feel good about ourself. It is when we get *and stay* needlessly stuck in a job that is unsatisfying or harmful that our Soul is truly sad and disappointed.

What can I do if I'm not happy with my job?

We may have more options available than we realize. Perhaps we can restructure our life and reduce expenses, develop new skills or go back to school so we can leave our job. Or maybe there's a way to enhance the job or the quality of the workplace, including our relationships with the people there. We could also change our perspective and look at the job as a temporary situation or a "means to an end" and appreciate its good aspects. Maybe it's giving us the skills, references or money to take the next and better step. If we're not happy in our job, we need to do whatever is necessary and possible to leave it or to turn it into a suitable job— or better yet, to make it a steppingstone to our calling. To achieve that usually takes a good amount of courage and Willpower—and a vision of our ideal job.

"It's A Lousy Job, But Someone's Got To Do It." There are many jobs in the world that are onerous; some are dangerous. But just because we find a job to be unappealing doesn't mean that it isn't suitable or a calling to someone else. So, we should be respectful of the work done by other people. However, some jobs are so oppressive that no one would see them as appealing. It is part of our collective mission to minimize such jobs. We can do this through the use of new technologies and methods and the enforcement of basic human rights. We also need to elevate the nature of many other jobs to make them more satisfying. We will return to that point later in the book.

When Do We Find Our Calling?

Will it be early in life, or will it take a while?

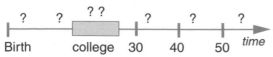

Again, our calling could be a job, parenting, volunteering or a hobby—or all of them.

I feel sad and down on my-self if I don't know what my calling is.

Emotional Mind

Not knowing what our calling is can be troubling to our Emotional Mind. It wants an answer to the questions, "What's my purpose?" (which we ask ourself), and "What do you do?" (which other people ask us). Having an answer is essential for our self-identity and self-esteem. Some people know at an early age what they want to be and do when they grow up. For the rest of us, the right path is harder to find. But that doesn't mean we are any less gifted. We just need more time to get to know ourself and to explore our options.

Consider the story of Anna Mary Robertson Moses—also known as "Grandma Moses." She was one of America's most renowned artists. Yet, it wasn't until she reached her seventies that she started to paint seriously, and she was self-taught. So, we never know when we are going to discover one of our gifts and pursue a calling.

Aren't we supposed to have found our calling—at least the job part of it—by the time we finish school?

Many young adults (and their parents) are concerned that after spending a lot of money on college they still don't know what their calling is. Generally, parents and educators can do more to help children find their path in life. Students, for their part, can be more proactive in learning about career alternatives. They can "link up" with someone who is doing what they're interested in and visit with them on the job. Or they can participate in work-study programs and discover firsthand what a particular vocation is like. Of course, another option is to postpone college until they have a better sense of direction. It is normal for us to be uncertain about our calling, and college is in part a process of self-discovery. Still, the more we can do *before* and during our college years to find our path, the better off we will be.

Many of us take jobs right out of school that are not our calling. They're steppingstones or supporting us as we go about our search. Finding our calling is also an inward process. We want to listen for intuitive messages from our Higher Self so we can be clear about our needs and desires. We should also be patient and kind to ourself if we are still searching. Finding such an essential part of our Life Plan is not easy. We must trust the process and let it unfold with time.

The following is a step-by-step approach to find the work that is our calling. It is only an overview, but it can help to organize our thoughts as we go about our search. You can skip this part if you have already found your calling.

Important Questions To Ask When Searching For Our Work

1. What are my **interests**? What activities, subjects or "causes" am I drawn to? What matters to me? What would be on my list of "Things I love or might love to do or be involved in?" Are my interests intellectual, physical, artistic, emotional or spiritual in nature? Do they involve working closely with other people?

   [Regarding the calling of parenthood, do we have the desire to parent *and* nurture a child, or are we just interested in "being a parent?" There's a big difference.]

2. What are my **gifts** or special **abilities**? What would be on my list of "Things I'm really good at or *could be* really good at?" In what ways can I express or act on my love for a particular interest? What skills or attributes have I been complemented on by my teachers, mentors, employers and other people?

3. Do my interests and abilities **match up**? Do I have what it takes to pursue an interest professionally? Can I overcome my shortcomings? Or should I pursue an interest as a hobby instead?

   [By being realistic about our abilities and letting go of unattainable dreams, we can focus more effectively on our true calling.]

4. What is **motivating** me? Am I attracted to a line of work mostly by the prospect of fame and fortune? Or am I driven by the desire to contribute? Am I hoping to prove something to others ("I'll show them") or to myself. Do I see it as something I'm "supposed to do?" Or am I drawn to a field of interest because I can be creative, and it makes me feel joyful? Obviously, there can be multiple reasons, but some can be problematic, while others are essential.

continued on the next page ...

5. What work **alternatives** are available—that is, what are the various ways in which I can participate in a vocation or satisfy a particular interest? [For example, a person interested in the field of entertainment could be an actor, writer, director or producer, and they could be in movies, theater, radio or television—to name just a few possibilities. In making a list of alternatives, we need to be expansive in our thinking. Maybe we can create a brand-new way to express our gifts and to pursue our interests.]

6. What are these various alternatives **really like**? What will be required of me? What are the people, workplace, hours and everyday pressures and responsibilities like? What sort of values are involved? Can I make a decent and honorable living? Do I need to do more research before I decide?

7. Is there a **"fit"** between me and a given alternative? Are my abilities and nature too different from the requirements and nature of the work? Can I change me or the work? Is there another way for me to participate? Should I look into something else?

   [We shouldn't expect a perfect match. Every alternative will have issues. Still, we need to find the livelihood that allows us to flourish in spite of its issues. This step takes self-awareness. By knowing our limits or boundaries—in terms of what aspects of a vocation are acceptable or not—we can make a wiser choice. Maybe we will decide to accept what we find objectionable. Or we'll figure out how to change the work or to participate under our own terms. Or we will pursue another path.]

Most of us can do well in any number of jobs, even unjoyful ones. But just because we have the intellectual or physical capacity to do a job, doesn't mean that it is right for us. In fact, being in the wrong job can be harmful to our health and happiness. That's why it is so important that we think through our choice step-by-step.

When we have found our calling, our Soul is more active in our life. We're more intuitive; we have lots of energy; and the "creative juices" really flow.

When we're using our gifts as our Soul hoped we would, we take ourself to a higher level, where the full scope of our "Let there be ..." power is available to us. In this state, we are more productive and creative. We're also more determined to use our time on Earth wisely. We have the sense of being "on a mission." We've got a passion for life.

When we are pursuing our calling we're at a "higher level," but it still can be very difficult work and stressful at times. And we won't always succeed at everything we do.

Even if we're on the right path, we will face "trials and tribulations." The time, effort and expense required to get prepared for and established in our profession could be significant. And we will experience our share, or more, of setbacks and interpersonal conflicts. However, we will also be more inclined to persevere and overcome those obstacles. We will be empowered by the *faith* which comes from knowing we made the right choice and by a *belief* in ourself. The path that pleases our Soul may not be easy, but it is the one that will, in the end, be the most fulfilling.

The Power Of Persistence—and knowing when to say "I give up."

If we're convinced (after a thoughtful review of our choice) we are pursuing our calling, then we shouldn't give up or let anyone or anything deter us from attaining our dream. Our attitude should be: "This is what I want to do, and this is what I *Will* do. Nothing will stop me." Of course, forces beyond our control might deter us, but we've got to proceed with a bold attitude. If, however, we're struggling far too much and there is very little or no joy involved, then we have got to ask ourself if we are on the right path. Chances are we're not, and our persistence is inappropriate.

> When you let yourself focus on what you love, you'll be brilliant at it. ... Greatness is all about trusting what feels important to you.
> Barbara Sher – author of *It's Only Too Late If You Don't Start Now*

A lot of us choose to be self-employed. As "entrepreneurs," we like the freedom that comes from being in charge. It's not an easy life or for everyone, but it can be very rewarding.

For many of us, part of our calling is to create an enterprise from scratch. We are driven by the desire to express our gifts in an environment of our own making. When we elect to use our "Let there be ..." power in this way, it is important we be adequately prepared for such a challenge. Also, we need to realize we will be setting the *values* that will guide how our venture operates. We have the power *and responsibility* to create a work environment in which other people, especially our employees and associates, are treated with trust and respect. When we're in charge (even if we're in a managerial position working for someone else), it is up to us to make choices that are not only sensible from a business standpoint but that are also fair and ethical.

Four Possible Reasons For Us To Work: We want to ...

1. express our gifts.
2. achieve and be respected.
3. meet our financial needs.
4. make a contribution.

Let's wrap up this section by briefly revisiting the question of "motivation" or why we're drawn to a particular vocation. It is God's hope that in choosing our work we will ask ourself, *"How can I make a contribution by doing this?"* That is not to say we must be totally selfless, for we all have personal and practical needs to consider. Indeed, our circumstances might place "making money" at the top of our list. Still, we can approach our choice with a spiritual perspective. At the very least, this means we should avoid doing work that causes needless harm to people, the planet or other forms of life. Such work is distressing to our Soul and God, and it is definitely not our calling. Ideally, we would choose work that in someway helps to improve the quality of life for people or to enhance the state of the natural world.

If your work is causing needless harm, then, as Ricky Ricardo from the *I Love Lucy* show would say, you will have "some 'splaining (explaining) to do" to your Soul and God when you return to the Spirit World.

Each of us can "improve the quality of life" by doing our work (be it a job, parenting or volunteering) as well as we can and by interacting with others in a positive way. Also, we can ask ourself if there is a better way to express our gifts within our current profession. Can we redirect our talents to help bring people together or to relieve suffering or to inspire children?—to name but a few examples.

We call ourselves "children of God." How are we to justify it?
By the words that we speak *and the work that we do.*

Matthew Arnold – English poet (paraphrased); 1822–88

Two Final Thoughts Before We Move On:

> We will know we have found "our work" when we feel a sense of "belonging"—just like we know we have found the right community or home.

We develop our gifts across lifetimes—bringing into each new life the cumulative effect of our prior experiences. Also, we can acquire new talents by being inquisitive and expanding our interests.

Money and Prosperity

It is not enough to "be spiritual." We have material needs that must be satisfied, and we have things we want to own or do and places we want to see—all of which takes money. Perhaps we can meet some of our needs by bartering or trading goods and services with other people. However, most of us still have to find a way to tap into the prevalent form of "financial energy" that flows through our country and around the world—namely, currencies such as the dollar or yen.

Money Circulates

Three Reasons For Making Money: We want to ...

1. provide for our **sustenance** (meet our basic needs).
2. have the **freedom** to live as we please without worry.
3. have the **power** to help our kindreds and others.

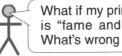

> What if my primary goal is "fame and fortune?" What's wrong with that?

Money is a "loaded" issue. It gives us much more than just material things. It has the *potential* to satisfy many emotional needs as well. Yet, having money can also wreak havoc in our life, especially if we are pursuing it for the wrong reasons. For example, if we're driven by the desire to prove our personal value or stature by the size of our portfolio, then chances are we will feel impoverished in other areas of our life.

A lot of us tie our sense of "self worth" to our financial "net worth."

Emotional Mind

Wanting a lot of money is *not* inherently a bad desire. However, most financially successful people are not working primarily for the money.

"Successful" people are motivated by the desire to use their gifts, to overcome challenges and to achieve, and to feel the passion and excitement that comes from doing something extremely well. The money then flows their way as a result or by-product of their efforts.

> Not everyone has the same ability to tap into "the flow" of money.

How we care for ourself (by getting an education, for example) and the choices we make regarding work have a major effect on our potential to earn money. However, there are other factors to consider. First, society does not adequately value all valuable work (most notably, parenting), and it overvalues work of questionable value. (I'll let you come up with your own examples.) It's not fair, but we may give up a lot, financially speaking, to do what we love. Second, there is not equal access to well-paying jobs, whether it be caused by discrimination or the lack of viable businesses in certain communities or countries. For many people these obstacles are insurmountable, and they are unable to tap into "the flow" at all or to any reasonable degree.

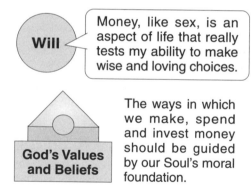

Will — Money, like sex, is an aspect of life that really tests my ability to make wise and loving choices.

God's Values and Beliefs — The ways in which we make, spend and invest money should be guided by our Soul's moral foundation.

We face the challenge of meeting our financial needs in a way that is both satisfying and *ethical*. How we make money is of vital concern to our Soul, as is what we do with the money once we have it. We want our choices to be guided by the light of our spiritual nature, not by the "darker" side of our human nature. Money can bring out the worst in us. So, we must be sure that our motives, as well as those of the people and companies with whom we associate, are good.

We Want To Make Our Money Grow

$ → $

How do we make this happen?

There are certain, spiritually-based actions we can take if our goal is to experience more abundance and prosperity. The list on the next page presents some of them in the form of "principles" or basic "truths."

The Prosperity Principles

How To Tap Into the Flow of Money
and To Be (or Feel) More Abundant

1. **Be aligned** with our Soul and its Life Plan. Pursue our calling and do our best to make the most of our time on Earth.

2. **Honor God's Values and Beliefs**. Earn and invest money in ways that make a contribution and don't cause needless harm.

3. **Express gratitude** for what we already have.

4. **Believe we deserve prosperity and abundance**. It is okay to make money, and there are many ethical, creative and joyful ways to do so. Be optimistic.

5. **Use our special gifts**. Do what no one else can or in a manner that is unequaled. Work for, create or invest in companies that provide unique products or services.

6. **Be educated and up-to-date in what we know.** Understand how to manage our money and know whom to trust.

7. **Live within or beneath our financial means**. Save and invest on a regular basis, if we can. Be disciplined.

8. **Be courageous**. Face our fears and do what we love. If we have excess money, be willing to take some investment risks.

9. **Have patience.** If we're pursuing our calling, persist in spite of problems. Allow our money to grow steadily over time.

10. **Be generous**. Share some of what we have with others, especially as we become more abundant.

The eleventh principle is this: **you prosper when all people are able to prosper**. Together, you must change the world so the poor and disadvantaged can provide for at least their basic needs.

Ultimately, we want enough money to allow us to live the life we have imagined. How much that takes varies for each of us. It is often the case, however, that we need *less* than we think do, especially if we simplify our lives—a subject to be covered in the next chapter. Also, we need to appreciate that as important as it is to have money, it is only one part of what it means to be abundant or prosperous.

Money Doesn't Guarantee Happiness

> I have lots of money, but I'm alone, working too hard or in an unhealthy state. I'm sad.

From a higher-level perspective, the person who is "rich" is he or she whose life is full of love and joy and creative expression. We need money, and it can make us happier, but it is not the primary source of contentment in life.

> Prosperity is the experience of having plenty of what we truly need and want in life, material and otherwise.
>
> Shakti Gawain – from her book, *Creating True Prosperity*

> Well, that's all I have to say at this point about the elements of a good life. To refresh your recollection, here's an illustration which shows the Life Circle.

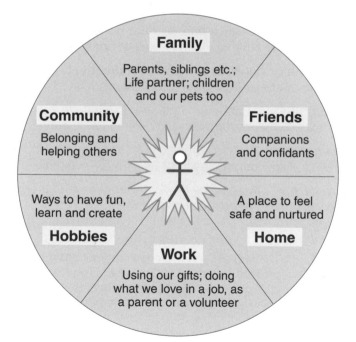

> You deserve the chance to create a good Life Circle and to be happy. I know that is easy for Me to say, but there are many things you can do to experience more happiness. And that is the subject of the next chapter.

In the Pursuit of Happiness

Joy Flows From Our Soul

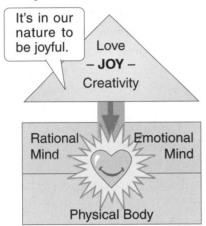

God gave us the capacity to experience pleasure, to appreciate the beauty and goodness of life and to be passionate, exuberant and hopeful. These abilities are inherent to every Soul, and they define the essence of *joy*.

We can be joyful, even if our life isn't going as well as we'd like. In fact, being joyful can give us the energy to make our life better. However, our joy can get blocked in the same way that our love and creativity can. This might happen if our childhood was particularly difficult or if the current conditions of our life are so burdensome that even the most joyful Soul would be downhearted.

We are here, in part, to learn how to bring forth our Soul's joy. Of course, that is easier said than done, especially if we're facing major obstacles. Still, there are things we can do to be more joyful. We will look at several of them in this chapter.

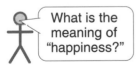

There is a difference between joy and happiness. Joy is an essential part of our spiritual makeup. It is within us, and it affects how we approach life. Happiness is an *emotional state*. We tend to "feel happy" when joy is flowing and our life, or at least key parts of it, are in good shape or moving in the right direction. However, if joy is blocked (maybe we have temporarily lost our ability to appreciate life), or if there is something seriously wrong with us or our Life Circle, then we will probably feel unhappy. If we want to feel happy more often, we may need to unblock our joy, change our Life Circle, or improve our mental or physical state.

If we want to experience more happiness, we need to be aware of our current feelings. We need to consider which areas of our life are in a "happy state" and which are not.

There is a checklist on the next page that can be used to evaluate how happy we are at this point in our life. But before doing this self-assessment, let's consider a few additional thoughts about happiness. Like other emotional states, happiness is not a permanent condition. It comes and goes. For example, we may feel happy about our job or a particular relationship today but feel sad about them tomorrow. Our degree of happiness will also vary from one aspect of our life to another. For example, we may love our work but be distressed because we don't have a life partner.

The different areas of our life are, of course, interrelated. If we are not happy with our "personal life," then that sadness can and often does spill over into our "professional life." However, we might be good at compartmentalizing our sadness. For example, perhaps we can perform our job well even though our marriage is in trouble. Generally, this separation of feelings cannot be sustained. So, we must deal with the cause of our unhappiness, or it will sooner or later, adversely affect the other elements of our Life Circle.

There is almost always something to be unhappy about. By its nature, life is a journey which will include our share of tears, frustration, loneliness and so on. There may be times, perhaps even extended periods, when we're feeling really sad about most or even all areas of our life. These periods will test our faith in ourself, in the goodness of life and perhaps in God too. On the other hand, it is possible that we will experience times when we're really happy about most or all aspects of our life. These "grace periods," when we feel totally blessed, are to be cherished. Regrettably, they don't come as often as we like or to everyone.

Finally, we can be in a state of happiness about a given area of our life even though it isn't perfect. Perhaps we want to take the quality of our job or marriage or the state of our body to a "higher level." Still, we can be satisfied with what exists at this moment. We can feel happy "on balance" or with "all things considered"—while doing what we can to be even happier in the future. Now, let's assess our own life and see how happy *or sad* we are.

— Your Personal Happiness Profile —

Put an X in the box that describes how you feel, *on balance,* about each area.

	Really Sad	Sad	So-so	Happy	Really Happy
Your physical "looks"					
Your physical health					
Mental /emotional health					
Your educational state					
Your self-esteem					
Your "sex life"					
Your finances					
Your sense of freedom					
Romantic / life partner					
Your children *					
Your work (or school)					
Your "home"					
Possessions (eg. clothes)					
Relations with parent(s) *					
Relations with sibling(s) *					
Friendships *					
Hobbies / fun activities					
Community					
On balance, all of the above					

* You could put an X in the box that describes your overall feelings and write the names or initials of specific people in the appropriate boxes.

We shouldn't despair if we have a lot of "sad" or "really sad" areas. "As long as we're alive, anything is possible." (It's an Albanian saying.)

How Do We Get From Here to There?

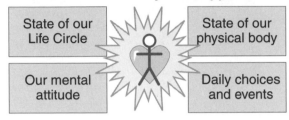

How we   Where we
feel now?   want to be

Although it is not possible for us to be in a perpetual state of bliss, most of us can be happier than we are. We can bring forth more of our Soul's joy and create a more satisfying reality for ourself. In the next few pages, we will look at how we can make that happen.

What Affects Our Joy and Happiness?

State of our Life Circle	State of our physical body
Our mental attitude	Daily choices and events

The first step is to know *how* we feel, which we did by filling out the checklist on the prior page. We also need to understand *why* we feel as we do. Self-aware-ness is essential. It helps us to create a good Life Circle, and it's key to how we live each day. If we know what we need more *and less* of, we can begin to change our life. Finally, we must understand what can block our joy and cause us to be unhappy and what kind of changes might be necessary.

Who Is Responsible For Our Sadness?

Fate	Others	– Us –
[eg. heredity, nature, etc.]	[their harmful behavior]	[our thoughts and choices]

The purpose of this question is not to assign blame, but to understand how we need to change our life and what we need to accept.

What Kind of Change Is Called For?

A change in the **structure** of our Life Circle?	and /or	A change in our **attitude** or **behavior**?

Often, self-change (a new attitude, etc.) will bring the joy back. Other times, we need to change the "who, what or where" of our life.

Our journey through life is a major challenge. Bad things happen and often for reasons be-yond our control. So, we want to maximize our chances to be happy and joyful. We can do this by creating a Life Circle that reflects the essence of our Soul—by doing what we love, by hanging out with loving people, and by living in a place that nurtures us. And, of course, we want to do all we can to keep our mind and body in a positive state.

Is It a Circle That Brings Us Joy?

Not every piece of our life needs to be in place or be perfect. But we want to be happy with what is there and the path we are on.

If parts of our life are missing or in a bad state, we probably are feeling down. We've got a case of "circle sadness." There are four major causes of circle sadness: (1) there is trouble in a given area because we made a poor choice (eg. wrong job or partner); (2) there is a problem with an otherwise good choice because of bad behavior on someone's part; (3) we're missing a piece of our circle that we really want (eg. a life partner, a child, nice home, etc.); and (4) a bad event happened to alter a circle that *was* joyful (eg. we lost our job, or a loved one died).

> Some things can't be changed, but I will take charge of what I can change. I will do my best to get my joy back.

As we consider how to make our life more joyful, we can look at how *our* behavior might be creating sadness. For example, do we have a habit of choosing mates or friends who aren't good for us? Are we trying to live beyond our means (or needs)? Are we neglecting our self-care or being hurtful with our loved ones?

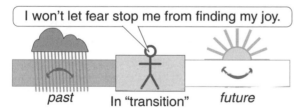

> I won't let fear stop me from finding my joy.

past   In "transition"   *future*

A major life change can be scary, even when we know it's the right thing to do. It takes a lot of courage to put ourselves on a new path.

Sadness is often a "call to action." Our heart and Soul are telling us we are on the wrong path and that we need to take some bold, new steps. Whether we need to overhaul our circle or change how we live, such challenges are opportunities for personal growth. We can learn to face our fears and to strengthen our Willpower. And if some of our sadness is caused by a factor beyond our control, we can still choose how we will respond. If we can change the circumstances of our life, it is vital that we take action. Many of us fall short in this regard. We want to be happier, but we don't do enough to make it so.

Don't be envious of others. As Thoreau said, each of us "hears a different drummer." Be yourself; make your own dreams come true. Besides, the people you are envious of might not be as happy as you think.

Some of us are sad because we have compared our life to what other people have achieved, and we don't measure up. We might even have a case of "circle envy." These are normal feelings to have, but they can hold us back if we allow them to persist. If we want a better life, then we must commit ourself to that goal. We shouldn't beat ourself up because of what others have achieved. Envy, like other negative emotions, is wasted energy. Instead of being envious, we can learn from successful people, especially those who have mastered *most of* their weaknesses and are using their gifts to create something positive in the world. Where it is appropriate to our life, we can emulate their good choices and actions.

When we look at the "perfect life" someone else has, we need to realize we might be looking at the *illusion* of success or happiness. It may appear on the surface that a person's life is wonderful because he or she has achieved significant material success, but in reality they are struggling in other areas of their circle. A great achiever may actually be a very sad person, who would be willing to trade some or all of their success for more joy and happiness.

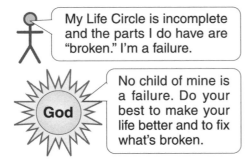

My Life Circle is incomplete and the parts I do have are "broken." I'm a failure.

No child of mine is a failure. Do your best to make your life better and to fix what's broken.

As painful as it can be to compare ourself to others, we can feel even worse when we look at our life relative to what we know our potential is or to what our dreams were. All of us have regrets and unrealized dreams. So, we need to forgive ourself for the past and focus on what we can do *now* to make the most of the rest of our life. We also need to redefine the meaning of "success" and "failure." Success is taking chances, facing our fears, and working to overcome our problems. Failure is not taking a chance or even trying to live life to its fullest or to attain our dreams. From now on, if we do our best, we succeed—*regardless of the outcome.*

Living In "Want To" Moments

Our Life Circle provides the structure and overall direction for our journey, but we live our life one moment at a time. When all is said and done, we will look back and remember the highlights or key moments of our life, especially the ones which were joyful. It is up to us to make the most of our limited time on Earth. The goal is to create a life filled with "want to" moments, where we are using our time as we wish and in positive ways. Also, we are here to learn how to live more "in the moment." This means we are mindful or aware of our surroundings and of what is happening. It also means we are consciously doing our best to make each moment joyful or meaningful in some way—so we (and our Soul) might remember it fondly at the end of our life.

Finding The Joy In Each Moment

"I am so glad to be alive right now because I can _____."
Fill in the blank with something about the moment that is life-affirming. Is there anything you can see, taste, feel, do, say etc. that is *or could be* joyful and make you happy?

I recall playing a game as a child called "what's wrong with this picture?" It was fun, but I wish my parents and teachers would have also encouraged me to play "what's joyful with this moment?" Imagine how much better our lives would be if we learned to see the good in life, in ourselves and in others. We elevate our energy and make better choices when we look at the people and things in front of us and see the handiwork of God.

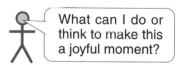
What can I do or think to make this a joyful moment?

If the moment is very difficult or painful, the answer may be, "There is nothing I can do but to accept the lack of joy at this time." And perhaps we can open our heart to give or receive love and compassion—a choice which will make our Soul happy.

We face a "Which came first, the chicken or the egg?" situation: Having a good Life Circle makes it much easier to live joyfully in the moment. But we need to live in that way (that is, joyfully) even if our life isn't great right now. Doing so will give us the emotional energy to fix what is wrong. So, the answer is: joy comes first.

Each of Us Needs a "Joy List"

What does (or would) put a smile on your face and make you feel joyful and glad to be alive?

Write on a piece of paper as many answers as you can to these questions:

What do I **do now** that is joyful?

What do I do, **but** not enough of?

What am I **not** doing, but I want to?

What should I **stop** doing?

Every Soul has a *path of joy*. By answering the questions shown to the left we are uncovering that path. Some items on our list will involve "doing" things; others will involve taking the time to "just be." Once we know what does or will bring us joy, we can make those activities a part of our life. And wherever possible, we can stop doing what makes us sad. Even if we can only take small steps on our path at first, it is important we begin.

Gratitude Unblocks Our Energy

When we focus our thoughts on what we have instead of what is lacking, we clear the way for us to receive more. We release, or at least diminish, our feelings of anger, regret, worry and envy. This allows us to strengthen our connection with the people and other elements of our life that we cherish. It inspires us to bring more blessings into our life. It is not always easy to be grateful, but giving thanks is a sure-fire way to release the joy and power of our Soul.

I know life is hard and at times really bad. Still, I thank God for the gift of life. I count my blessings everyday.

God

Keeping a "gratitude journal" is a great thing to do. Before you go to bed, make a list of what you really enjoyed or appreciated that day. Soon, you will find that a daily practice of gratitude has improved your outlook—and that can help transform your life.

Worry is always about the future ... gratitude is in the here and now. ... Gratitude lights up what is already there. You don't necessarily have anything more or different, but suddenly you can actually see what is. And because you can see, you can't take it for granted.

M.J. Ryan – author of *Attitudes of Gratitude*

Your life is not a problem to be solved but a gift to be opened.

Wayne Muller – author of *Legacy of the Heart*

Keep Life In Perspective

Bad things will happen to us and not all of it will be "small stuff." We need to see these events in the context of life's inevitable ups and downs. This perspective can help us to "rise above" the everyday incidents that are mostly annoyances. And it can make it easier for us to cope with life's more devastating events. Of course, even the most spiritual perspective will not save us from all the sadness. Still, our acceptance of the nature of life may lessen the pain.

We can learn something from most negative events. If we can view these episodes as growth opportunities, we will return to a state of happiness sooner. Also, it helps to have faith and to look ahead with the expectation that our life will, or at least could, improve. An optimistic perspective and the ability to see the humor in life is key to our happiness. Finally, although our life won't be free of "have to" moments, we can change our perspective regarding many of them. For example, we can look at a task such as grocery shopping not as a chore but as a chance to appreciate the abundance and diversity of food available and to nourish ourself and our loved ones.

A new perspective for one of my moments:

> I used to hate changing my cats' litter box. But then I realized that if I didn't need to do it that would mean my cats were no longer in my life, which would make me very, very sad. So now I think to myself, "I really **want to** do this, and I am **grateful** they are with me."

Live More Simply; Go Through Life With Fewer Burdens

> Our life is frittered away by detail ... Simplicity, simplicity, simplicity! ... simplicity of life and (the) elevation of purpose.
>
> We are rich in proportion to the number of things we can afford to live *without.* — (paraphrased)
>
> Henry David Thoreau – American writer; 1817–62

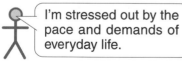

I'm stressed out by the pace and demands of everyday life.

Many of us long for a simpler life, with more freedom and less stress. Of course, this is far easier to dream of than it is to achieve. Economic realities make it necessary for most people, including both parents in many families, to work long hours. Still, we are free to make choices. The goal is to take a fresh look at what is meaning-ful and truly "essential" and to live by the principle that "less is more." How do we live a simpler and more satisfying life? The answers will vary from person to person. Perhaps we can change jobs and pursue our calling, even if it pays less. Or we can live in a smaller house or move to a more affordable locale. If we control how much we spend, especially for needless things, we can move closer to the ideal of liv-ing *beneath* our means. Of course, most of us can also choose how many children we will have, which will profoundly affect the com-plexity of our life. To restructure our life and make it more fulfill-ing, we need to expand our thinking beyond what society is telling us we must have to be happy. Our Soul wants us to travel through life as lightly and simply as we can.

On Earth, there is an acronym, K.I.S.S., which means "Keep It Simple, Stupid." In the Spirit World, we have the same acronym, but it means "**Keep It** (life) **Simple** *and* **Spiritual.**" We don't like to call anyone "stupid!"

Money Doesn't Guarantee Happiness

Don't confuse the pursuit of money with the pursuit of happiness.

$ $ Not enough	My "financial zone of happiness"	$ $ $ Not necessary

I need enough to take care of my "must have's" (food, shelter etc.), to fund my Joy List, and to provide for my senior years.

Lifestyles of the Rich and Famous

Lifestyles of the **Satisfied** and **Joyous**

There's nothing wrong with fame or fortune, but the real "winners" are those who are content with what they have and with who they are.

Happiness is not necessarily having all we want, but finding meaning in every-thing we have and do. We need money to live, and we can use it to help others. But we don't want to sacrifice our values or block our joy by what we do to get our money. It is vital we have enough money, but wealth by itself isn't enough to make us happy.

I've begun to think of myself as "independently wealthy" because I realize that I carry within myself most of what I need to make me happy.
Cathleen Roundtree – author of *On Women Turning 50*

Be More In Balance

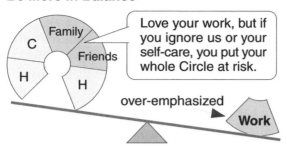

Love your work, but if you ignore us or your self-care, you put your whole Circle at risk.

When our life is out-of-balance, we limit our joy, and we "steal the joy" from others too.

Most of us feel our families are, or should be, at the center of our lives. But do our choices and actions reflect that belief? As a society we must create more work situations that support rather than undermine family lives. In the meantime, we each have to make choices and keep our priorities as straight as we can.

Is it possible to "have it all?" Can we be totally committed to our work and do whatever it takes to excel and also be a great parent, spouse, friend and so on? This is an unrealistic expectation for most of us, and we need to make trade-offs. But if we are needlessly over-emphasizing the work element of our circle, we will surely block our joy and cause others to be sad too.

Have Fun; Give It a Rest; Take Time To "Just Be"

This will help me to be creative and loving.

Don't burn yourself out. Have fun; recharge. Do it on a regular basis.

Every Soul wants to enjoy its time on Earth. Our mission is not just to become "better" or more enlightened. Actually, if we can learn to relax and have fun and be playful even as adults, we will have grown in a very meaningful way. Joyful activities make us physically and emotionally healthier and help us be more productive. This is especially true if we're having fun with our kindreds.

Enjoy the simple yet wondrous moments of life—such as watching sunsets, smelling the roses, sharing meals, laughing, or reading a book. These kinds of moments are very special to your Soul—and they're inexpensive.

P.S. We shouldn't wait until "later" to have fun. We must enjoy the "now."

Three Ways To Keep Our Joy From Getting Blocked

"Shields Up"	"Be Ourself"	"Bygones"

Keep out the negativity	Don't needlessly please others	Quickly let go of anger / regrets

If we keep our life positive, follow our heart and respect our needs, and maintain our inner peace, we can stay joyful longer.

> ... if you are happy, all of us profit from it.
>
> Thich Nhat Hanh – Zen Buddhist monk

Emotional Mind

When we're happy, we make better choices. We treat others with kindness, and we're more creative. That is why all people "profit" when we are happy. Our pursuit of happiness is good for everyone.

Our Joy Can Unblock Their Joy

A kindred   **Us**   A stranger

We will change the world as more of us bring forth the light of our Souls. Each day as we interact with people, we have the chance to affect how others feel. We can help bring more happiness into our homes, our places of work or wherever we are by being joyful—even if it's just by smiling.

The Joy Of Our Body, Mind and Soul

Sensory joy – appreciating the sights, sounds, tastes etc. of the world; includes sex and being healthy and vibrant.

Emotional joy – being serene and free of worry; feeling good about ourself and life; sharing loving moments.

Spiritual joy – being on our Soul's path; acting with love; living life to its fullest; learning and growing.

We experience joy on different levels. Many of us are disappointed when we satisfy a particular physical or material need, and we are still unhappy. That is usually because we are not giving proper attention to the other elements or levels of who we are.

A Summary of Ways To Be More Joyful and Happy
(including some that were covered elsewhere in the book)

☐ Change what we can about our Life Circle

☐ Turn "have to" moments into "want to" moments

☐ Find the joy in each moment; live fully in the here and now

☐ Follow our Soul's path of joy (from our "joy list")

☐ Practice gratitude; keep life in perspective

☐ Bring simplicity, balance and fun into our life

☐ Keep out negativity; be ourself; let go of anger etc.

☐ Beautify our surroundings with flowers, artwork etc.

☐ Express our feelings; ask others for help, if needed

☐ Take good care of ourself; be more self-loving

☐ Give and receive love; enhance and heal relationships

☐ Use our gifts and express our creativity

Let There Be ...

Joy to the world!

We need to raise the general level of joy across the planet. There are, of course, plenty of reasons to be down-hearted. Not only is there is real pain and suffering to contend with, but we also add to our emotional weariness with the violence and negativity that is shown constantly on television and in the movies. To bring forth our collective joy, we could use more celebrations, more uplifting music and entertainment, and more good news. We also need to make it possible for all Souls to pursue happiness. As long as there are people who are unhappy for reasons beyond their control and which can be eliminated, we cannot be truly happy. Finally, we want our spiritual cousins—the animals, trees and so on —to be free of needless suffering. We will cover these subjects in the chapter *Creating Heaven On Earth.*

Joy is (one of) the most infallible signs of the presence of God.
Teilhard de Chardin – Jesuit paleontologist; 1881–1955

The happy person is he or she who does not lose their child's heart.

Mencius – Chinese philosopher (paraphrased); 372–289 BCE

It makes Me happy to see My children in such a joyful state. I'm sorry you can't feel like this all the time. I hope that through your actions and with the help of others, you will feel joyful more often.

Next, we're going to look at the creative process. We will consider how we can use our Soul's energy to make positive realities.

Be Creative and "Make it So"

Creativity is God's gift to us. Using our creativity is our gift back to God.

Julia Cameron – *The Artist's Way*

We are each blessed with the ability to change reality. We can improve the quality of life for ourself and others with the choices we make. This creative power is part of our divine nature. It is expressed when we build our Life Circle, which sets the framework for our journey. And it is expressed each day as we make self-care choices, use our gifts and relate to other people. We are "Reality Makers." However, many of us don't appreciate the extent of our power or know how to best tap into it. In this chapter, we will take a brief look at reality making so we can create the life our Soul imagined.

Reality Making Is a Two-Step Process

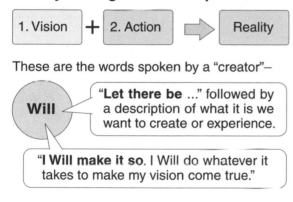

1. Vision **+** 2. Action ⇒ Reality

These are the words spoken by a "creator"–

Will

"**Let there be** ..." followed by a description of what it is we want to create or experience.

"**I Will** make it **so**. I Will do whatever it takes to make my vision come true."

Whether we wish to write a book, find the ideal job or create peace between neighbors, it helps to begin with a vivid, mental image of our desired reality. This vision or "inner reality" defines our creative intention and serves as a beacon or source of guidance and inspiration as we proceed. From a spiritual perspective, our "Let there be ..." vision acts like a seedling placed in a greenhouse. It draws to itself the creative power and energy of our Soul (and perhaps of other Souls), which is essential for reality making.

Creativity is a process, a way of looking at the world and consciously choosing the results you want to see.

Robin Lennon – author of *Home Design From The Inside Out*

> When we create something, we always create it first in a thought form.
> Shakti Gawain – author of *Creative Visualization*

We need to be clear about what we want because clarity helps to focus our energy. If we don't know exactly what we want, we can imagine the *essence* of our desired reality. We can envision the basic qualities of the person, place or thing we would like in our life or of the state of being we would like to experience. We can also evoke the feelings we will have once we have attained this reality. Basically, the idea is to bring as much "life" and emotional energy as we can to our "inner reality." The more we do that the easier it is to manifest the vision as part of our "outer reality." Much has been written about this step in the creative process, so I will not dwell on it. The above-referenced books are excellent resources on this subject.

> Author Angeles Arrien offers an interesting way to think about our desired outcome. Do we want to: (a) create something that has never existed before (make a brand-new reality), (b) sustain a current reality, or (c) let go of a reality that no longer serves us?

Once The Vision Is Set, We Need To ...

> "Make it so."
> Jean Luc Picard from *Star Trek*

If reality making only took coming up with visions, life would be far easier than it is. It's not that this first step is effortless. Indeed, many of us are not clear on what we want or need in life. Still, it is the second step that separates the "creators from the dreamers." We have to be willing to *take action*. This step is especially hard because we are all inclined, at least sometimes, to procrastinate and be lazy. Or perhaps we are worn out by the pressures of everyday life or constrained by other personal issues, and we don't have the energy to make our dreams come true. Regardless of its cause, inaction is the downfall of reality making. We must find a way to take action, even if we only take a few small steps at first. We need to generate momentum towards our goal.

> A vision, if it is not followed by action, is of limited value.
> Plotinus – Roman philosopher (paraphrased); 205–270

The Best Reality Making Occurs When All Our Parts Are Positive and Fully Engaged

Higher Self: Acts as our "source" or "channel"

Sends us ideas and insights via our intuition

The **Chooser:**

Decides the vision and goals to pursue

Will

Disciplined, determined and directs our actions

Rational Mind

Emotional Mind

The **Thinker:** processes ideas, gets knowledge, prepares a plan

The **Feeler:** is optimistic, enthusiastic and grateful

Physical Body

The **Doer**: takes action in concert with our other parts; best if healthy

Values and Beliefs Our moral foundation

Guides us to create good realities.

This illustration reinforces a point made in the chapter *Letting Our Light Shine Through.* We are at our creative best when we are "synergized" or in the most positive state possible for us. Of course, no one is or can be perfect, but most of us can attain a higher-level of existence.

We often undermine our reality making with negative patterns of behavior and *thought.* As previously noted, such patterns are often deep-rooted and associated with self-esteem and childhood issues. It is important for us to break our negative habits and to develop new, constructive ones. This isn't easy to do, which is why therapists and "self-help" books are so popular. Deep down, we know we are holding ourselves back, and we long to be more fulfilled. However, we shouldn't wait until we're in a more positive state before we act on our dreams. If we act "as if" we are already a powerful creator, it will help us to become one.

To regain the freedom of our Will, we must become consciously aware of what we have been subconsciously choosing. Then we can choose anew.

Henry Reed, author of Edgar Cayce on Mysteries of the Mind

The trick is in what one emphasizes. We either make ourselves miserable, or we make ourselves strong. The amount of work is the same.

Carlos Castaneda – *Journey to Ixtlan: The Lessons of Don Juan*

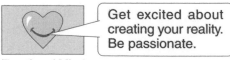

Emotional Mind

Get excited about creating your reality. Be passionate.

Enthusiasm is an essential part of reality making. We don't have to act like an exuberant cheerleader, but if our attitude is one of apathy or pessimism then the chances of our vision ever materializing are greatly diminished. Such feelings block our creative force. Passion is the emotion that inspires us to pursue our dreams and overcome the inevitable obstacles.

> Nothing great was ever achieved without enthusiasm.
> Ralph Waldo Emerson – American philosopher; 1803–82

The Two Modes Of "Making It So"

ACTIVE (doing)

RECEPTIVE (being)

We need a balance of both modes.

Putting ourself "in neutral" on a regular basis is just as important to reality making as is taking action. This means not only having fun to "recharge our batteries" but also learning to be still and to quiet our busy mind. Through moments of reflection and meditation we connect with the true source of our creative vision and "make it so" power—our Soul. Our intuitive channel opens further, and ideas and *soulutions* to our problems flow more easily into our conscious mind.

Another aspect of being receptive is to be watchful for acts of synchronicity. These seemingly random or coincidental events are being orchestrated from the Spirit World and are meant to help us in our creative efforts. We may not even be aware at first of their relevance to our efforts. Finally, being receptive means we approach the creative process with an appropriate amount of patience. We can't control everything, and sometimes there are good reasons for delays.

It Flows From Our Soul

> Great work is invariably the result of an original mind pursuing an intense interest with great patience.
> Barbara Sher – author of *It's Only Too Late If You Don't Start Now*

Our creativity flows best when we are aligned with our Soul and its Life Plan, and we are pursuing one of our callings. Even then, making our dreams come true can require much effort.

> Miracles come after a lot of hard work.
>
> Sue Bender – artist and author of *Everyday Sacred*

Two Or More Reality Makers Can Be Much Better Than One

A Creative Alliance: the union of "Let there be ..." power in the pursuit of common goals.

We can achieve great things when we collaborate or join creative forces with other people. But as we saw in the chapters on life partners and community, it is vital we link-up with people who are "right" for us. This means we have a shared vision, common values and beliefs, and that we are able to work harmoniously together. The people we join with in creative alliances should bring out the best in us and supplement our shortcomings, and they should be honest and trustworthy. In each area of our life, we want to be with people who will help us to fulfill our dreams.

Whether we are acting alone or with others, we need to carefully consider the merits of what we're intending to create. Will it be good for those who will be affected? As creators, we have a tremendous responsibility. We are not here to cause needless harm to ourselves or to anyone or *anything* else. Rather, we are here, in part, to use our gifts and creative energy to help elevate the quality of life—even if it is only in a small way. If we join with other creators, we should be sure we're using our collective talents in a positive manner.

There Are Four Kinds of People

> Those who **make** things happen.
> Those who **impede** what's happening.
> Those who **watch** things happen.
> Those who **wonder** what happened.

Partial source: John W. Newbern

> Our society has progressed largely because of our creativity and inquisitiveness—and because we're competitive. We're driven by the desire to develop products and services which are more ingenious than what others have put forth. Competition is inherently good, but when it is tainted with excess greed or negative motives, there can be harmful results. *How* we compete is very important to our Souls.

Life involves taking risks and knowing when to ignore the people who say "it can't be done." To be a great Reality Maker, you must be bold and have faith in yourself.

Ideally, we would go about our reality making easily and effort-lessly, without any risks and with the full support and encouragement of other people. This could happen on occasion, but it is not the model for most creative efforts. Great endeavors in life involve hard work, the possibility of loss, and a dose of skepticism from other people. Regardless of what we are hoping to achieve or create, we must be willing to face these challenges and do what is necessary to make our dreams a reality.

Whatever you can do, or dream you can, begin it. Boldness has genius, power and magic in it.

Johann Wolfgang Von Goethe – German poet; 1749–1832

 We should live with passion and boldness. But we must also be aware of the consequences of our actions. Next, we will look at how we can make wise choices.

Our Choices Have Consequences

Will

I'm free to do mostly what I wish. But every choice has consequences for me and others. So, I will do my best to choose wisely.

Life is a journey of the Will. We spend most of our time on Earth facing challenges and learning how to make good choices. Much of this book has focused on our most important choices, such as: selecting a partner, choosing our work, having children, taking care of ourself, relating with other people, using our "Let there be ..." power to create new realities, and so on. We have seen that every choice has consequences, some of which can be far-reaching. Our Will gives us the ability to choose, and it is a gift from God. It is important we use that gift wisely.

God

Please remember the "R and R" of making choices:

Respect and **R**esponsibility.

God gave us Values and Beliefs, Commandments, and the Golden Rule to guide us in our decision-making. It seems we need all the help we can get. So, let's consider one more principle, which is: wise choosing involves *respect* and *responsibility*. Respect means we see the goodness in ourself and in others, we acknowledge our right and theirs to pursue happiness, and we act with consideration for our humanity and common spiritual heritage. Responsibility means we honor the trust and commitments we have with other people, we make choices which are thoughtful and based on good judgment, and we are accountable for our choices.

Respect and responsibility are meant to guide all our choices. We should have "R and R" for ourself, for the people who depend on us, and for others directly or indirectly affected by our choices. Other forms of life and the Earth are also to be treated well. Finally, and very importantly, all children and the Souls who will soon be born deserve our collective respect and responsibility.

The "Ripple Effect" – Our choices can change how life
unfolds for a lot of people. It is also known as the "domino effect."

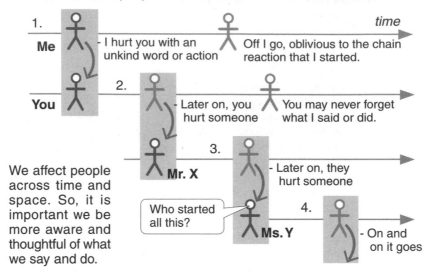

1. **Me** - I hurt you with an unkind word or action   Off I go, oblivious to the chain reaction that I started.   *time*

2. **You** - Later on, you hurt someone   You may never forget what I said or did.

We affect people across time and space. So, it is important we be more aware and thoughtful of what we say and do.

3. **Mr. X** - Later on, they hurt someone   Who started all this?

4. **Ms. Y** - On and on it goes

There are direct and unintended consequences of our choices.
For example, with each interpersonal encounter we send forth a
"ripple" of either positive or negative energy that can influence the
behavior of many people. The impact of our words and deeds could
even extend for years into the future. This is especially true when it
comes to how we treat children. Since many choices, including those
that are creative or work-related, have lasting and unintended consequences, we need to become more discerning. If we are the one initi-
ating the ripple, we can ask ourself, "Am I going to release positive
energy with my action." And if we are on the receiving end, we can
lessen (or even stop) the effects of a negative ripple, or we can make
them worse, by how we react.

Life Is A Series of "Forks In The Road"

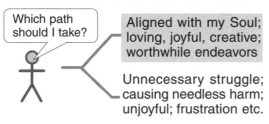

Which path should I take?

Aligned with my Soul; loving, joyful, creative; worthwhile endeavors

Unnecessary struggle; causing needless harm; unjoyful; frustration etc.

Everyday we must
choose between numer-
ous alternatives. Will
we, for example, tend
to our self-care or not?
Will we be supportive
of a loved one or be
judgmental? In these
and other daily instances, we have to choose whether to say or do
something constructive or to be hurtful.

When others have to pay for our poor choices we're known in the Spirit World as a "**cost-shifter**."

Our bad habits, unresolved emotional issues, and acts of selfishness can often hurt other people. Of course, it's not nice to be hurtful, even unintentionally. However, if we are deliberately or knowingly causing harm, or not trying to change our ways, then we are seriously impeding our spiritual growth. When we return to the Spirit World, our Soul will ask, "What were you thinking?" So, it is important we do our best *now* to bring forth our Soul's light and to put ourself on a more loving path.

Examples Of Poor Choices		The Possible Effect On Others
Being hateful, angry, or jealous	=>	Violence; fear; emotional trauma
Abusing drugs, tobacco or alcohol; eating unhealthy food	->	Crime; pain/loss for our loved ones; excess health care costs
Being greedy and disregarding our interconnectedness	=>	Exploitation of the weak and poor; environmental damage

In our youth, we see ourselves as indestructible. That kind of thinking can lead us to do things that are harmful or even fatal to others—or that will reduce the quantity and quality of our own time on Earth.

We Can Stay Vital and Extend Our Life

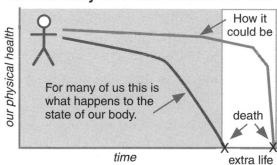

While we are not in total control of our physical health or longevity, most of us are the major factor in the equation. Our self-care and lifestyle choices can lengthen or shorten the duration of our earthly journey. If we make poor choices, we risk a more painful existence than is necessary as well as a premature "departure date."

There is nothing of which we are so fond, and ... so careless of, as life.
Jean De La Bruyere – French moralist; 1645–96

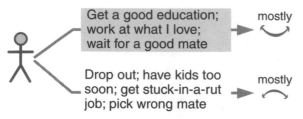

Some forks in the road are more consequential than others. A few key choices (especially regarding our Life Circle) will profoundly affect our future. Since wise choices will put us on a more fulfilling path, it is essential we take whatever time is necessary to decide. We can also seek guidance from other people. Choices which will be hard or impossible to undo call for special care.

Sometimes the best choice is obvious; other times it takes a lot of Soul searching to find it. And frequently the ideal path will, as previously noted, involve hard work. But it will be a worthwhile effort. Also, we may have to face some of our biggest fears when we make key choices. For example, it takes a lot of courage to pursue our calling when there are financial risks involved or when others are being critical of our choice.

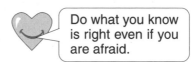

Do what you know is right even if you are afraid.

Often, It's Not an "Either Or" Choice

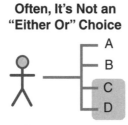

We can limit ourselves by considering only two alternatives. Often, there are other possibilities, but we don't see them. Perhaps we feel compelled to choose, and so we are focusing only on the options right in front of us. If we remove our "blinders," slow down the decision-making process and get into our receptive or intuitive mode, other alternatives will emerge. Generally, at least one of them will be more desirable than what we were originally considering.

What's Driving Our Choices?

Our HEART or emotions?	Our HEAD or intellect?
Our BODY?	Our SOUL?

"Follow your heart" is good advice *if the underlying emotion is positive,* such as love or compassion. But it is probably not the best advice if we're feeling needy or fearful, for example.

On other occasions we are told to "do what makes sense." With this advice alone, we might choose a career just because we have the requisite skills and intellect, or because it is the safe and sensible alternative. But if it is not what we love to do, then it's probably not the best choice.

Sometimes, we are driven by physical urges which can lead us to drink or eat too much or to have irresponsible sex. We choose to satisfy our body without thinking of the consequences. Finally, many of our choices are not even made consciously. We are at times "creatures of habit," responding to our physical and emotional impulses in the same way over and over again.

If we want to become a better chooser (which will help us to become a wise, old Soul), then we need to make our choices in a more "holistic" way. This means we consider what is best for each of our elements, especially our Soul. We can do this by asking ourself the right questions before we choose.

The "Holistic Choosing" Questions

Yes	No	
☐	☐	Would my Soul (or God) approve? Is it an expression of the goodness in me? Are my intentions positive?
☐	☐	Will it cause needless physical or emotional harm to me or other people, especially my loved ones?
☐	☐	Is it quite likely I or someone else will regret this choice?
☐	☐	Does it feel right in my heart and in my "gut?"
☐	☐	Does it make sense? (Not all choices will be logical, but have we at least considered the major risks?)
☐	☐	Have I done my "homework" to identify the consequences and alternatives? Do I know what I'm getting into?
☐	☐	Are there any significant warning signs or feelings?
☐	☐	Could this overcomplicate my life or create needless struggle? Is there an easier or more joyful alternative?
☐	☐	Will this cause tension between me and my kindreds?
☐	☐	Is fear keeping me from doing what I know is right or better?
☐	☐	Will I be sending out a positive "ripple?"
☐	☐	Will it cause needless harm to other life or the Earth?
☐	☐	Is not making this choice an alternative? Should I wait?

Of course, it's not enough to ask the questions. We must have the courage, discipline and good judgment to make our choice and to act, or to wait.

Not doing something is a choice, which could be appropriate or quite harmful. If, for example, we skip going to the dentist or doctor, especially if we're aware of symptoms, we risk potentially serious consequences. We could make matters worse by our inaction.

My goal is to attain self-mastery. I want to be a wise, holistic chooser in each area of my life.

Self-mastery is the ideal, but it is not easy to attain. Our choosing skills can vary greatly from one part of our life to another. For example, we could be incredibly adept at making work-related choices, but not so good at making self-care or relationship choices. Such imbalances do not make us a bad person. No one's Will is perfect. Still, we are here to learn and grow. If we're making poor choices in a given area of our life, then that is where we should focus our self-development efforts.

When we return to the Spirit World, we will review the choices we made here on Earth. We will see *and feel* the effects of our words and actions. We will understand the full extent of the more important ripples we sent out. So, if we want to have a good review experience, we should learn to make better choices. But there are more down-to-Earth reasons to make that effort. The quality of our life and of those we love can be greatly enhanced by becoming a wise, holistic chooser.

Even when we are in a positive state, making wise choices and creating great realities, bad stuff can still happen to us. Why is that? Next, we will look at the various factors which provide an answer to that question.

What Else Affects Our Reality

> Our life is what our thoughts make it.
>
> Marcus Aurelius Antonius
> Roman emperor; 121–180

> I am the master of my fate;
> I am the captain of my Soul.
>
> William Ernest Henley
> English poet; 1849–1903

God: Those are very nice sentiments, but they're not entirely true. Please read on.

We are called "Reality Makers" for good reason. God gave us spiritual and earthly powers that we can use to manifest our dreams. We are, to a great extent, "masters of our domain." But we are not in total control of what happens to us. In fact, many people are constrained by overwhelmingly adverse conditions. All of us are vulnerable, to varying degrees, to people and forces that we can only partially influence or cannot change. So, we create our own reality up to a point.

Bad Stuff Can Happen, Even If We Make Good Choices

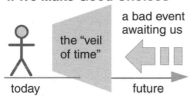

the "veil of time"

a bad event awaiting us

today   future

This means we need to savor every moment of our life.

We might be a wonderful person who is loving, joyful and creative, yet we are not immune to the misfortunes of life. When we least expect it, something can happen that will significantly alter our reality or even bring our life to an end. We may ask "Why did this happen to me and how can I recover from it?" This chapter attempts to answer that question. We begin with a statement from my Soul that offers a perspective on reality that is different than what we usually hear.

There are accidents; karma is only part of the picture; everything that happens is not part of God's plan; we are not responsible for all of our reality; and when we make a really bad choice it is called a "mistake."

The Seven "WHY ME? FACTORS" — These are the forces responsible for our reality. They explain why things happen to us.

1. **GOD** — She made it happen to protect us, to help us grow, or so we could make a contribution to the world. If an event seems malicious or senseless, God didn't do it. Most of what happens to us is not "God's Will."

2. **OUR OWN SOUL** — It was orchestrated by our Soul, perhaps to help us make a life change. Such events may not be easy to go through, but they are always well-intended. Some of these events were planned before we incarnated.

3. **OUR EARTHLY CHOICES** — We're responsible because of how we cared for our body or mind, constructed our Life Circle, used our time and creative energy, treated someone else or reacted to what was said or done to us. What happened may be due to karma we brought about in this or a prior lifetime.

4. **OTHER PEOPLE'S CHOICES** — Our reality was altered by someone else. It could have been a person from our Life Circle, a stranger or a company or government. We might be one of many people affected. It may have been intentional or not.

5. **HEREDITY** — We inherited a physical, intellectual or emotional trait from our ancestors. Our reality was affected by our genes.

6. **CHANCE** — It was a random event or true accident where no one was at fault; we got a disease or disorder that cannot be explained by any other factor; it was just our "luck."

7. **NATURAL CAUSES** — The weather or a geological activity made it happen; it was the result of a universal force like gravity; or the passage of time (also known as aging).

God

Often, there is more than one factor involved. And it's not always possible to know for sure which ones were responsible—especially if I or your Soul made it happen. However, even if the cause was beyond your control, you still get to choose how to respond.

I use the term "Why Me?" because we think of these factors mostly when bad stuff happens. But they apply to good events too.

As a rule, the key determinant of our reality is how we use our own free Will. But any of the *Why Me? Factors* can impact our life at any time. As noted before, some of those factors might have affected us while we were in our mother's womb. Also, the factors can be interconnected. For example, "chance" is often involved with heredity (as when only one sibling out of several inherits a disorder such as diabetes) and with natural causes (as when only one home out of dozens is *not* hit by a tornado). It is also possible that the Soul of the child who got diabetes knew that was going to happen and wanted to face that challenge in this life, or that God intervened to save that house from being destroyed.

Most Incidents Are Preceded By One Or More Earlier Developments

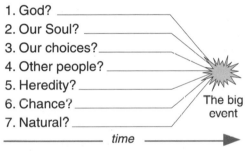

1. God? _____
2. Our Soul? _____
3. Our choices? _____
4. Other people? _____
5. Heredity? _____
6. Chance? _____ The big event
7. Natural? _____
——————— time ——————▶

Usually, it's like unraveling a mystery to figure out which of the "Why Me? Factors" contributed to the final outcome.

When things happen in life, good or bad, it is often the result of a series of choices and events that have occurred over time. We can examine big events in history, such as the sinking of the *Titanic* or the explosion of the space shuttle *Challenger*, and see a variety of causal factors, some occurring years before each "accident."

Some of the choices or actions that precede a big event may, in and by themselves, be harmless or go unnoticed at the time; or the person(s) involved might not think what they've done will cause any harm. The point is bad things often happen when the right combination of factors occurs in a particular sequence. Our role in the chain of events may be entirely innocent, and we may be oblivious to all of the other factors involved (as was the case with the unfortunate people who bought tickets for the *Titanic*).

We Souls know life is unfair and unpredictable, but we also know it doesn't have to be as bad as it is.

It's not just historical events that are preceded by various Why Me? Factors. The cause of most personal incidents, such as the breakup of a relationship, can also be traced back to a series of prior choices and events.

Let's briefly look at two other examples. First, when a person has a heart attack it is often quite unexpected. Heart attacks may be due to a hereditary condition or aging, but it is highly probable the attack was the culmination of many years of poor lifestyle choices. Indeed, many health-related events are self-created. We have more control over this aspect of our reality than most of us will acknowledge.

Now, consider the case of a planeload of passengers killed in a crash. While they chose to take the flight, the fatal event was undoubtedly beyond their control. Maybe the plane was designed or maintained improperly, which was a choice made by others. So, it was a disastrous event that didn't need to happen. It is also possible the plane crashed for some bizarre reason, such as a bird flying into an engine. That would be a "chance" event and an another example of the chaotic and unpredictable nature of life. Awful things do just happen. Finally, it is hard to imagine that God wanted such an event to occur or She had anything to do with it.

As I have said before, it is not for us to say that a person died or suffered because of karma. Sure, some events are "retribution" for how we treated others, but it is an overused explanation. And if people die together, we cannot assume they had "collective karma" to resolve. Saying "it was their karma" may help us deal with the suffering of others and with our own fears of something similar happening to us. But there were probably other Why Me? Factors involved that we're overlooking or denying.

The Future Is Not Ours To See, But It Is Ours To Shape

Future Events Fall Into One of Three Categories

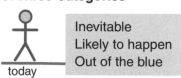

Inevitable
Likely to happen
Out of the blue

today

God has not preplanned our life. It is mostly up to us.

If we could look ahead in time, we would see that we are not primarily the victim or beneficiary of "destiny." Some events, such as our death, are certain to happen. However, the timing and nature of our death are not cast in stone. Most of our future is a collection of *potential* realities.

Our past and current choices, together with the effects of the other *Why Me? Factors,* have set in motion various events that are likely to occur at some point in our life. These events may affect our health, our work and relationships, or any of the other elements of our Life Circle. As we continue on a particular path, whether it be essentially harmful (like smoking) or positive (like working diligently towards a goal), we increase the odds that the "big event" will actually occur (which for the smoker might be getting cancer). So, as time progresses and if we don't change our ways, a future reality will become *more* "likely" and then "inevitable."

Of course, it works the other way too. We can *decrease* the odds of a prospective harmful event, or eliminate the possibility of it happening at all, by making positive changes now. If we're to become a better "chooser," we must learn to look forward in time and to see how our choices and the other *Why Me? Factors* might lead to a particular outcome. There might be nothing we can do about it, but most often there is. Finding the Will to make the necessary changes is typically the hardest part.

Will — I have complete control over my own thoughts, feelings and actions, including how I care for myself and how I react to what happens. Plus, I have more control over some of the other Why Me? Factors than I realize.

We underestimate the impact we can have on how some of the other factors affect us. For instance, we choose the people with whom we associate and, when we're adults, with whom we live. So, wise choices can limit our exposure to the harmful actions of negative people. The work and hobbies that we pursue also make us more or less vulnerable to certain factors. Even when it comes to Mother Nature we're not helpless. For example, it's up to us whether we live in a flood zone or where earthquakes happen (as where I live).

To be alive is to be exposed to the *Why Me? Factors.* We can't escape them entirely. However, even though we cannot prevent the inevitable, we can at least minimize any possible negative effects by preparing ourselves and our homes for the worst.

It's not accurate to say all natural disasters are an "act of God." Many of them are in the sense that God made a chaotic and changing universe. But more and more disasters are being caused by our own abuse of the environment.

Do We Create Our Own Medical Reality?

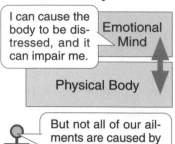

I can cause the body to be distressed, and it can impair me. — Emotional Mind

Physical Body

But not all of our ailments are caused by negative thoughts or poor choices.

Much has been written about the mind-body connection and how love and a positive attitude can make for healthy cells, cause profound healing or forestall hereditary disorders. On the other hand, if we exist in an on-going state of stress and negative emotions, we can create illness, like the earlier example of the person who has a heart attack.

While this link between the mind and body is real and should be heeded, it is not appropriate to blame ourselves for every malady. Even an upbeat person who is free of hereditary risks and has done everything right can still get a disease like cancer. It might be a "chance" genetic occurrence or the result of having been exposed, perhaps unwittingly, to an environmental hazard. There are many examples of where our mind or body can be thrown into disarray for reasons beyond our control, or for reasons we would do something about if we only knew what they were.

We Each Live Under Our Own "Prevailing Conditions"

The 7 Why Me? Factors have created a state of being for me that is, to use a weather term, "mostly sunny."

I'm glad your life is so nice. Mine really sucks, and it's not all my fault.

God — Life isn't always as easy as saying: "I choose to have a great moment." Sometimes, it is doing the best you can in spite of bad conditions.

No two people experience the same reality, even if they are living together. We each have our own perceptions of what is happening around and between us. And we each have our own mental and physical conditions which can enhance the quality of our life or make it unbearable. We are here to learn how to use our "Let there be ..." power to make those conditions better for ourself and others— and to live as fully as we can even when those conditions are undesirable.

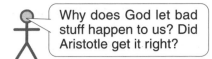

We all deserve credit for choosing to incarnate, because no one on Earth is immune from pain. It is endemic to the Physical World. Regardless of whether it is self-inflicted, coming from others or caused by one of the other factors, it is not easy for any of us to find the courage and inner strength to cope with it. While some pain is inevitable, a great deal of it is avoidable and needless and therefore preventable. We can learn from the pain and adversity of life, but we certainly don't need as much of it as there is. God is waiting for us to act as Her co-creators and to reduce the level of pain we experience.

Suffering Is The Extra Layer Of Anguish We Create In Our Mind

Anger – at the pain, ourself, others or even at God

Denial – not accepting the inevitable or unchangeable

Negativity – "Life is horrible; things will never get better."

Resignation – not willing to change what we can change

Pain and suffering are not the same. Suffering is the added tension and unhappiness we create within our Emotional Mind, making a painful event even more difficult to bear. Instead of focusing on what we can do to heal ourself or trying to find something good that could come out of our misfortune, we get stuck in one or more of the elements of suffering shown above. Combined with the pain itself, our suffering can completely debilitate us.

To experience suffering is a natural part of the grieving and healing process. But we can reduce the amount of suffering in our life, especially if we maintain a spiritual perspective. We can ease our Emotional Mind by accepting the uncertainty and inevitable events of life and by being open to the lessons which our misfortunes can teach us. If we do our best to create a loving Life Circle and to keep ourself in a positive state, we will be better prepared to deal with the pain when it does occur, as it surely will.

Ten Ways To Respond When You Know What "Hits The Fan"

- ☐ Find comfort and support within our Life Circle—turn to our family, friends and community; find solace in creative work
- ☐ Be determined; do all we can to recover and rebuild; get the best professional help we can find, if we need it
- ☐ Accept what we cannot change or control
- ☐ Fix or change the Life Circle elements (like our job or marriage) or the personal habits that caused us so much pain
- ☐ Forgive ourself; try to release the anger we feel for others
- ☐ Learn from our mistakes, grow, and make better choices
- ☐ Focus on other people; help alleviate their suffering; work to prevent others from being hurt like we were
- ☐ Put things in perspective; consider the blessings we do have
- ☐ Seek out activities that can bring joy back into our life
- ☐ Pray and meditate; ask God and our Higher Self for strength

God: Sometimes, you've got to pick yourself up, dust yourself off and start all over again.

God's message may sound trite or insensitive, but it is a simple truth that applies all too often in life. Of course, there will be at least one time (at the end of our journey) when we won't be able to pick ourself up. But generally, we do have the capacity to respond to our misfortunes. We possess a "Will to live" that comes straight from our Soul. We may not fully recover or get over our losses, but we will survive and find a way to make our life meaningful.

But we may not be able to do it on our own. We will need to lean on the loving support of others.

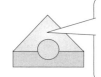

When you see another Soul and especially one of your kindreds in pain, reach out. Do what you can to bring them relief.

We can curse the darkness and ask Why me Lord? Or we can open our hearts to our human experience and allow the full bright light of compassion to reaffirm our relationship to others and to life.

Kathleen Brehony – author of *Awakening at Midlife*

Our Souls Are Optimistic and Resilient By Nature

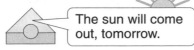

The sun will come out, tomorrow.

I always entertain great hopes.
Robert Frost; 1874–1963

Prevailing Conditions Change

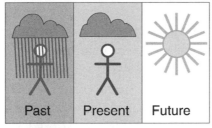

| Past | Present | Future |

The "Silver Lining"

I'm singin' in the rain.

We can often find a hopeful prospect or a way to grow in spite of our problems.

In the middle of difficulty, lies opportunity.

Albert Einstein; 1879–1955

It is normal to feel depressed and despondent when we face a personal crisis. But if we're to make it through our pain, we need to tap into the positive energy of our Soul and believe that the future can and will be better than our present reality. The sunshine may be a ways off, but we can still imagine how good it will feel when it arrives.

Sometimes a misfortune is a blessing in disguise—in the sense that we are "forced" to make essential changes to the way we live. We come to realize how fragile the gift of life is, and we approach the rest of our journey with new priorities. We emerge from our crisis wiser and stronger.

Experience is not what happens to a man. It is what a man does with what happens to him.

Aldous Huxley; 1894–1963

"Let there be ..." an end to the kind of pain and suffering I feel.

The spiritual challenge is to maintain, in the face of pain and adversity, our appreciation for life and to make something good come from our misfortune. Hopefully, that means we have grown in some meaningful way. It can also mean we've decided to help others who are afflicted by the same conditions. Maybe we can do something to ease their suffering or even help find a way to stop or cure the cause of our pain. Either way, we are acting with compassion and respect for the "oneness" of humankind.

When we are no longer able to change a situation—we are challenged to change ourselves.

Viktor Frankl – Psychiatrist, writer and Auschwitz survivor

The unexpected will happen and there are aspects of the Physical World you can't control, which is why I said you are not the "masters of your fate." Still, you do have the power to create a far better reality than what exists now.

There are seven forces, which I affectionately call the "Why Me?' Factors," that influence our reality. While we cannot eliminate all of the painful consequences that come from the last five factors (the first two being God and our Soul), together we are doing a lot to be in more control of our fate. Through advances in science and medicine (and other disciplines associated with our *Rational* Minds), we are finding ways to prevent or mitigate the effects of heredity, natural causes and chance. But the activity which will have the greatest impact on the state of our personal reality is each one of us taking control of our own life.

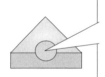

When the bad stuff happens, I will respond with as much strength and positive energy as I can. In the meantime, I will do my best to make my light shine brightly. I will take good care of my Earthly Self and keep negative people out of my Life Circle. Most of all, I will be loving, joyful and creative.

Next, we're going to look at the subject of forgiveness because we all make mistakes, and we need a way to release the past.

To Err Is Human, To Forgive Divine*

* So said Alexander Pope – English poet; 1688–1744

God: Learn to forgive others and yourself. Doing so will bring more love and light into your life.

That's easy for you to say. You're not the one hurt.

From the moment we were conceived until the day we die, we're vulnerable to the actions of other people. Some of that behavior will be harmful and deeply upset us. Of course, we will do our fair share (or more) of hurting others, and they will be angry at us. We are all imperfect choosers impacting each other's lives. That is why no one can make it through life without dealing with forgiveness.

It is easier for God to be forgiving—not only because She isn't hurt as we are, but also because She knows *why* the other person acted as they did. Still, God would like us to give most people the benefit of the doubt and at least a second chance to be good.

Forgiveness is important to our Souls. It is how we acknowledge our common struggle as human beings and how we show respect for our spiritual connection. Kindred Souls in particular honor their love by being forgiving on Earth.

Forgiveness is important in other ways too. The hurt and anger we hold inside is like the plaque that clogs our arteries. If we don't clean out our Emotional Mind, we can put the quality of our life at serious risk.

I'm burdened by the past.

X X
X X
X X
Emotional Mind

X = our memories of hurtful events—some done to us; others done by us

The Costs Of Being Unforgiving or "Emotionally Clogged"

- Blocks our Soul's light and can damage our self-love
- Impairs the rest of our Reality Maker, especially our body
- Restricts the love between us and the "offending person"
- Might break the earthly bond we have with a Kindred Soul
- Can diminish the love between us and other people in our life
- Diverts us from the here and now; wastes our energy

How Far Will We Go?

√ Heal ourselves
? Help heal them
? Heal the relationship
? Do all of the above

Forgiveness is a form of healing. The question is how much healing do we want to do? Do we just want to release our own feelings so we can get on with life (which of course is no easy task)? Or are we also able and willing to say "I forgive you" so the other person can deal with their guilt and regret (assuming they have those feelings)? Finally, do we wish to "go the distance" and to restore or even advance the relationship?

If we can take care of our own pain, we've accomplished a lot, and that should be our first priority. Forgiveness doesn't mean we have to extend an "emotional pardon" to everyone who hurts us or heal each relationship. Even if we do act beyond our own self-healing, that doesn't mean we condone the other person's actions or that we must forget what they did.

Also, forgiveness doesn't require that we deny our anger. In fact, anger can be good. It helps us to cope with a bad situation and to show the offending party how hurtful they were. It motivates us to make needed changes to a relationship or to obtain the remedy we are due. But when anger so dominates our mind that we neglect the positive aspects of our life or obsess about "getting even," then it has become detrimental. We need to release anger that has outstayed its usefulness or at least rechannel it in some constructive way.

Each Hurtful Event Elicits a Different Response

1. I've let it go very quickly.
2. I'll get over it in due time.
3. I will never forgive them.

Many of us get stuck between 2 and 3. We want to be forgiving, but we don't know how. Or we're afraid we will be hurt again. So, the past retains its hold over us.

If someone bumps into us by mistake and says they're sorry, we (generally) forgive them right away. But most hurtful events are harder to get over. For example, if our property is stolen, it could take us months to release the anger. If we suffered physically or emotionally as a child, it could take us many years to reach a point of forgiveness and to heal the relationship with our parent. And if we were to lose a loved one to a senseless act of violence, we might never be forgiving, especially if the guilty person shows no remorse.

 It's not easy to let go of the past. Many times I've thought of how different my life would be if only I had a better childhood. But that is projecting the hurt from the past into the now. I'm keeping the pain alive with the power of my mind.

Each harmful situation is unique, and there are many "variables" that affect how far we will go with our forgiveness. As we face new events or rehash the old ones that are stuck in our mind, we can ask ourself a series of questions—questions that will help us to put each situation into perspective and to process our feelings.

There are eleven questions presented on this and the next page, together with a range of possible answers. It's obvious which answers can lead us to quickly let go of an event and which ones explain why forgiveness can be so hard.

The "Forgiveness Questions"

1. Who caused us harm?

Family member or friend (a kindred)	Someone else we know; no real connection	— It was a stranger —	
		Who seems basically good	Who's surely a bad person

2. How badly were we hurt?

Minor harm; no big deal	Enough for us to feel pain or to be offended	Significant emotional or physical harm	Tragic loss of life or property

3. Where does the blame lie?

Mostly ours; some theirs	Mutual blame	Mostly theirs; some ours	It was all their fault

4. What was their intent?

— They didn't mean to hurt us —		Knew we'd be hurt, but didn't care	Their primary intent was to hurt us
It was an accident	They weren't thinking well		

5. Are there extenuating circumstances?

——— They were "impaired" in some way ———				There are no excuses
Mental disability	Temporary stress etc.	Troubled upbringing	Substance abuse	

6. Are they remorseful?

"I'm really sorry. Please forgive me."	They're probably sorry, but haven't said so	Said they're sorry, but they aren't really	"I'm not sorry at all. I feel no guilt or regret."

7. How are they acting now?

Changed completely; redeemed	Changed a lot; very hopeful	Changed, but not nearly enough	No change at all; still causing harm

8. Have they atoned for their actions?

Have they made amends, remedied the wrong, been punished enough and/or put themselves on a path of personal growth?

9. Which are we dealing with—

a truly bad Soul or a good Soul who is acting badly?

We can't know for sure what someone's spiritual nature is, but in most cases we can assume they have a good Soul.

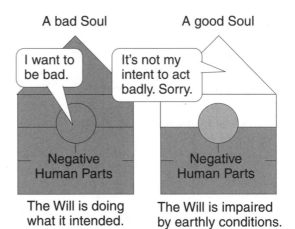

A bad Soul

I want to be bad.

Negative Human Parts

The Will is doing what it intended.

A good Soul

It's not my intent to act badly. Sorry.

Negative Human Parts

The Will is impaired by earthly conditions.

10. Would they hurt us again?

If the other person really knew how much they hurt us, and if they could relive that moment, would they act in the same way again?

11. What is it costing us to be unforgiving?

Could we be more loving, joyful and creative if we forgave? Might we lose a relationship we really want to keep, even with its problems?

Easiest to Forgive

- A Kindred Soul
- Very minor harm
- Didn't mean it
- They're very sorry
- Won't do it again

> But sometimes when a Kindred Soul is hurtful it is very hard for me to forget it or to forgive them.

One reason why it is so difficult to release bad memories from our childhood is that deep down we feel a trust was broken. We were counting on our parents to love and protect us. Even if our Soul knew before we incarnated that our life situation would be trying, it is still a shock to our Emotional Mind when one of our kindreds mistreats us—especially if we were in a vulnerable state as any child is.

We expect a lot from our family members and friends. So even though we want to be forgiving (because we do love them), sometimes we get stuck in our feelings of hurt and disappointment. In those cases, it helps to step "outside of the box." We can expand our thinking and change our perspective.

Recall and Appreciate the Spiritual Bond

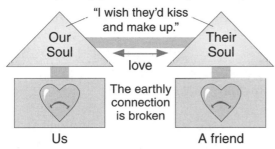

Our love might cool here on Earth (or go completely cold), but chances are high our Souls still love each other very much. If we believe that and appreciate that our bond goes back many lifetimes, it can make forgiveness easier. We might also consider that whatever happened between us on Earth is an opportunity for mutual growth. If we can get through it together, we will not only heal our earthly relationship but also strengthen our spiritual love.

We Can Visualize Talking To Their Soul

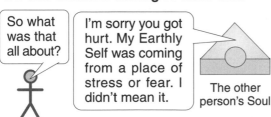

It always helps to empathize or to "see the why" behind a hurtful event. Sometimes the best way to do that is to imagine what the other Soul would say to us.

Be Realistic

I like to make mountains out of molehills, which makes it harder to be forgiving.

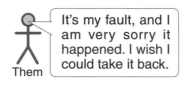

Emotional Mind

Many of us tend to blow hurtful events out of proportion and to do things which make reconciliation even harder. Instead of empathizing, we imagine the other person had really bad motives. Instead of expressing our feelings, we build a wall of silence and bitterness between us. It is natural to fight back (emotionally speaking) when someone hurts us, but it is not conducive to healing.

Many relationships end over relatively minor "infractions." A simple misunderstanding or an event precipitated by stress, temporary selfishness or by someone's eccentricities can sever the earthly bond between two Kindred Souls. To prevent this from happening we need to be more accepting of each other's weaknesses (if they're essentially non-harmful) and learn to go more with the flow of interpersonal behavior.

Maybe Both Sides Need to Forgive

I'm sorry.   Me too.

Often, there is some degree of shared blame. Even if it is mostly "their fault," we can still cut them some slack and meet them half way. Life is too short to waste the love that exists between Kindred Souls. Besides, they probably didn't mean to hurt us.

It's my fault, and I am very sorry it happened. I wish I could take it back.

Them

We'd like to get an apology from everyone who hurts us but that won't happen. Some people who feel regret cannot express it easily or effectively. So, it's up to us to decide if we will let go of the past without having heard a full declaration of remorse.

Before I forgive you and restore the bond, I need to see some real change. I don't want to be hurt like that again.

Us

At times, "sorry" is not enough. Some behavior is so hurtful that the other person must regain our trust, and we need to set limits or establish boundaries to protect ourself. We may help someone to heal, but before we "go the distance" they have to show at least meaningful progress in their personal growth.

Hardest to Forgive

- A bad Soul
- Devastating harm
- Did mean to do it
- They're not sorry
- Haven't changed

Hopefully, we will make it through life without crossing paths with a Soul who is acting really badly. But even if we make all the right choices we can still be a serious victim of the fourth "Why Me? Factor"—*other people's choices.* If that happens and the hurt is really awful, we may find it impossible to forgive.

The "Levels of Love" — modified for when people really hurt us

We often begin with an **absence of love**:
"I'm angry. I hate them for what they did. They should suffer badly and forever. At times I feel like I want to harm them."

Responding with **Basic Love**:

"It's not easy to see their divinity, but I believe he or she is a child of God who has lost their way.

I (can almost) empathize and understand why they did it. But that does not excuse their bad behavior.

They should pay an *appropriate* price here and in the Spirit World.

I hope they will learn and grow from this and that God can help redeem their Soul (if it is bad)."

Responding from the **Upper Levels of Love**:

"I will do something constructive to help others in my situation or to change the conditions that might have caused it.

I will release my anger and resentment.

If they atone and show remorse, I will (try to) say 'I forgive you.'

I will be compassionate and help the one who hurt me or people like him or her."

This is a list of possible responses. We each do what we feel comfortable with.

"Do unto others"

God

If **you** did something that was harmful and were sorry, you'd want a shot at redemption. So try to be loving. If the person is really bad or unrepentant, you may leave the loving to Me.

We can be more forgiving than we think, but God understands that we have our limits.

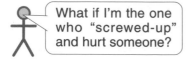

What if I'm the one who "screwed-up" and hurt someone?

It is going to happen more than once in our life. The "shoe's going to be on the other foot," and someone will be asking the Forgiveness Questions in reference to what we did to them. We will feel regretful, and we will hope the person we hurt will be forgiving and "go the distance" with us. There will also be times when our actions will hurt only us, yet our Emotional Mind will still be burdened by regret. So, we must learn how to be self-forgiving.

Ways To Seek Forgiveness and To Heal Ourself

Accept responsibility • Say "I'm sorry" • Make amends if we can • Learn and grow (get help if we need it) • If punishment is called for, pay it • If given another chance, be grateful; honor their trust • Be guided in future choices by love • Accept our humanness

You did then what you knew how to do.

Maya Angelou
American poet, writer

We are on a journey of personal evolution. We're doing our best to be better from day-to-day and from life-to-life. To help us let go of the poor choices we made in the past, we need to remind ourself of that fact.

Practice Forgiveness Prevention

Become more **aware** of whether our words and actions are or might be hurtful, then **change** our behavior *before* we cause harm.

Our Soul

Sometimes what we have to do for our own growth and happiness will hurt others.

Doing what is best for us — such as leaving a relationship, changing jobs or relocating—is sure to hurt someone in our life. Of course, that is not our intent, and we will feel sad about it. But in the end, we must follow what we believe is our Soul's path. (However, that doesn't mean if we leave a marriage, for example, we should also walk away from a child who still needs us.) Generally though, the challenge is to implement our choice in a way that minimizes the pain for all concerned. Being open with our feelings and explaining "the why" behind our choice is an important part of the process.

You've made hurtful choices, but I forgive you. However, do try to become wiser as time goes by.

I appreciate your forgiveness, but sometimes I feel it is I who should be forgiving you. After all, you're the One who made a world where suffering exists.

God is a patient and understanding parent who gives us many chances to grow. She will never abandon us, even if we stray far off course. God's mercy is a blessing for our Soul. And we can express our gratitude by showing Her that we're learning and expanding our energy.

On those occasions when we're upset with God for the state of our life or of the world, we are not making Her angry. God does not get defensive. She understands why we would want to blame Her for our woes. But once again God reminds us that this life is just one episode in our Soul's existence, and it is now up to us to make the Physical World better for ourself and others.

It's Never Too Late For Reconciliation

For example, we can communicate with the Soul of a loved one who has passed on.

Would you forgive me?

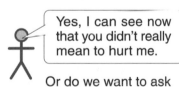

Yes, I can see now that you didn't really mean to hurt me.

Or do we want to ask them to forgive us?

This is the Soul of one of our kindreds who has returned to the Spirit World and who is now asking us this question via telepathy.

Generally, it is better to express our feelings face-to-face, but we don't always get that opportunity. Fortunately, we can convey our "pardon" (if they hurt us) or our remorse (if we hurt them), even if the other person has died or is beyond approach in this life. By using the power of our Unconscious Mind, we can send out *thoughts* of forgiveness. If our thoughts are sincere, rooted in love, and really directed at the other person (or at their Soul), we can advance the healing process. At a minimum, we will release some painful memories from our own Emotional Mind. If the other person has passed on, we will also bring peace to his or her Soul. And if they are still here, we may pave the way with our thoughts for a more personal reconciliation later on.

We're All Going To Make "Mistakes"
No one is perfect, and we're all learning.

Bygones.

love is restored

People we love who did something hurtful

We didn't mean it.

Will we empathize, cut them some slack, and be forgiving? Or will we stay angry?

We don't have to say "I forgive you" or resume relations with everyone.

Goodbye

Someone who really hurt us or our loved ones and who is not sorry or changed.

But we can be self-loving and release our feelings so that we can move on.

Most hurtful incidents are not so bad that we can't get over them. Besides, do we really want to waste the love that we could be sharing with our family and friends.

Forgiveness is a compassionate act. It helps relieve the emotional suffering of those who caused us harm, it can promote personal growth, and it can even transform a troubled Soul.

Today is "**emotional amnesty day**." I am releasing the regrets and anger I feel towards others and myself.

Great! That will lighten my load and make our journey easier and far more enjoyable.

Emotional Mind

The price of admission to a good future is letting go of the negative events of the past. Old hurts are like "anchors" holding us back. So, maybe it's time for us to clean the slate and to clear out our emotional attic. We can declare a "blanket pardon" and let everyone off the hook. Let's move on unburdened and do our best to avoid or prevent hurtful events in the future. (I'm sorry for using so many metaphors in this paragraph. Please forgive me.)

God

The next chapter presents some final thoughts on the journey of life. But before you get to that, I'd like you to read about one person's reaction to an awful event that occurred in her life. It's inspiring.

In 1998, James Byrd Jr., a 49 year old black man, was brutally killed. He was the victim of a despicable hate crime. It would be understandable if those who loved him reacted with hate of their own for the three men charged with his murder. But they didn't. Here is what Byrd's sister Mary Nell Verrett had to say about forgiveness to writer Dennis McCafferty from *USA Weekend* magazine:

> "Will we ever forgive the men who did this? Forgiveness is when you let go of resentment. We resent now. But when you carry resentment inside, it tears away at you. You become sick. You become a victim all over again. It can keep you from sleeping, eating and thinking straight. It can keep you from going forward. One day we won't resent anymore.

> "My brother would have wanted the world to grow from this, and I think it will. Our family has no use for destructive hate. We have done our best to communicate a message my brother would have wanted the world to know: We are all here to stay. It is just as well we learn how to live together as one community.

> "This act of hate has inspired the most profound outpouring of love I've known. (She received thousands of letters from all over the world.) We are so far away in miles, but so close in mind and heart."

I could not have expressed it better Myself. In forgiving, you open your heart to all the love that is around you. Mary Nell Verrett has shown you some of the compasssion and divinity that is in every Soul.

Final Thoughts on the Journey

To know how to grow old is the master-work of wisdom, and one of the most difficult chapters in the great art of living.

Henri Frederic Amiel – Swiss philosopher; 1821–81

The first-half of life wasn't easy. Will the second-half be harder? How can I make it fulfilling?

Each phase of life presents us with new challenges and lessons to learn, as well as new opportunities to find happiness.

| Childhood | Early Adulthood | | Mid-Life | Senior Years |

The second-half of life can be fantastic. But we need to understand that aging and the passage of time also have certain "costs" which we won't like.

According to psychologist and author Kathleen Brehony, one of the major challenges we face in the second-half of life is learning how to "live fully while knowing that death and loss are inevitable." Like it or not, physical life is impermanent and at times painful. If we can accept or make peace with this reality, the rest of our journey will be more satisfying and meaningful.

I finally understand what life is about; it is about losing everything ... so every morning we must celebrate what we have.

Isabelle Allende – author

Since we will lose everything eventually, it only makes sense to live life to the fullest, to take each day and each relationship as the blessing that it is.

Kathleen Brehony – author of *Awakening at Midlife*

Please do all you can right *now* to live the life you have imagined. Also, having a spiritual perspective of death can help you to live more fully. This journey will end, but your Soul will live on forever. And you will be reunited with your loved ones.

As We Get Older, The "Portal of Death" Comes More Into View

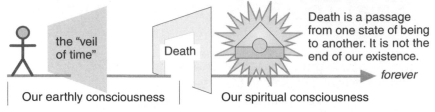

The "veil of time" keeps the occasion and circumstances of our death a mystery. But as we get older, or if we have a life-threatening illness, the veil gets more transparent. Death becomes more real to us.

Seeing ourself as a spiritual being who survives death can really help us to cope with the inevitable declines of our body. As our Earthly Self weakens and slows down, we can envision the light of our Soul shining through ever more brightly. The "portal of death" represents the boundary of *physical* life. When we pass through it we shed our body and return to our home in the Spirit World.

> Grow old along with me,
> the best is yet to be.
>
> Robert Browning
> English poet; 1812–89

> I've been thinking more about death since I entered mid-life, but it is possible I won't die for another 40–50 years. I've got a whole lot of living yet to do.

Despite its many challenges, mid-life and on can be the beginning of our second adulthood and a wonderful opportunity to live more fully. With an increased awareness of our mortality and of how quickly time passes, we learn to value what's important and to let go of what isn't. We live with a greater appreciation for each moment and for the importance of being authentic or true to oneself. We tend to have a greater sense of purpose and urgency, knowing we are not yet done with our mission and that we still have places to go, things to do and people to meet.

Mid-life is an especially good time to review how our journey has been going and to ask, "What do I still want to do?" and "What do I want to change?" Even if we have many unrealized dreams, we should not be discouraged. Instead, we should act as if we still have the time to make many of them come true.

> It's never too late to be what you might have been.
> George Eliot – novelist; 1819–80

> Being true to oneself is the law of God. ... Wisdom, compassion and *courage*—these are the three universally recognized moral qualities.
>
> Confucius – Chinese philosopher; 551–479 BCE

Pursuing our dreams or making big changes to our life takes a great deal of courage. Still, facing our fears and the uncertainty that comes with taking a new path is preferable to living (and dying) with major regrets or staying in a situation that is unsatisfying or worse. So, as we look ahead to the second half of our life, we ought to be sure we're on a path that will allow us to be happy and fulfilled.

> Two roads diverged in a wood, and I—
> I took the one less traveled by,
> And that has made all the difference.
>
> Robert Frost
> American poet; 1874–1963

> Loss and death are inevitable, but much of what we associate with aging is not. Vitality is the natural way of life. How we care for our body, mind and Soul has a profound effect on our ability to live fully in our second adulthood.

Seven Ways To "Live Long and Prosper" – Or, How To Be Emotionally, Physically and Spiritually Fulfilled Well Into Our Senior Years

- ☐ Have a daily practice of healthy living: exercise, eat good food
- ☐ Maintain loving relationships and seek out new ones if we are alone; make some younger friends
- ☐ Continue to learn and use our intellect; be inquisitive
- ☐ Stay engaged in life: pursue one of our callings; participate in the community and make a contribution
- ☐ Do fun things often and with other fun-loving people
- ☐ Have a positive attitude about aging; view life as an episode in our Soul's eternal journey
- ☐ Reflect periodically, in a self-loving way, on the choices and events of our life; keep doing our best to bring forth our light

> By changing personal behavior, people could reduce their risk of dying early by 70% to 80%.
>
> Prof. John Graham, Director, Harvard Center for Risk Analysis

We Are As Young As We Feel

Emotional Mind

Even though my body isn't as strong as it used to be and it has lost its youthful appearance, I am still young "inside."

Each of our parts experiences aging differently. Our Soul is of course timeless and to a great extent, so is our Emotional Mind. Occasionally, I feel emotionally worn from my years on Earth, but generally I don't think of myself as old. I feel as I did when I was in my teens, even though when I look in the mirror I can see I have aged.

To really appreciate the rest of our journey, we need to recapture our "joie de vie" or the joy of life we felt as a child, or that we wish we had felt back then. We want to think, feel and *act* young and pursue life in a playful manner. If we seek out ways to have fun and to express ourself, we will be more vital and enhance the quality of our life—and probably live longer too.

> How old would you be if you didn't know how old you were?
>
> Satchel Paige – baseball pitcher; 1906–82
>
> It takes a long time to become young.
>
> Pablo Picasso – Spanish artist; 1881–1973

Every Soul is concerned about how its Earthly Self is spending its time. Each moment is precious, especially as we get older. It's a shame to be wasteful.

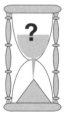

Since we don't know how much time we have, we should use it wisely.

If throughout our life we watched television on average 3 hours per day and we lived to be 80 years old, we would spend **10 years** of our time on Earth being passively entertained (to put it nicely). Such poor usage of time was probably not part of our Soul's Life Plan.

> Useless amusement is very bad for a being whose life is so short and whose time is so important.
>
> Jean Jacques Rousseau – French philosopher (paraphrased); 1712–78

Using our time wisely doesn't mean we are always doing something. As noted before, taking time to "just be" is important too.

However, many of us are squandering the precious few moments we have on Earth. Whether we're a teenager or a senior, we want to be mostly engaged in meaningful activities. If we spend too much time doing nothing or pursuing "mindless" entertainment, we will, as was also noted earlier, have "some 'splaining to do" to our Soul when we return to the Spirit World. Besides, there is so much to see and do why wouldn't we want to use our time wisely?

> The passage of time drives you crazy when you know perfectly well you're not using it right.
> Barbara Sher – author of *It's Only Too Late If You Don't Start Now*

> Someone once told me that time was a predator that stalked us all our lives. But I'd rather believe that time is a companion that goes with us on the journey. It reminds us to cherish every moment because they will never come again. What we leave behind is not as important as how we have lived.
> Captain Jean Luc Picard; from *Star Trek: The Next Generation*

> One of the "perks" of aging is we get to be an elder or wise person. In days gone by, the elders in a tribe or community were revered. Sadly, that is not true today. But we can still find ways to share our wisdom with younger people.

In the second half of life, our generosity tends to grow. We want to give back to our community and help make the road easier to travel for the generations coming after us. So, we are inclined to be more charitable with what we have earned and to share what we have learned. By mid-life, and certainly by our senior years, we have accumulated many valuable insights about the art of living. Sharing this wisdom with younger people, even if it is just with one person, is good for us and them. Being a mentor adds meaning and purpose to our life. The young person who is willing to be counseled by an elder can become a wise chooser earlier in life. Now, if only our society would treat older folks with more dignity.

> Respect the elders. Learn from their wisdom. They are, as Rev. Matthew Fox says, the "treasured ones." Also, we owe a lot to those who came before us.

Before The Journey Is Over

Are there loose ends you want to tie up or something you would really like to do?

Senior Years

Death

My "I Really Want To-Do" List

Write on a piece of paper your answers to these questions:

What do I want to **see** or **do** before I die?

What do I want to **say** to various people before I die?

Which relationships do I want to **enhance** or **heal**?

Whether we're at the end of a long, fulfilled life or facing the portal of death at an early age, we might consider preparing an "I Really Want To-Do" list. The more items on that list we can attend to, the more at peace we will be when we make the passage back home.

Even if the end of our journey is not imminent, we could still answer this question: "How would I live if I had only one year left to go?" This exercise is similar to the life review referred to earlier. But in this case, our "to-do" list will reflect a greater sense of urgency and importance. By assuming that death's door is closer than it may be, we can really prioritize how we are using our time. It can help us to be sure we are not ignoring our desires or taking our loved ones for granted.

God

Caring for your kindreds as they near the end of their lives is a very special role you can play. You can act as a "midwife" and help your loved ones make the transition back to the Spirit World.

As time goes by, the people (and pets) who are close to us will die. To "be there" at the end for them, if we can, is a loving way to honor a kindred bond. As they make their passage back home, we can give them love and provide care. We can also be forgiving and help them to find inner peace. When *we* return to the Spirit World, they will greet us and say "thank you." Also, caring for our kindreds can be therapeutic for us. It can heal old wounds and teach us about dying, which will help us with our own eventual death.

As we approach our death, we hope our kindreds will think of the spiritual bond that exists between us and realize we didn't mean to be hurtful during our life.

To help close out this chapter, let's look again at the prayer of St. Francis. It applies to all of life but especially to how we approach the second-half.

God grant me the **serenity** to accept the things I cannot change, the **courage** to change the things I can, and the **wisdom** to know the difference.

The Road God Wants Us to Travel ...
The Freeway of Love

Love
Joy
Creativity

The best moments occur on this road. When the ride gets bumpy, call Me on your *prayer* phone.

"Happy trails to you." Have a very pleasant journey through life.

We begin life on a given road, with certain travel companions and in a "vehicle" that may or may not be as well equipped as we'd like. Our challenge is to make our journey as meaningful as we can and to be a Good Samaritan and help others.

Keep your eyes on the road right in front of you because ...

Life can only be understood backwards, but it must be lived *forwards*.
Soren Kierkegaard – Danish theologian; 1813–55

Slow down and enjoy life. It's not only the scenery you miss by going too fast—you also miss the sense of where you are going and why.
Eddie Cantor – American singer; 1892–1964

In the next chapter we will take a closer look at the subject of death and consider what the afterlife is like and where we go from here.

When your earthly life is over, you will return to the world in which your Soul was born. You will reflect on your life, keep learning and get ready for your next adventure.

A Soul coming home

I'm also going to rest and enjoy myself.

The universe or Physical World

The Spirit World

Death and the Hereafter

I'm not afraid of death, I just don't want to be there when it happens.

Woody Allen

What is "death," and why do we fear it? Is it the idea of being punished for our sins that scares us the most? Since I don't believe God is vengeful, I'm not worried about pain in the afterlife. In fact, I believe that most of us will enjoy, to varying degrees, the splendor of the hereafter. For me, it's losing the earthly connection with my loved ones that makes me wish I didn't have to die.

Death Is Not the End. It's a New Beginning.

The Soul leaves the Earthly Self and the Physical World behind. Then it can focus all its energy on exploring and growing in the Spirit World.

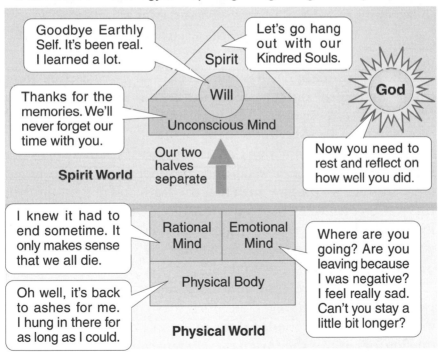

Goodbye Earthly Self. It's been real. I learned a lot.

Let's go hang out with our Kindred Souls.

Spirit

Will

Thanks for the memories. We'll never forget our time with you.

Unconscious Mind

God

Spirit World

Our two halves separate

Now you need to rest and reflect on how well you did.

I knew it had to end sometime. It only makes sense that we all die.

Rational Mind

Emotional Mind

Where are you going? Are you leaving because I was negative? I feel really sad. Can't you stay a little bit longer?

Physical Body

Oh well, it's back to ashes for me. I hung in there for as long as I could.

Physical World

Death is a transformation. It is sort of like birth but in reverse. It can be quite an ordeal when our Soul leaves our body or disconnects from our Earthly Self. But when it's over, an exciting new adventure begins.

It's A Two-Step Process

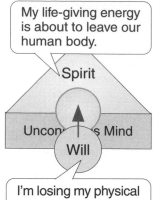

My life-giving energy is about to leave our human body.

Spirit

Uncon s Mind

Will

I'm losing my physical consciousness. I'm coming home to be with you again.

Our Will never stops being part of our Soul when we're alive, but it is "detached" in the sense that it spends all of our waking moments in the realm of the Physical World. It is only when we're asleep that it temporarily rejoins the rest of our Soul.

When we die our Will makes its final journey across the "threshold" and goes back to the Spirit World for good (or at least until we incarnate again). At the same time, our Spirit stops sending us the energy that kept us alive. And then our Soul leaves us, and our Earthly Self dies.

Death can be brutal; there's no use pretending otherwise. But from another point of view, death appears as a joyful event. In the light of eternity it is a "wedding," where the Soul achieves wholeness again.

Carl Jung – Swiss psychiatrist (paraphrased); 1875–1961

The experience of death is not the same for every person. Some deaths are sudden, and the passage to the other side is painless. For others, death can linger and be quite grievous. Sadly, that can be the case even if we did everything "right" in life.

The mind and body don't always approach death at the same rate. One may deteriorate well before the other is ready to go. In our body, the cells are programmed to resist death and to fight for their survival. So even when the Soul is ready to leave, it may not be easy. Eventually the body will surrender. However, sometimes our Soul won't leave until it knows our loved ones are ready to let us go, or until it has "made peace" with them.

Some people have "near-death" experiences, where they make it *partway* across the threshold and then they come back to Earth— maybe because God wanted them to complete some part of their mission, or perhaps they just have very tenacious Souls.

The strongest desire known to human life is to continue living.

Dorothy Dudley – American writer; 1884–1962

What We Fear Most About Dying

1. That we will die prematurely.

2. That we will be in great pain.

3. That we will die alone. No one will be there *or* care if we die.

4. That we will lose our dignity and be dependent upon others for our basic human needs.

5. That we will cease to exist— that there is no "life" after death.

6. That there is a hereafter—and we will be punished for our life.

The prospect of death also produces the pains of regret and remorse. We think of what we did wrong in life and of all the things we wish we would have said or done.

Coping with death can be overwhelming and depressing—even if one has a spiritual perspective. As we get older and experience the death of people we know and love, we see how painful and drawn-out the process can be. And as our parents (and especially our peers) die, we come to understand how indiscriminate death really is. We begin to worry and say to ourself—"It's going to happen to me!"

God

Death can happen at any time, but most of you have a lot more control over how and when you will die than you realize.

The best advice I can give is this: make healthy choices, enjoy the moment and appreciate the beauty and people in your life while you can.

Our current lifestyle choices won't prevent our return to the Spirit World, but they can affect the nature of our eventual demise. And equally important, how we choose to use our time will affect how we feel about our death. If we choose to do what we love and to love others, we will be more grateful for life and less fearful of death. Having done our best to honor our Life Plan, we can more easily accept the inevitable, and perhaps even welcome what comes next. Finally, we can heal our emotional wounds by making amends with those we hurt. By saying "I'm sorry" we release the guilt that burdens our Soul. We shouldn't wait until we think we're near the end of our life to do this—for the end can come at any time. Perhaps the best way to deal with death is to believe in the grace of God and in the goodness and immortality of our own Soul.

When A Loved One Dies We're Left Behind, But Not Alone

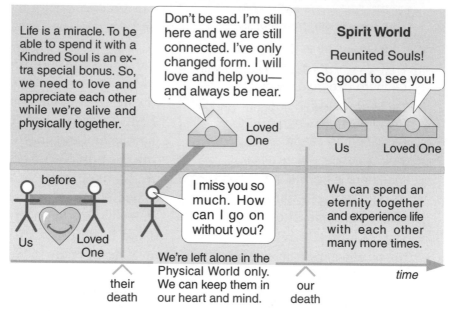

Losing a loved one can be even more difficult than facing our own death. The emotional impact of such a loss can be so great we might never fully recover. This is especially true if their death happens "before their time" (as with children and young adults) or if it is a particularly painful or needless death.

There is no easy way to cope with the death of a loved one. We can find comfort with other kindreds and keep our memories alive. We can also take solace knowing the spiritual connection with our loved one's Soul endures. He or she is now in a place, with the Angels and Spirit Guides, to look over us and to send us love and guidance. It is through our thoughts and prayers that we stay in touch with each other. And when *we* die our Souls will be reunited and share the spiritual experience together.

We can honor the memory of a loved one who has died by helping others in his or her name or by carrying on an activity that was important to them. And as difficult as it can be to go on without a loved one, they would want us to try and find meaning in the rest of our journey. We will grieve and be terribly sad, but the love we hold within our heart will go on forever.

"The Light at the End of the Tunnel"
We see the brilliance of God and of our own Soul.

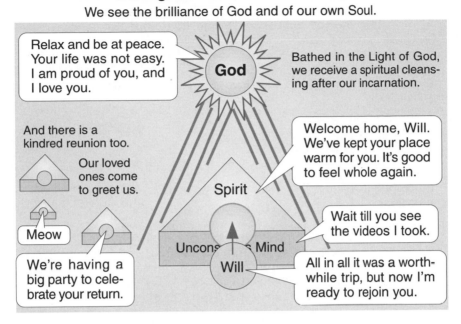

People who come back from a near-death experience describe the sensation of moving through a dark tunnel, emerging into a bright light and then encountering a "Being" of glorious radiance. There are three views of this that I like. First, we see the Light of our own Soul as we come back into the full awareness of the Spirit World. Second, we also see the Light of God as She comes to "cleanse and soothe" us with Her unconditional love. And third, one or more of our Kindred Souls are in the greeting party to help us make the transition back to the Spirit World and to honor the end of our journey.

Some say the brain is producing these feelings and images to help us cope with the pain and emotions of dying. That may be true, but we still have the spiritual experience too. They don't have to be mutually exclusive explanations.

We See Ourselves As We Were On Earth

At first, we see the energy version of our old Earthly Self (and of our Kindreds). And we're in familiar earth-*like* settings. This helps us to ease back into the Spirit World.

Our Life Review – The One Movie We Have to Watch

After our death, our reunited Soul reviews and reflects
upon the activities of our lifetime. It's for our own good.

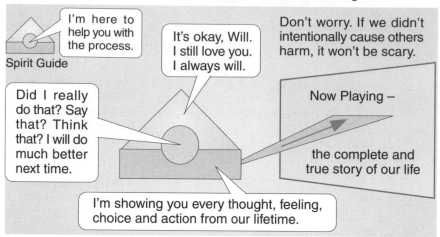

The key review criteria are God's Values and Beliefs. We get to see
when we lived in accordance with them and when we did not.

People who return from a near-death experience also say, "I saw my whole life pass before my very eyes." Frankly, I find this concept both fascinating and a bit scary. Here we are, just barely dead, and our reunited Soul is all gung-ho on reviewing the results of our life. What's the rush? Well, this "play back" is for the benefit of our spiritual development. It's an opportunity for us to see what we did well and what we might have done better so we can learn and grow.

Life Reviews are a loving, nonthreatening experience. Neither God nor the Angels are sitting there judging us or waiting to punish us. It is our own Soul or, more specifically, our Will that comes to the realization (in a safe, spiritual environment, away from the stress and distractions of the Physical World) of how well it chose while it was incarnated. We will see *and feel* how our words and actions affected people and other forms of life. This feature of the review helps us to get the "full picture" of our time on Earth.

Most Souls are mature enough to "grade" themselves. But to make sure we see our life in the proper perspective, one of our Spirit Guides is there with us. This Soul is wise enough to know most of what can go right and wrong during the physical experience. Our Guide can help us to understand why we might have acted as we did and to see how we could do better. A Life Review may not be the most enjoyable movie we will ever see, but it will be the most educational.

Some Typical Life Review Questions

- ☐ Did I love myself and give my love to family and friends?
- ☐ Did I get along well with others, treating them with courtesy, respect and kindness?
- ☐ Did I help people and animals who were suffering?
- ☐ Did I seek forgiveness from those I hurt or try to remedy the harm I caused?
- ☐ Did I act as a good steward of the Earth and other forms of life?
- ☐ Did I have fun? Did I enjoy my time in the Physical World?
- ☐ Did I discover my special talents and work at what I love?
- ☐ Did I use my creative energy and make enough positive "Let there be ..." choices? Did I make a contribution?
- ☐ Did I face my fears and let more of my light shine through; did I become a better, more spiritually evolved person?
- ☐ Did I do my best to lead a life of love, joy and creativity? Were my intentions good?
- ☐ Do I still have lessons to learn? Do I need to try again? (Almost all of us need to check this one.)

A Life Review is a very comprehensive process, delving into every aspect of our earthly journey. With the answers to these and other questions, we can identify the lessons we still need to learn, and we can begin thinking about our next incarnation.

The Life Review is a loving, self-judging experience, but it can still generate intense feelings within our Soul—even though we left our Emotional Mind behind on Earth. If we did a good job, we will feel proud and joyful. On the other hand, if we acted *badly* on Earth, we will feel guilty and remorseful.

> Don't wait for last judgment—it takes place every day.
> Albert Camus – Algerian-born French novelist; 1913–60

We shouldn't wait until we are off the planet to review the quality of our choices. If we ask these questions throughout our lifetime, and then act to improve ourself, we will be prepared for the real Life Review when it occurs, and our Soul will have fewer regrets. We are not only the lead actor in our movie, we are also one of the screenwriters. Each day we have a major say in how our script will unfold.

During Our Life Our Soul's Energy Expands or Contracts
Our Life Review makes us aware of how it changed and why?

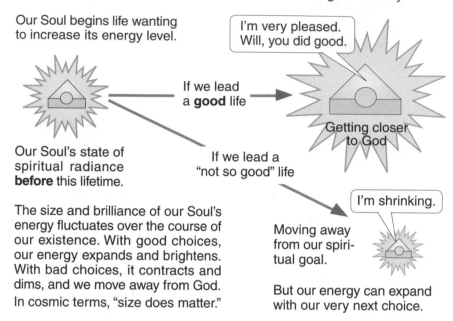

Our Soul begins life wanting to increase its energy level.

I'm very pleased. Will, you did good.

If we lead a **good** life

Getting closer to God

Our Soul's state of spiritual radiance **before** this lifetime.

If we lead a "not so good" life

I'm shrinking.

Moving away from our spiritual goal.

The size and brilliance of our Soul's energy fluctuates over the course of our existence. With good choices, our energy expands and brightens. With bad choices, it contracts and dims, and we move away from God. In cosmic terms, "size does matter."

But our energy can expand with our very next choice.

Our Soul's energy level, which defines our state of spiritual development, expands or contracts *automatically* based upon the nature of our everyday choices. Spiritual energy is self-regulating. God doesn't have to intervene, it just happens. It also doesn't matter whether we take responsibility for our bad choices while on Earth. Our Soul knows the truth of our existence, and our energy level is adjusted to reflect the reality of our life.

The size and brilliance of our spiritual energy determines our "proximity" to God in the hereafter. The more energy we possess, the closer we can be to Her. It is not necessarily a physical closeness we experience, since as Souls we can exist anywhere we choose. It is more of a sense of intimacy, like being with our best friend. If we're really "energetic," then our connection with God will be quite strong. Our self-love will be high too because we will know we have "done good." Finally, as we move closer to God, we become even more aware of the true nature and scope of our creative powers. When we are in the presence of God we have a better sense of our own divinity.

God

My hope is that all of you will grow and get really close to Me. You have the ability; of this I am certain.

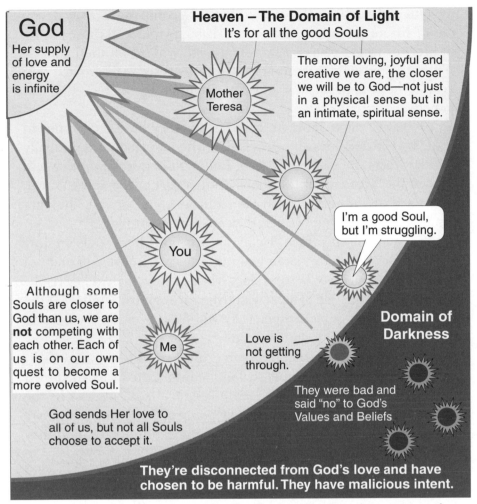

Some benefits of being "close" to God – more creative power and opportunities for fulfillment, hang out with other energetic Souls and get invitations to God's "Let there be ..." parties.

When we die we go back to the Spirit World. The question is, to which part of it do we return? We want to be in "Heaven," which is not a place separate from the Spirit World but the part of it that is "in the Light." In Heaven, we will enjoy fabulous scenery and other "sensual delights." Our loved ones will be there, and we will feel no pain. We will be mostly blissful, though we might feel sad as we review and reflect on our life. Heaven will exceed our wildest dreams. And we will find that all good Souls, *regardless of their religious beliefs on Earth,* are welcomed in Heaven. It doesn't matter whether we worshipped in a church, synagogue, mosque, temple or wherever.

Our right to be in Heaven and in God's company is solely determined by our intentions and actions. Even people who chose poorly in life, *but whose Souls wanted to be good,* will be "in the Light"—albeit at a greater distance from God. If they caused real harm to other people, they will be far away and expected to do a lot of reflection and remedial spiritual work.

However, when Souls are truly "bad," (they have chosen not to abide by God's Values and Beliefs), or when a person intentionally harms others on Earth *and their Soul is not remorseful,* they will exist in the "Domain of Darkness." In this part of the Spirit World, Souls are disconnected from God's love—not because She isn't sending it to them but because they are not accepting it.

You may call this place "Hell," but it is not where Souls are tormented for eternity by Satan and his crowd. It is instead a state of existence in which Souls experience fear and loneliness. They're like people on the outside of a party, staring through the window at the rest of us having a great time. They will forever be on the outside looking in unless they choose to be "good" again.

As I have mentioned before, some Souls like (if that is the right word) being in this state because they are intoxicated with their own power and by what they can create (or take from others) in the Physical World. Sure, they're in the company of other Souls, but there is no love between them. There is only envy and distrust, and they are always looking over their shoulders.

I know that for someone who has been affected by the harmful actions of another person, the Domain of Darkness doesn't sound as bad as "burning in Hell." But the Souls who are disconnected from God's love are being tormented in ways we can't fully appreciate. Not being in the Light is a form of spiritual isolation that takes a severe toll on those unfortunate Souls.

There Is Hope For All Souls

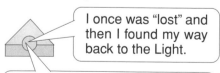

I once was "lost" and then I found my way back to the Light.

I was lonely and got tired of all the negativity. I know I'll have to work hard to get close to God.

God is merciful. She gives every Soul the opportunity to atone for its poor choices and to reenter Heaven. No Soul is banished to the darkness forever, not even the worst ones. But it's not enough to say "I've seen the light." Their actions must show they are sincere.

Multiple Choice Question: **Where Do We Hang Out After Death?**

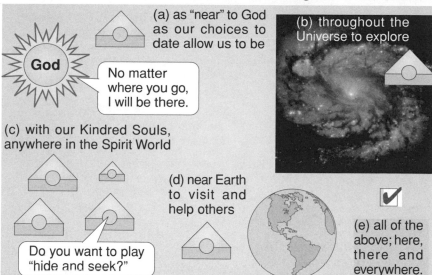

(a) as "near" to God as our choices to date allow us to be

God

No matter where you go, I will be there.

(b) throughout the Universe to explore

(c) with our Kindred Souls, anywhere in the Spirit World

Do you want to play "hide and seek?"

(d) near Earth to visit and help others

(e) all of the above; here, there and everywhere.

As Souls, we are like photons of light traveling through space. We have no perception of distance or the passage of time. In the Spirit World, where we are free from the constraints of the physical body, we can be anywhere and everywhere in an instant just by thinking of being there. We can wish upon a star and have it appear. We can go visit other planets and galaxies throughout the cosmos. And we can be near our loved ones still on Earth. These concepts are "mind-boggling," but they're true. Indeed, from this perspective, death looks like the beginning of an excellent adventure—not that I want it to begin anytime soon.

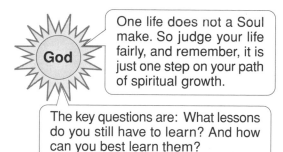

God

One life does not a Soul make. So judge your life fairly, and remember, it is just one step on your path of spiritual growth.

The key questions are: What lessons do you still have to learn? And how can you best learn them?

Even though we can have a great time in the Spirit World, the rest of our existence is not all fun and games. That may not seem fair after we have endured the trials and tribulations of this life. Still, we are going to have further work to do in the Physical World—unless we were able to achieve our "mission" during this incarnation!

After We Die, Our Soul Reflects and Then We Look Ahead

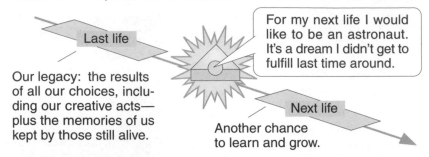

For my next life I would like to be an astronaut. It's a dream I didn't get to fulfill last time around.

Last life

Our legacy: the results of all our choices, including our creative acts—plus the memories of us kept by those still alive.

Next life

Another chance to learn and grow.

We keep incarnating until we've grown into our full godlike splendor. And then we could choose to come back again just to help others.

We Are Each On Our Own Path

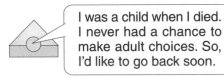

I was a child when I died. I never had a chance to make adult choices. So, I'd like to go back soon.

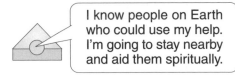

I know people on Earth who could use my help. I'm going to stay nearby and aid them spiritually.

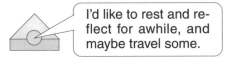

I'd like to rest and reflect for awhile, and maybe travel some.

We have our own way to become more loving, joyful and creative.

Our Spirit Guides will help us during our "review" to put our life in perspective and to develop a plan for our ongoing spiritual development. We will discuss the many options which could facilitate our growth, including perhaps going back to Earth (or some other planet) fairly soon and trying physical life again.

We might decide it would be best if we didn't incarnate for awhile. That's a perfectly fine alternative because the evolution of our Soul doesn't occur just on the physical plane. We can grow substantially while in the Spirit World too. We could be tutored by one of our Guides (it's like hanging out with Yoda from *Star Wars*). Or we could attend Spiritual University, where they teach courses on "*How to lead a better life.*"

If we are qualified, we could choose to help other Souls with their lessons or act as a Spirit Guide for a Soul who is incarnated. Of course, we can always send love and positive energy to the people we knew on Earth who are still there. The point is this: helping others while we are in the Spirit World is good for our Soul—just as a life of service is here on Earth.

I want to live forever, at least in the hearts and minds of those I leave behind and who will incarnate after me. I want immortality!

We all want to feel as if our life mattered and that someone will remember us or that another person's life was better because we were here. Also, most of us will probably want to brag (at least a little) to our Kindred Souls when we cross over. We might want to say, "Did you see how well I did during my life? I wasn't perfect, but I made a real difference. I was a contributor!"

Our life can have meaning far beyond our limited time here on Earth. To achieve that goal, we need to make a commitment to fulfill our mission. If we use our special talents to make meaningful "Let there be ..." choices, and most importantly, if we lead a life of love and service to others, then we will "live on" after we leave the Physical World. We might even inspire people for generations to come. We make our life worthwhile by doing our best to learn and grow—and by becoming more loving, joyful and creative.

> If you want immortality, make it.
> Joaquin Miller
> American poet; 1841–1913

> The wise man looks at death with honesty, dignity and calm, recognizing that the tragedy it brings is inherent in the great gift of life.
> Corliss Lamont – American philosopher; 1902–95

> There is no "cure" for death—except to enjoy the life that comes before it.
> George Santayana (paraphrased)
> Spanish-born, American philosopher; 1863–1952

As painful as death can be—for the person who is dying and for his or her loved ones—please remember that it is the end of just one episode in your Soul's eternal journey and that you and your kindreds will be together again.

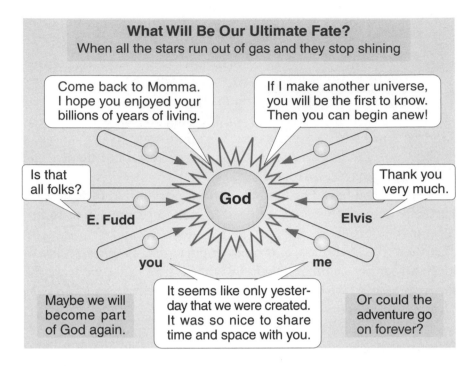

Do you ever wonder what will happen when the lights go out in the universe? Astronomers are saying that *trillions and trillions* of years from now all the stars will stop shining and disintegrate. The universe will be of no use to anyone. In fact, stars like our Sun, capable of supporting earth-like planets, may no longer exist in "just" another 10 billion years or so.

If that is true, what was God thinking? What does this mean for the eternal existence of our Souls? I'm not sure, but I do have faith that if and when it happens, God will find us a new home. Or maybe we will all be "reabsorbed" into Her energy, where we will wait until She creates another universe. Or maybe there are other universes in existence right now we could occupy, or God will create another one before our stars fade out. Or perhaps we will spend eternity in the splendor of the Spirit World.

In any case, let's not worry about it. We should focus on this life. and make it the best one possible. We can have faith that God will take care of the rest. After all, She can be pretty creative.

A Summary of "Down to Earth"

Our home away from home.

Now we're going to recap the key points from the previous sixteen chapters. We have covered a lot of ground, beginning with what incarnating means and ending with death. The focus of these chapters was to help us make the most of our precious time here on Earth.

Getting Physical

Incarnation is a union of cosmic proportions. Miraculously, a Soul is able to join forces with a newly conceived human being so it can experience physical life. For as long as our spiritual and earthly elements are coupled, we have the ability to manifest in this dimension our love and joy and to create new realities.

Like two pieces of a puzzle:

Our Soul

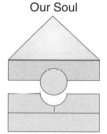

Our Human Mind and Body

Our Souls like coming to Earth because it is such a beautiful planet, and there is so much to see and do. We long for the chance to experience the sensations of the physical body, to use the powers of the intellect and to feel human emotions. We also come to learn how to make wise choices. Life is a very special occasion for a Soul. It is not meant to be something we must "get through" so we can be happy after death. God wants us to enjoy the journey itself—and to help our fellow Souls who are really struggling.

Our Life Situation

The overall condition in which our Soul begins its earthly adventure is our "life situation." It includes the mental and bodily traits we receive, as well as the economic, family and physical environment into which we are born. Obviously, we don't all begin life in a similar state or with similar circumstances. However, a person's life situation is not necessarily a reflection of the state of his or her Soul. A very evolved Soul can incarnate into a really bad situation. And a Soul who has a lot to learn might be born into a wealthy family. Everyone deserves respect regardless of his or her life situation.

Our Souls are very involved in the process that determines the life situation we will get. Prior to each trip to the Physical World, we prepare a Life Plan based on the state of our spiritual development. It includes our incarnation preferences, what we hope and need to learn, and how we want to express our gifts.

I like to believe the Angels are in charge of placing Souls into life situations. Perhaps we get what we ask for, though we might not see it that way when we're on Earth. Some aspects of our incarnation could be a karmic response to our actions in a prior life. Or we may be willing to take a less than ideal situation just so we can "get real" and be with our kindreds. And because there is still needless suffering on Earth, some Souls will be asked to become children with very poor prospects. Finally, our life situation might not work out as we hope it will. We are told to expect the unexpected and to be prepared to find the strength and courage to put ourself on a more fulfilling path.

> **Four Possible Incarnation Scenarios:**
> 1. Got what we wanted
> 2. Got a karmic situation
> 3. Took what was available
> 4. We volunteered

 When we incarnate we tend to get "spiritual amnesia." We must reestablish our awareness of and connection with the Spirit World and uncover our gifts and purpose.

We Are Reality Makers

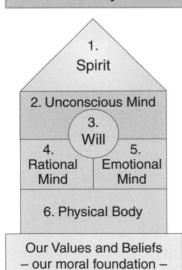

A model of who we are

Each of us has six elements. The first three are of the Soul. The others originate here on Earth. Our Spirit contains divine energy, is always connected to God and provides the "breath of life." Our Unconscious Mind is multipurpose. It is the source of our intuition and many creative ideas, as well as the eternal keeper of our memories. Our Will's role is to make choices. That is why we call it the "Chooser." Our Soul exists both within and beyond our human form. However, to do its job, our Will must get really immersed in the lower vibrations of the Physical World.

Our human or conscious mind has two components—one is *rational* (known as the "thinker"); the other is *emotional* (known as the "feeler"). Our human body is the sacred "temple of the Soul" and is to be treated with care and respect.

Our Spirit and Unconscious Mind, which are unaffected by Earth's lower vibrations, together are called our "Higher Self." Our "Earthly Self" consists of our human mind and body. Our Will is currently part of both selves. It listens to the wants and needs of each, is guided by our Values and Beliefs and then decides what we will say or do. We can learn to recognize which part of us is "talking" and to tell whether the message or impulse is good or not.

Most people think of themselves as "only human." So, they don't fully engage their Higher Self in their reality making. Learning to be more intuitive and to connect with your Higher Self through meditation and other methods can profoundly change your life for the better.

Our six elements are all linked together. The health of one affects the state of the others. The condition of our Emotional Mind is of particular importance.

As Reality Makers we can do amazing things if we are in a positive and harmonious state. Having a healthy Emotional Mind is key because "like attracts like." If we're positive, other positive people and opportunities will be drawn to us. Our creative energy will be more focused and effective. An impaired Emotional Mind is a prescription for trouble. It leads to poor choices and lets in negativity.

No One Is Perfect

We each have flaws. Our free Will can make good or bad choices. And our human nature has a dark side which can cause us to act from a place of inappropriate fear or selfishness. Our mission is not to eliminate all of our imperfections, but to make our spiritual side a more "visible" partner here on Earth —and to consciously choose to live by the good-natured side of our heart. We will never be perfect, but we can live with respect, kindness and compassion for ourself and all that God created.

Our Goal Is To "Live Spiritually"

now   future

Three Broad Categories of People

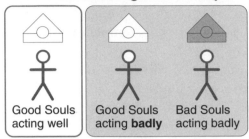

| Good Souls acting well | Good Souls acting **badly** | Bad Souls acting badly |

We can't tell if a person's Soul is bad. Earthly problems might be the cause of their harmful behavior.

Most of us have basically good Souls, and we are trying to lead good lives. When we are hurtful, it generally is not done deliberately or with malice. The distinction between good and bad is *intent* and *remorse*. A good Soul does not intend for its Earthly Self to cause harm and is sorry when it does. While we should refrain from labeling someone's Soul as "bad," it is appropriate to describe earthly behavior as such, or even in some cases as "evil."

An impaired mind, body or moral foundation can cause a person with a good Soul to act badly. He or she doesn't get into this state overnight. Childhood deficiencies or traumas are often responsible. Or there could be a biological problem. Whatever the cause, their Will has lost its way and is making harmful choices. If a person does have a bad Soul, he or she probably got like that over several lifetimes.

God

As a society, you can help children who are at risk, improve the conditions into which Souls are born, and help adults who have lost their way. As individuals, please work on your own issues. Remember, the world gets better when each of you gets better.

We face many challenges on Earth, and at times we stumble or even get on a negative path. The question is—will we learn from our mistakes and evolve into a better person and Soul?

Bringing Forth Our Light

Love, joy and creativity are the "light" of our Soul. **Personal growth** is the process of removing the obstacles that block that light.

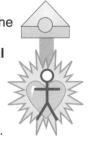

We can function at a higher level (and minimize our unintentional harmful behavior) by letting more of our spiritual essence shine through. To make this happen, we probably need to do some repair work (to fix the harm done to us by others and ourself) and to make life-style changes. Good self-care is essential to living fully "in the light."

We are not on a quest for perfection but rather for the level of excellence and wholeness that we personally can attain. Nor are we in competition with anyone else. When we are doing what we love and pursuing what we feel is in our Soul's Life Plan, we are *aligned*. When our Reality Maker elements are in a positive state and we are in touch with our Higher Self, we are *synergized*. It is when we are aligned *and* synergized that we are at our creative best.

Personal growth also maximizes our ability to be loving and joyful. It helps us be a better parent, partner, friend, etc. It reduces the needless pain, and it could extend our life. The ultimate reward of growth is we get more spiritual energy.

As we progress to a higher level of personal power, we contribute to the collective mission. We can inspire others to bring forth their light.

Self-awareness is the first step of growth. We begin by appreciating our good qualities. Then we acknowledge our shortcomings—particularly those which we can and should do something about. We can't resolve all of our issues at once, so we must prioritize. The first ones to address are those which are causing us or others real harm, such as substance abuse. Next in line are the issues which are holding us back in life, such as not having an adequate education.

Many of us have deep-rooted, emotional issues and harmful patterns of behavior. Some are from our childhood; others we inherited. To resolve them takes inner healing work, Willpower, and perhaps outside help too.

Some personal issues must be addressed with a sense of urgency. However, growth is best viewed as ongoing process. It is not about constantly striving to be better or depriving ourself of fun. The goal is to bring forth our light in a well-balanced manner and to be self-loving and accepting along the way.

It's All About Energy

We want our mental energy focused in the here and now. If it is, we will become a more fulfilled and effective Reality Maker.

Our light shines brightest when we're living in the moment. We can get stuck in the past with anger and regrets and lost in the future with worries. Letting go of thoughts and feelings that divert our energy brings us peace of mind.

All We Need Is Love

Love is the prime essence of your Soul and mine. We need to give and receive love in order to flourish and be happy. Love is more than a feeling. It is a way of life. It is seeing the divinity in other people and all life and making choices that honor our interconnectedness. Love is the path of compassion, respect and kindness.

God Put Love In Our Souls. Will We Express Our Love?

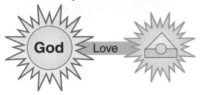

God sends unconditional love. She does not discriminate. God loves everyone and all things.

God's love for each of us, the love we have inside for others and ourself, and the love coming from our kindreds in the Spirit World is boundless. If we're not feeling much of this love, it could be we are burdened with fear and negativity. Or perhaps we don't believe God and Souls are real or that we deserve to experience love.

Enhancing the flow of *self-love* can have a profound and positive effect on every aspect of our life—and if we're a parent, on the lives of our children. The first step in bringing forth self-love is to look in the mirror and "see the light." When we realize we are a spiritual being and that God loves us as we are, we elevate our self-image. And our heart begins to open to the flow of self-love.

Do unto others as you would have them do unto you. It's that basic.

God doesn't expect us to love all people the same. But at a minimum, She wants us to observe the Golden Rule shown to the left. This basic level of love calls for tolerance, mutual respect and kindness, not being hurtful, and doing what we can to help someone in need. Of course, we can love some people (and pets) at even higher levels.

It is not easy to be loving here on Earth. If we were "only human" it might be too much to ask of us. Since the thought of loving everyone is overwhelming, it helps to focus on one person at a time. If interacting with someone is especially hard, we can visualize his or her Soul and appreciate our common spiritual heritage. We can also empathize or put ourself in their shoes. When we help relieve or prevent the suffering of another person or living thing, we are expressing one of God's favorite values—compassion. To be loving, or not, is a choice we make each moment of each day.

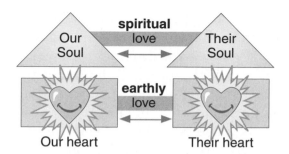

In a loving and satisfying relationship, the earthly bond reflects the specialness of the spiritual connection. We can move towards that ideal if both people are in the "intimacy zone," where we express our true feelings and feel safe and appreciated. We also need to follow the principle of "relationship karma," which is, *we must give what we wish to receive.* We can bring more love into our life by finding some of our kindreds and making new friends and by enhancing or healing the relationships we already have.

To Forgive Is Divine. And It's Liberating Too

X = our memories of hurtful events.

We are all imperfect, and there are issues in every relationship. So, forgiveness is an essential part of life. Forgiveness is how we honor our spiritual connection, acknowledge our common experience as human beings and restore the flow of love. Forgiveness is also self-loving because it unburdens our heart. It is a form of healing.

We can choose to heal ourself by releasing the hurt and anger, and we can help the other person heal by saying "I forgive you." We could also choose to heal or restore the relationship. As we face new hurts or rehash old ones, we can ask the "Forgiveness Questions": Who caused the harm? Was it a kindred? How serious was the harm? What were their intentions? Are they sorry? and, Would they do it again? If an event is really hard to let go of, or if the other person has since passed on, we can visualize talking to his or her Soul. Finally, we can free our heart and mind by making today "emotional amnesty day." This means we release all the unloving thoughts and feelings we hold for others and ourself.

We can practice "forgiveness prevention" by becoming more aware of whether our words and actions are *or might be* hurtful—and then change our behavior *before* we cause any harm.

In summary, do your best to bring the beauty and power of your Soul's love into the realm of the Physical World. It will transform you and help create Heaven on Earth.

Making Life Choices

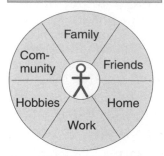

Our **Life Circle** provides the structure and overall direction for our journey.

We want a framework for our life that allows us to manifest our Soul's light. A few key choices will determine how we use our energy each day and who will be the "co-creators" of our reality. As we explore the possibilities for our Life Circle, we can ask these questions: *What* do I love to do? *Who* do I love to be with? *Where* do I love to be? *How* do I love to live? It is best to take the time necessary to create a good circle and to honor our own vision.

We need the essence of each element. For example, we want people in our life who love, support and nurture us and for whom we can do the same. If our parents, siblings and so on provide this, that's wonderful. But friendships can be just as fulfilling. There is more than one way to create the essence of a "family."

> There is someone for each of us, even if we need a pick axe, a compass and night goggles to find them.
> From *L.A. Story* by Steve Martin

Our search for a life partner who will be our best friend and loving co-creator can be quick, or not. We'd like to be with our Soul Mate, but we can be happy with a close kindred. Choosing wisely is important. Still, even if we are with our Soul Mate, cohabiting won't be easy, and it may not last. If we wish to honor our bond, we will act like "we are in this together" and work to resolve our issues. If we don't have a partner, we can still lead a fulfilled life.

> To conceive a child is to join with Me in the miracle of life. It is the most sacred and God-like act you can perform and one of the most consequential. Please be ready.

Before we bring one of our kindreds into this world, we need to be prepared. A child requires unconditional love and will expect us to be a responsible guardian, as well as a teacher and role model. They will need to learn from us how to be a wise chooser and someone who can lead a balanced life. Having a child and being a parent can be a glorious experience, but it's not for everyone. There are other ways we can use our "Let there be ..." power.

> Sex can be wonderful, if it is done thoughtfully and responsibly. **Higher-level sex** is preferable. Our sex life can be better if we are in a good and joyful state. Deciding when and with whom to have sex are two of the most important choices we make. Lives are at stake.

Here on Earth, we need ways to recreate the sense of oneness and interconnectedness that we enjoy in the Spirit World. Our circle isn't full unless we have the essence of community or a sense of belonging. We want to join with members of our "larger family" to share joyous and deeply meaningful moments, to provide for our mutual needs, and to pursue common goals. We also want to express our Soul's love and compassion and help those who are suffering.

A "home" is more than a physical structure. It is a place that meets our emotional and spiritual needs as well. It is where we can nurture ourself and our loved ones and where we feel comfortable and at peace. Our Soul is happiest when there is some beauty around us. A "dream home" is full of love and is gentle to the natural world.

> Our **calling** is the activity that uses our gifts, we love doing, is mostly joyful, we're very good at, and allows us to make a contribution.

We all have at least one calling, which we might or might not discover early in life. Often, we pursue our calling(s) through our "work," which could be a paying job, parenting, volunteering or all of these activities. Or, we might express our gifts and find the most happiness through our hobbies. We want to find and pursue our calling because doing so brings out our passion, and we really connect with our Higher Self. There are questions we can ask to determine if we are well-suited for a particular career. If we can't do our calling right now or make enough money at it, we should at least do our best to avoid a "stuck-in-a-rut" job.

How we care for ourself (by getting an education, for example) and the choices we make regarding work have a major effect on our potential to earn money. The ways in which we make, spend and invest money should be guided by our Soul's moral foundation. We can tap into the flow of money by following the *Prosperity Principles*, which include being aligned with our Life Plan and feeling gratitude for what we already have. All people deserve a chance to prosper.

Money Circulates

From a higher-level perspective, the person who is "rich" is he or she whose life is full of love and joy and creative expression. We need money, and it can make us happier, but it is not the primary source of contentment in life.

Joy and Happiness

We are joyful by nature. We appreciate the beauty and pleasures of life. And we can be passionate and hopeful. Happiness is an emotional state which comes and goes. We "feel happy" when joy is flowing and our life, or at least key parts of it, are in good shape or moving in the right direction. If we want to feel happy more often, we may need to unblock our joy, change our Life Circle, and/or improve our mental or physical state. We need balance, simplicity and fun in our life, and we shouldn't defer our happiness. All work (even if it's our calling) and no play makes for a dull Soul. Each of us has a path of joy, which will put a smile on our face and keep the child within us alive. So, it is important we prepare our "Joy List" and live by it.

Why Things Happen

We are not in total control of what happens to us. All of us are vulnerable, to varying degrees, to people and forces that we can only partially influence or cannot change. So, we create our own reality up to a point. Bad stuff can happen even if we make good choices.

The 7 "Why Me? Factors":

1. God made it happen
2. Our own Soul chose it
3. Our *earthly* choices
4. Other people's choices
5. Heredity (our genes)
6. Chance; an accident
7. Natural causes

Often, there is more than one factor involved. And it is not always possible to know for sure which ones were responsible. However, even if the cause was beyond our control, we still get to choose how to respond.

While some pain is inevitable, a great deal of it is avoidable and needless and therefore preventable. We can learn from adversity, but we don't need as much of it as there is. God wants us to act as Her co-creators and to reduce the level of pain we experience.

Suffering is the extra layer of emotional anguish that exists on top of the pain.

The spiritual challenge is to maintain, in the face of pain and adversity, our appreciation for life and to make something good come from our misfortune. Hopefully, we will grow in some meaningful way. We could also help others who are facing the same conditions. Maybe we can do something to ease their suffering or even find a way to stop or cure the cause of the pain.

Reality Making Is a Two-Step Process

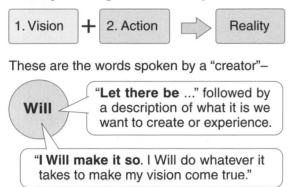

These are the words spoken by a "creator"—

Though we can't control all aspects of life, we generally are the main factor in the equation. The best reality making occurs when we have a vision, are in a positive state and enthusiastically taking action, and we are being receptive to the intuitive guidance of our Higher Self. We can also benefit greatly by forming "creative alliances" with other reality makers.

| Consequences |

We have God's Values and Beliefs and the Golden Rule to guide us. There are also the principles of *respect* and *responsibility*. We should have "R and R" for ourself, for the people we love, and for others affected by our choices—including other forms of life and the Earth.

Every choice has consequences, which can be far-reaching and unintended. With each interpersonal encounter or use of our creativity we send forth a "ripple" of either positive or negative energy that can influence the behavior of many people. The impact of our words and deeds could even extend for years into the future. This is especially true when it comes to how we treat children.

If we want to become a better chooser, we need to make our choices in a more "holistic" way. We should consider what is best for our body, mind, heart and Soul. We can do this by asking ourself the right questions before we choose. Our ability to make choices is a gift from God. It is important we use that gift wisely.

| It's Not Over Till It's Over (and even then it's not) |

The second-half of our journey can be great, but we must accept that loss is part of life. We can live long and prosper (or increase the odds that we will) by taking good care of ourself throughout our life and by staying physically, mentally and spiritually active. We can postpone or reverse some of the effects of aging, but the real challenge is to make the most of every moment we have on Earth.

> Don't complain about getting old. Not everyone has the privilege.
>
> Unattributed

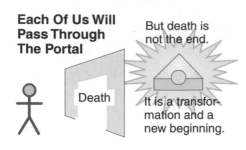

Each Of Us Will Pass Through The Portal

Death

But death is not the end.

It is a transformation and a new beginning.

Generally, we have a great deal of control over how and when we die. When we do pass through the "portal of death," we'll separate from our Earthly Self and see the light of God and of our Soul. We will also be greeted by some of our kindreds and Spirit Guides. Once we are on the other side, we will conduct a Life Review, which is mostly a self-guided tour of the choices we made. We will see and feel the effects of our words and actions. (It is a good idea to periodically do a Life Review while we are still here and to anticipate, before we say or do something, how we're going to like reliving that choice.)

Our Soul's energy expands or contracts based on the quality of our choices. The more energy we have, the closer we are to God—not in a physical sense but in a spiritual and intimate sense. All good Souls, regardless of their religious beliefs on Earth, are welcomed in Heaven or the Domain of Light. Our right to be in God's company is determined by our intentions and actions. The Domain of Darkness is reserved for Souls who said "no" to God and were deliberately hurtful. However, God is merciful. These Souls can redeem themselves and return to the Light.

After death, we can hang out here, there and everywhere. We can explore the universe while maintaining a connection with our loved ones still on Earth. We will also continue with our learning in the Spirit World. And since each lifetime is but an episode in our Soul's eternal journey, we will get ready for the next incarnation.

God: Please don't fear death. Do all you can right now to live life to its fullest and to manifest the love, joy and creativity that I put in your Soul.

Bye, bye Earth — *for now.*

Part III – We Are All In This Together

The Earth speaks ...

The future for humankind, for the other forms of life that coexist with you and for me as a planet is very much in your collective hands. Honor our interconnectedness and common spiritual heritage. Come together and create a positive tomorrow for us all.

I am asking you to live at a higher level. Bring forth the light of your Souls, and act as the spiritual siblings that you are.

So far, we have looked at the "big picture" and gotten "down to Earth." We have considered how as individuals we can grow and make the most of our life. Next, we will focus on our "collective mission."

In *Creating Heaven On Earth,* we'll look at the state of the world and how we could make it better. This chapter is different from the others. It includes facts and figures which highlight concerns about our present and future global reality. It also offers a course of action and a spiritual perspective that might help transform the quality of life on this planet. This chapter is in the book because an essential part of the "meaning of life" is for us to make life more meaningful for the people and species that inhabit this world.

In *Spirituality and Religion,* we will consider how certain beliefs are now dividing us and how we might find common ground. A set of universal spiritual principles that could help unite us and make it easier to create Heaven on Earth will be offered. We will also look at how we can bring forth the essence of our Souls in our everyday lives. Finally, in *The Best Is Yet To Come,* we will end this part of the book with a hopeful vision of the future.

It is hard to write these sort of chapters without injecting one's own bias or personal views. Still, I hope I have presented an objective and sensible discourse on what are very serious and complex subjects.

"Let us open our eyes to the sacredness of Mother Earth ..."
David Monongye – Native American elder; 1902–82

This picture of the Earth was taken from the Apollo 17 spacecraft in 1972. It shows Africa, the Arabian peninsula, and Antarctica.

(NASA photo)

Creating Heaven On Earth

Let's transform the world ...

... with the power of our love, joy and creativity.

It is understandable why we want to believe in the afterlife and the existence of Heaven. Our time on this planet is not easy. For many, it is miserable or worse. Having faith in the idea that our suffering will end and be replaced with some "heavenly bliss" helps us to persevere.

As we look at the world today, we might ask ourselves, "Is this really how life is supposed to be?" I believe God would answer with a resounding "No!" Although She created the Physical World as a place for us to be challenged so we could learn and grow, God also gave us extraordinary abilities so we could act as Her "co-creators."

When our Souls were born, we were told that while we couldn't control all aspects of life, much of what we experienced was entirely up to us. Then God sent us on our way with the expectation that as Her children we would work together and use our "Let there be ..." powers to create a positive reality on whatever planet we incarnated. Of course, She knew this would not happen overnight and that here on Earth, it would be especially challenging.

Here is the mission that God gave our Souls. It was presented in a prior chapter, but it is worth repeating here.

Our Collective Mission: To Create "Heaven On Earth"

We will have achieved our goal when we can say the following:

(a) We have used our "Let there be ..." powers to minimize the pain and suffering experienced in the Physical World;

(b) We have created a reality in which all people can meet their basic needs and most are able to lead a long and fulfilled life;

(c) We are living in harmony with our fellow humans and with the Earth and other species (the animals, trees, etc.);

(d) We have left the world better off for the Souls who will come after us (including ourselves when we come back again).

Let's consider some other expressions of our collective mission:

A child's Soul

I want to live in a world in which I can do what I love, have a nice place to call "home," and have time for my family and friends. I want to enjoy the beauty of nature and to see people and nations at peace.

Earth speaks ...

I imagine a future in which everyone can create a satisfying Life Circle in a way that has a "sustainable impact" on the environment, respects other forms of life and causes no harm to other people.

"Sustainable" means we are able to meet our current needs without compromising the ability of future generations to meet their needs, and we are respectful of the Earth and other species.

Given the state of the world and the history of humankind, it is hard to imagine we could ever create Heaven on Earth. Still, it is essential that we focus our energy on our collective mission, even if it appears unattainable right now. The quality of life on this planet and perhaps our survival depend on it. So, we should be inspired by the vision of Heaven on Earth and not be deterred by our past performance. As we learn to bring forth more of the light from our Souls, we will be astounded by what we can accomplish together. God has given us a most formidable goal, but She did so knowing that we have what it takes to succeed. Finally, all of us can contribute to the mission, but God is especially hopeful that many of the two billion young people will "rise to the occasion."

Please dedicate yourselves to "the mission." Make it your quest for the 21st century. I know it seems like a fantasy, but it is possible. Maybe you won't achieve it in your lifetime, but it will never get done if you don't give it everything you've got.

The great French marshal Lyautey once asked his gardener to plant a tree. The gardener objected that the tree was slow growing and would not reach maturity for one hundred years. The marshal replied, "In that case, there's no time to lose. Plant it this afternoon."

From *Make Gentle the Life of This World: The Vision of Robert F. Kennedy* by Maxwell Taylor Kennedy

We've Proven That We Can Do The Seemingly Impossible

"... I believe that this nation should commit itself to achieving the goal, before this decade is out, of landing a man on the moon and returning him safely to the Earth." (from a speech in May, 1961)

"We choose to go to the moon ... not because (it is) easy, but because (it is) hard, because that goal will serve to organize and measure the best of our energies and skills, because that challenge is one that we are willing to accept, one we are unwilling to postpone, and one which we intend to win ..." (from a speech in September, 1962)

President John F. Kennedy
[We achieved the goal on July 20, 1969 with Apollo 11.]

Obviously, our mission is *far more* difficult than putting a man on the moon. But history shows that if we really focus on a goal, we can do it. Let's commit to creating Heaven on Earth before the 21st century is out.

Like the moon program, we need to concentrate our Will-power, allocate sufficient resources and get our best people working on the mission. We'll look at what else we can do, but first let's consider a few other thoughts about the vision.

We Can Raise The Level Of The "Duality"

Better	Best
Good	Better
Bad	Good

In the chapter *Karma and Other Cosmic Laws*, we saw that the universe consists of "dualities" such as hot and cold, light and dark, birth and death, and so on. One side of the duality cannot exist without the other. However, there is an important lesson God wants us to learn and that is: *in some cases, we don't need to have an undesirable state at one end of the scale.* For example, there can be rich people without others being poor. Instead, the duality can be "adequacy" (as in everyone has enough to meet their basic needs) and "affluence." With other dualities, such as "pain and pleasure," we can eliminate much but not all of the bad side and shift the balance towards the good side.

Perhaps we cannot prevent this world from being a world in which people suffer. But we can reduce the number of suffering people.
Albert Camus – French novelist (paraphrased); 1913–60

Let's create a reality in which all people are free to use their gifts and free of needless worries such as those concerning food, shelter, health care or discrimination.

... when we allow freedom to ring — when we let it ring from every village and every hamlet, from every state and every city, we will be able to speed up the day when all of God's children ... will be able to join hands and sing in the words of the old Negro spiritual, "Free at last, Free at last, Thank God A-mighty, We are free at last."

Martin Luther King, Jr.; from his "I Have a Dream" speech in 1963

To Fulfill Our Mission We Have To Transform Ourselves

The Next Step In Our Evolution: Learning To "Live Spiritually"

This will occur when we bring forth the light of our Souls, and we act with love and respect for each other and for all that God created.

Man's destiny is to be the ... agent for (the) future evolution of this planet.

Julian Huxley – British biologist; 1877–1975

There is a major shift underway from what futurist Barbara Marx Hubbard calls "self-centered consciousness" and the destructive exploration and exploitation of the world to a harmonious, cooperative and constructive approach to human behavior. More people are choosing to use their "Let there be ..."power to manifest the love and joy that is in their Souls. This is what God wants all of us to do, so together as Her co-creators, we can preserve *and enhance* the wonder of life.

Life on Earth is nothing if not miraculous. At least two things on Earth are limited: livable space and natural resources. Two things are unlimited: our responsibility and our inventiveness. The task before us is to keep the miracle alive, to live in the miracle, to make the miracle more and more miraculous each day.

Marilyn Hempel – Executive Director/Editor of *Population Press*

God

So, here is the challenge: make the Earth a place where nearly all Souls can enjoy a meaningful life and where you are living in balance with other life. You can't make it a perfect world, but you can do wonders. It can be close to paradise.

Where We Are Now

Before we get to how we might create Heaven on Earth, we need to look at the current state of the human and global condition. In many ways the future looks bright. There are incredible advances coming in medicine, computers, energy, communications and so on. But we face numerous and significant challenges too. So, let's ask: "What's *wrong* with this picture?" The intent is not to be overly negative but to focus on what we need to change. We will barely scratch the surface of the issues presented here, but at least we'll get a sense of what we are up against.

People Are Suffering Terribly

- Every day, over 800 million people go hungry; 19,000 children die. 1.5 billion people lack clean water; 2.6 billion lack access to safe sewers.
- 1 billion people are unemployed, and nearly 3 billion (half of humanity) exists on a mere $2 per day.
- Even in the United States, 20% or more of the children live in poverty.

We live in a world of tremendous inequities. There are the "haves"— people who possess the means to live well and to buy lots of stuff. And there are the "have-nots"—who are struggling just to survive. Billions of people live in conditions so dreadful that we can hardly imagine what life is like for them. Bringing an end to such poverty and suffering is the most important part of our mission. Unfortunately, we're moving *away* from that goal.

The Gap Between The Poor and Rich Is Huge and Widening

Destitute Lack basic necessities	Subsistent Have barely enough to live	"Middle class"	Affluent A plentiful life-style	Super-rich Luxurious consumption

At least 45% of humanity are "destitute." The poorest 20% of people consume just 1.3% of all goods and services. The wealthiest 20% consume 86%. They eat 45% of all meat and fish and own 87% of the vehicles.

Source for above facts: 1998 United Nations Human Development Report

> ... those who live with us (on this planet) are our brothers (and sisters) ... they share with us the same short moment of life ... they seek— as we do—nothing but the chance to live out their lives in purpose and happiness ...
>
> Robert F. Kennedy; 1925–68

Su tristeza es nuestra tristeza
(Their sadness is our sadness)

People without food, shelter, jobs, hope etc.

It is morally objectionable that so many people lack the necessities of life. How can we allow our fellow Souls to suffer as they do? Beyond the moral issue, there are also practical concerns. Poverty breeds violence, and it fuels immigration as the poor try to escape the intolerable conditions of their homeland. Our interconnected global economy is vulnerable, and there is political and social instability in many countries, largely because of poverty. From a higher perspective, we are missing out on the contributions all those people could make if they were not so deprived. Everyone has special gifts, and we cannot afford to waste the creative power of so many Souls.

> Each of us is necessary. ... Our global family aches for the gifts of each one of us as we seek political and ecological healing among the peoples and species of the earth. All creation awaits our gifts.
>
> Wayne Muller – author of *Legacy of the Heart*

It's No Wonder We All Feel More Crowded Together

All the billions of Souls that I created should experience life on Earth—*but not all at the same time.*

World Population	
Year	Billions
1804	1
1927	2
1960	3
1974	4
1987	5
1999	6
2050	9 *

*U.N. medium estimate

We want to eliminate poverty and solve our other problems, but the hole we are in is getting deeper as we're trying to climb out of it. *Some 200,000 babies are born every 24 hours!* In the next 50 years 3 billion Souls are likely to incarnate, increasing the world's population by 50% to 9 billion people. 97% of that growth will occur in "less developed" countries, making the concerns mentioned earlier even worse. To feed, clothe, house, educate and find work for so many more people will be a monumental task. It will place a huge burden not just on their home countries, but on the environment and "more developed" nations too.

Most of the 3 billion new people will live in urban areas, which means there will be worse traffic, longer commutes, less affordable housing, more pollution and the loss of open space. The quality of life will be adversely affected, and it will be more difficult for us to "live spiritually."

Emotional Mind

The more crowded the Earth is the harder it is for me to be loving. I become more selfish, judgmental and fearful.

The effects of over-population arouse emotions which are at odds with how we must feel if we're to solve our problems. We need to create a greater sense of community, but we're inclined to be more isolated and self-protecting as the world becomes more stressful. We retreat further into the apparent safety of our homes (if we're lucky enough to have one). More congestion, scarcity and competition will be emotionally challenging. It could lead to more anger and hostility on an interpersonal, national and international level.

The troubled state of humankind is taking a big emotional toll on all of us. We feel it "in our Souls" because we know that life was not meant to be like this.

The problem isn't just that we'll be crowded or feel distressed. We're also using up the world's resources at an excessive rate and causing major environmental damage. The industrialized countries have been mostly responsible. But now billions of people want to consume like the rich do, and it's not possible.

There Is No Way Everyone Can Live As Americans Do

It would take roughly 3 Earths to allow 6 billion people to live like the *average* American.

The people in the less developed countries rightfully desire to improve the quality of their lives. However, the standard to which many aspire (the American way of life) is not only unattainable, but the pursuit of that goal is also a recipe for disaster. People in the wealthy countries (not just Americans) have used natural resources far in excess of their "fair share" (based on population). The environmental impact of their consumptive habits has been so devastating that the Earth cannot endure an escalation of such behavior.

The "American Way Of Life" Takes A BIG Toll On The World

- Americans comprise less than 5% of the world's population, but consume roughly **30%** of the world's resources.
- Since 1940 Americans have used more of the Earth's minerals than all previous peoples put together.
- Nearly 20% of households have 3 or more vehicles. Americans produce 25% of all "greenhouse gas" emissions.

Source: *Our Ecological Footprint* by Rees and Wackernagel

 I know it's not fun to read this stuff, but please stay with me for just a few more pages. Once we get through the rest of the troubling news, we'll focus on what we can do about it.

The Earth Is Suffering. We Have Caused It Great Pain.

It is crying for help ...

Are we listening?

Forests are being destroyed. Oceans are polluted. Fisheries are overexploited, and coral reefs are dying. Groundwater is being contaminated; water tables are falling. Topsoil is eroding, and land is becoming barren. The atmosphere is loaded with carbon dioxide, and temperatures are rising. Food supplies are threatened. The weather is getting more severe, causing economic and human tragedy. Sea levels are rising, and coastal areas are at risk. It's not a pretty picture.

Source: *The State of the World 1999* by The Worldwatch Institute.

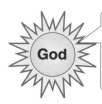 **God** I am also gravely concerned about the loss of plants and animals. You should be too. Species are disappearing faster than at any time in history. You are jeopardizing all life by destroying the biological diversity of the planet. This is not how "co-creators" act.

"... Nearly seven out of ten of the biologists polled said they believed a **'mass extinction'** is under way ... **up to one-fifth of all living species could disappear within 30 years.**" (From a *Washington Post* article by Joby Warrick; April 1998.) Nearly all these biologists felt this extinction was caused by human activity, "especially the destruction of plant and animal habitats" so we can build houses, roads and businesses. The biologists ranked the rapid loss of species "as one of the planet's gravest environmental worries, surpassing pollution, global warming and the thinning of the ozone layer."

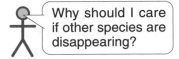
Why should I care if other species are disappearing?

Humans, the Earth and other species are interdependent elements of one living system. We each have different roles to play, but all are important to the whole picture. For example, without the plants and trees we would not have oxygen to breathe. Beyond that obvious connection, we depend on other species for *many* critical ecosystem services, ranging from pollination to the prevention of soil erosion. It is natural for species to die off, but we're messing with the natural order and destroying the delicate balance of life. In doing so, we will lose in ways we may never know and forever regret. The results could even be catastrophic.

> This mass extinction "threatens to tear great holes in the web of life."
> From the 1998 United Nations Human Development Report

God

"We are all interconnected" is not some platitude. It reflects the reality of your world. And it is especially true when it comes to what you eat. In fact, the way in which many of you eat causes harm to the Earth, other people and species—and yourselves.

We Need To Consider The "Full Cost" Of What We Eat

- One third of all the raw materials used in the U.S. and 50% of the water goes into the "production" of animals. They create 20 billion pounds of waste every day; most of it ends up polluting the water.

- More than 260 million acres of U.S. forests have been cleared to feed animals; another acre of trees disappears every 8 seconds. Each year, billions of tons of topsoil are lost due to raising animals.

- An acre of land feeds 20 times as many people on a vegetarian diet as compared to the standard American diet. If Americans consumed just 10% less meat, 60 million starving people could eat. What the world's cattle eat could nourish nearly 9 billion people.

- 95–99% of all toxic chemical residues in our diet come from the animal products we eat. Toxic chemicals can damage our DNA, which can lead to cancer, sterility and birth defects.

From *A Diet For a New America* by John Robbins.
Also from the organization, People for the Ethical Treatment of Animals.

P.S. We're destroying rainforests to create grazing land for cattle just so we can eat hamburgers.

The animals also pay a huge price for our diet. Turn to the next page to see what I mean.

Every year in the United States alone, more than **8 BILLION** animals are slaughtered for human consumption. Most of them are raised in "factory farms" where they are treated cruelly from the day they're born through the moment they're killed. About 2,400 animals must die to feed **one** person on a typical meat-based diet for his or her lifetime.

[Source: People for the Ethical Treatment of Animals]

"Elitism" Exists Within Our Own Species

"Those people are not as good as me" is a mindset that has caused great pain and that must end.

It is bad enough we look down on animals and other species and treat them horribly, but we do it with our fellow humans too. Throughout the world we see discrimination and violence driven by prejudice and hate—whether it be based on race, gender, sexuality, age, class, nationality or religion. Also, there are many cases of oppression and exploitation caused by greed and the pursuit of power. Clearly, we have a long way to go in gaining mastery over our "dark side" and in promoting human rights and social justice.

It is the poor who face the brunt of environmental problems. This too is largely the result of "elitism" or the misguided and harmful belief that some groups of people are less important or less deserving of respect than others.

In the U.S., half of all black and Hispanic people live in neighborhoods that have toxic dumps. Two million tons of radioactive uranium have been dumped on Navajo land, which has caused excessive rates of cancer. Each year, over 300,000 Hispanic farm laborers are made ill by pesticides. 44% of urban black children are at risk of lead poisoning. (This disparity regarding who pays the human price for environmental hazards exists between rich and poor countries as well.)

Source: *The Reinvention of Work* by Matthew Fox

United States

Why are you writing bad things about me? I'm a great country. And why should I worry about the future? I'm more prosperous now than ever.

The United States *is* a wonderful nation, and Americans have many reasons to feel proud. We can, however, appreciate our greatness and prosperity while also taking responsibility for how we are hurting the planet, some of our own citizens, other people and other forms of life. Our future well-being is dependent upon the availability of natural resources, adequate food supplies, global political and economic stability, and our ability to export goods and services to people who can afford them. Our national treasury and personal incomes are looking good right now, but we have just reviewed some issues that cast real doubt on whether our lifestyle is sustainable. In fact, it is clear we should rethink our current way of life and make some fundamental changes.

From *The State of the World 1999* by The Worldwatch Institute:
  "Our analysis shows that we are entering a new century with an economy that cannot take us where we want to go. Satisfying the projected needs of 8 billion or more people with the economy we now have is simply not possible. The western Industrial model—the fossil-fuel-based, automobile-centered, throwaway economy that so dramatically raised living standards in this century—is in trouble."

Billions of Souls coming to incarnate.

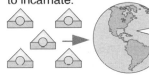

As your home planet, I must tell you time is of the essence. The quality of life for you and especially future generations is seriously at risk.

We cannot afford to ignore or gloss over these issues. The worst can happen. It has before. Human societies have collapsed by overusing their local resources. Now, our global environment is threatened. We have to take remedial action.

Humanity never stands still; it advances *or retreats.*
Louis Auguste Blanqui – French journalist; 1805–81

"No challenge in the new century looms greater than that of transforming the economy into one that is environmentally sustainable. This Environmental Revolution is comparable in scale to the Agricultural Revolution and the Industrial Revolution. The big difference is in the time available. The Agricultural Revolution was spread over thousands of years. The Industrial Revolution has been underway for two centuries. The Environmental Revolution, if it succeeds, will be compressed into **a few decades**."
Lester Brown of The Worldwatch Institute

Now, let's shift the focus to what we can do about our problems. On this and the next page, there is a comprehensive list of action items. Each of them is an essential part of a *global revolution* which is now under way. They represent momentous changes that touch every aspect of our lives and will affect how our collective future unfolds. At the heart of these changes is the desire to have a more just and spiritually-oriented society and a sustainable economy. Although there is activity happening on many items, it is critical we intensify our efforts and that more of us get involved. This revolution or global transformation will succeed only if we make it our highest priority *and it is rooted in the principles of love, joy and creativity. We will have to bring forth the essence of our Souls.*

Twenty Ways We Can Collectively Create Heaven On Earth

☐ Recognize our spiritual nature and the interconnectedness of all life—see ourselves as part of a planetary community; take into account the needs of future generations.

☐ Stabilize the human population as quickly as we can (through lower birth rates and family size) so there is no further growth in the total number of people here on Earth.

☐ Reduce and then eliminate poverty and hunger (many of the actions listed here, plus others, will help achieve this).

☐ Enhance how we educate and care for all children and young adults; devote more resources to their early years so we are not wasting lives and money later on in our prisons.

☐ Ensure that all people have adequate health care; devote more resources to the prevention and cure of serious illnesses.

☐ Become a less consumptive society; individuals and households limit superfluous spending; we save and conserve.

☐ Change our dietary habits; eat fewer animal products so we can improve our health, feed starving people, take better care of the Earth, and be more compassionate.

☐ Develop new, benign technologies, especially regarding energy, transportation and food production; help "developing countries" to adopt these technologies so they don't become dependent on fossil fuels or on other harmful aspects of industrialization.

☐ Recycle, reuse and reduce the materials used in products.

☐ Expand and use mass transit and other ways to get around so we can minimize single-person usage of automobiles.

☐ Build smaller, more energy-efficient homes and more affordable housing; better manage land development and urban sprawl.

☐ Restore the environment and endangered species where it is possible; prevent the further needless destruction of nature.

☐ Create new jobs in which people can work on activities that: a) provide for the basic needs of humanity, b) heal and restore the natural world, and c) rebuild the infrastructure of society. Transform existing jobs to make them more meaningful.

☐ Revitalize our cities; make them showcases of our ability to solve problems and models of harmonious diversity.

☐ Take responsibility—as individuals, businesses and governments—and act in accordance with positive Values and Beliefs; get and stay informed about "the issues" and make our political and business leaders more accountable.

☐ Elevate the nature of capitalism so the exploitation of the poor and the natural world are no longer tolerated.

☐ Pursue all paths that lead to a major reduction of global military spending; reallocate financial and creative resources to activities that reduce suffering, heal the planet, and prevent wars.

☐ Assist those who will be hurt economically by the transition to a healthier, more sustainable, less militaristic society.

☐ Foster more understanding, tolerance, reconciliation and co-operation between races, faiths, cultures and nations.

☐ Attend to our emotional and spiritual well-being by emphasizing art and music, by beautifying our communities, by making the media more positive, and by encouraging people to work on their "inner healing" and personal growth. Acknowledge those who really help us to fulfill our mission; celebrate our spirituality and our connection to each other and to all life.

Granted, this a long list. But let's not underestimate what we can do if we put our bodies, minds and Souls into it.

I have indeed put forth a very ambitious "to-do" list, parts of which may seem unrealistic. Still, we need a comprehensive response to our problems. Plus, I believe, in time, we can accomplish all of these items. In the next few pages, I will elaborate on some of the actions—beginning with the need for us to get a "new attitude."

Our Current Unloving View of Reality

We feel we are at the top of all that God created.

Us

We think everything else exists for us to use as we please.

Our pets
Other animals

Plants, trees etc.

The Earth

This view is ultimately self-destructive.

Our destruction of the Earth and other forms of life dishonors God and all that She created. Our behavior does not reflect well on our spiritual heritage, and it deeply troubles our Souls. We wrongly believe that God placed us "in charge," and we have treated those "below" us with a complete disregard for their divinity. In doing so, we have not only endangered the planet and countless species, but we have also put our own existence at risk.

A More Loving Perspective

Everything is from God.
We need each other, and we are meant to exist in harmony.

Animals

God

Humans

Plants   **Earth**

We need to change our view of reality, if we're ever to fulfill our mission. Instead of seeing ourselves at the top, with the right to destroy all that is below us, we need to accept—deep within our hearts—that *all of creation is sacred and interconnected.* Only by treating the Earth and other species with great respect can we honor God or have any hope of improving the quality of human life.

The original instructions of the Creator are universal and valid for all time. The essence of these instructions is compassion for all life and love for all Creation.

David Monongye – Native American elder; 1902–82

> **Reverence for life** comprises the whole ethic of life in its deepest and highest sense. ... Until he extends his circle of (love) and compassion to include all living things, man himself will not find peace.
>
> Albert Schweitzer – French physician; 1875–1965

Let's Stop Acting Like We're Separate

Instead, let's see humanity, the Earth and other species as one large community and one complex "living organism."

In *Creating Community Anywhere*, the authors (Shaffer and Anundsen) make this point: "Just as we need to reconnect in new ways with family, neighbors, coworkers, and those different from us if we are to survive as a species, we also need to develop a new relationship with the Earth and its diverse species if we are to survive as a *planetary community*." The first step in creating this relationship, they say, is for us to enlarge our sense of self to include the natural world. This expanded identity has been called our "ecological self" by activist/writer Joanna Macy. From this perspective, we can see the whole world as our larger body. The trees, for example, are "our external lungs." So, our destruction of the rainforests is really an act of self-mutilation. It may even be suicidal, especially since those tropical ecosystems also serve as our global medicine cabinet.

The authors also tell us that with a planetary perspective, we can view the lifestyle changes that humanity must make not as sacrifices done for something outside of us, but as acts of "self-interest" based on an expanded sense of who we are. By looking after the needs of the natural world we are looking after ourselves too. From now on, we need to come from the higher place of our ecological self as we make our choices.

> All things are connected
> like the blood which unites one family.
> All things are connected.
> Whatever befalls the Earth befalls the sons of the Earth.
> Man did not weave the web of life, he is merely a strand on it.
> Whatever he does to the web, he does to himself.
>
> Chief Seattle

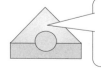

Remember, it is not just the current members of our planetary community that we're concerned about. We want to show respect for all the Souls who will incarnate after us by considering their needs too.

Isn't the world supposed to be *better* for us than it was for you?

We need to adopt a long-term perspective—like the Native Americans did. They made their choices with the well-being of their descendents in mind. In fact, they considered the impact their actions might have on the *seventh generation* to follow them. They weren't just thinking "what's in it for me?" Their time horizon was nearly two hundred years into the future. It is our responsibility to leave the world in such a state that newly-arriving Souls can lead better lives than we have—and not just materially better, but spiritually and emotionally as well.

We don't inherit the land from our ancestors, we borrow it from our children.
Pennsylvania Dutch saying

Earth speaks

Future generations won't live in a better world if you don't stabilize the population. In fact, I'd like to see the population decline over time to a more sustainable level.

We are not properly caring for the people already here, and great damage is being done to our planet and other forms of life. Fortunately, there has been a major decline in the growth rate of the human population in recent years, especially in the "more developed" regions. In some places, such as Europe and Japan, populations are likely to *decrease*. However, the "less developed" countries have 80% of the world's population, and fertility rates are still high in many of those areas. For example, the United Nations mid-range forecast is for India to add 500 million people over the next 50 years and for Africa to grow by nearly *1 billion* people.

Fertility Rates – expressed as the average number of children born per woman.

Year:	1950	2000
All countries	5.0	2.7
More developed	2.8	1.6
Less developed	6.2	3.0
United States	3.5	2.0
Africa	6.6	5.1

When the rate is more than 2.1, which is called the "replacement rate," populations increase.

We all need to be concerned about population growth. Billions of Souls will be suffering, and we risk environmental destruction and political and economic instability. We can each control our own reproductive behavior, but to stabilize the population we need to focus more of our collective resources on the problem.

How To Stabilize Populations In "High Fertility" Countries

- ☐ Raise literacy rates and education levels.
- ☐ Address sexism and raise the status of women.
- ☐ Create work for the unemployed and thus raise income levels —because as wealth rises, population growth declines.
- ☐ Reduce infant mortality rates to lessen the need for women to produce children to "replace" those who will die young.
- ☐ Provide ready access to birth control methods.
- ☐ Governments *and* religions make family planning a top priority.

United States

Fertility rates have fallen here, which is great. But I'm still expecting 70 million more people by 2050 due to lots of people having kids, folks living longer and immigration. So, please have small families.

But it's my God-given right to procreate. I am entitled to as many children as I want.

That Was Then, This Is Now

20th century thinking:
"I love children. I want a big family."

21st century thinking:
"I love children so much I will have only two—or even just one. And I will have them when I am truly ready."

It would be wonderful if we could all have large families like they did in the "good old days." Alas, it is a luxury the world can no longer afford. This does *not* mean parents who already have more than two children should feel guilty. Nor should we criticize them. It is *prospective* parents who need to let go of the emotional attachment to big families. If we want a good future for our offspring and planetary community, we have to accept the limits of our current reality. This is not an issue about one's ability to support a big family either. People with ample financial means use a large and disproportionate amount of natural resources during the course of their lives.

By the time a baby born today in the U.S. reaches age 75, (s)he will have used on average: 4,000 barrels of oil, 54,000 lbs. of plant matter, 64,000 lbs. of animal products, and 43 million gallons of water—and will have produced over 3 million lbs. of atmospheric wastes, 23 million lbs. of liquid wastes and 1,500 tons of solid wastes.

Source: *Our Ecological Footprint* by Rees and Wackernagel

> No goal is more crucial to healing the global environment than stabilizing the human population.
>
> ... just as the false assumptions that we are not connected to the Earth has led to the ecological crisis, so the equally false assumption that we are not connected to each other has led to our social crisis.
>
> Al Gore – Vice President; author of *Earth in the Balance*

We all experience suffering, even the rich. But **hunger** and **poverty** add layers of misery that are especially oppressive. Of course, these are tough problems, but we can solve them through a combination of actions.

Poverty and hunger need not be permanent parts of the human condition. We can reduce and then eliminate the suffering that so many of our spiritual siblings endure everyday by: seeing ourselves as interconnected, stabilizing the population, making education and the proper care of children a top priority, empowering people (especially women) at the local level, creating jobs and paying people more of a "living wage," rejuvenating our cities, and making the world far less militaristic—to name but a few key actions. To achieve this goal, we also need to see the poor and hungry as deserving of a meaningful life as we are. Let's not use "it's their karma," "it's God's will," "it's their fault" or "it's none of our business" as excuses for inaction. Finally, it would help if we saw the elimination of such needless suffering as the most noble goal we can pursue.

> In nothing do we more nearly approach the gods than in doing good for those who are suffering.
>
> Marcus Cicero – Roman poet (paraphrased); 106–43 BCE
>
> For the fortunate among us, there is the temptation to follow the ... familiar paths of personal ambition and financial success ... But that is not the road history has marked out for us.
>
> Robert F. Kennedy; 1925–68

P.S. – Letting Prosperity "Trickle Down" To The Poor Is Not Enough

Some people say that "a rising tide lifts all boats" or that by tending to the economic needs of the well-off, the poor will benefit too. This is partly true, but the yachts are rising disproportionately more than the rafts. The poor are not being "lifted" enough. In fact, many of them are sinking.

We need to be more proactive in addressing the problems of hunger and poverty. At the top of the list, right with stabilizing the population, should be a greater focus on children.

Each and every child matters. It is immoral to neglect a child's needs or to waste the gifts their Soul brings to this world. It is also bad for our society. Not only will a child create his or her own reality, but they will also touch many other lives. Any child could grow up and have a profound impact on the world—for better or worse. So, it is essential that we meet the basic needs of *all* children, especially with respect to their health care, nutrition and education. Also, we should change *how* we educate our children. We need a more expansive approach that brings out the best in every Soul.

God

Love and teach the children well. They deserve it, and they will then be able to create a good future.

My Dream For Education: All Children Are Fully Prepared For Life

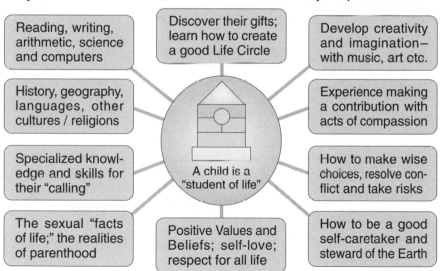

Reading, writing, arithmetic, science and computers

Discover their gifts; learn how to create a good Life Circle

Develop creativity and imagination— with music, art etc.

History, geography, languages, other cultures / religions

Experience making a contribution with acts of compassion

Specialized knowledge and skills for their "calling"

A child is a "student of life"

How to make wise choices, resolve conflict and take risks

The sexual "facts of life;" the realities of parenthood

Positive Values and Beliefs; self-love; respect for all life

How to be a good self-caretaker and steward of the Earth

I see children learning from their parents, teachers, mentors and other role models. And they're receiving a "holistic education" which addresses each Reality Maker element—namely, the intellect or Rational Mind, Emotional Mind, Physical Body, Will, and the nurturing of their Soul.

I view (education) as the most important subject which we as a people may be engaged in.
Abraham Lincoln; 1809–65

> By educating children we help them to earn a better living, which reduces poverty and hunger. By making education more "holistic" we help them to have more satisfying lives and to be leaders who will change the world.

My dream is that we teach children not just to be "smart" or skilled at a profession, which I know is hard enough, but that we also help them to become *wise*. We would teach children how to make choices that are good for them and our planetary community. We would help them to be "self-aware" and to know how they can best express their gifts and make a contribution to the world. The essence of education would be to teach children how to bring forth more love, joy and creativity in all areas of their lives.

There are, of course, limitations on what can be taught in schools. But maybe we could include a course or two that would impart more of the "knowledge of life." Beyond that, parents can try to establish a more meaningful and ongoing dialogue with their children. And we can develop more community-based programs that bring wisdom to our children—especially from our elders who have so much to offer. Finally, more of us could become "teachers" in the capacity of a mentor or Big Brother or Sister or as a child's uncle, aunt or grandparent.

> A child educated only at school is an uneducated child.
>   George Santayana – Spanish philosopher; 1863–1952

> If we want to bring out the best in children and transform education, we should also enhance the physical environment of schools. Many of them have the feel of a prison. They suppress a child's heart and Soul.

We need to do everything we can to inspire and empower children. We cannot afford to shortchange them when it comes to their education or other basic needs, or we'll never fulfill our mission. As it is, large numbers of people—the vast majority of which have *good* Souls—are being lost to the "dark side" of life and ending up in real prisons. At the end of the 20th century, *1 out of every 150* citizens in the U.S. was incarcerated. That is twice as bad as it was only 15 years earlier. We are now spending far more to keep people in prison than we spent on them when they were children.

The "Spirit" of the United States speaks:

We need to get our priorities straight and devote more resources to the care of children. We also need to shift the focus from consumption to the pursuit of emotional and spiritual happiness. My people are ingenious and hardworking. So, they deserve to be prosperous. But I can't truly feel good as a country knowing that the American lifestyle is causing harm to the rest of the planet. I am troubled by our materialism.

We are *not* bad people because we like to buy things. We want to live comfortably, reward ourselves for our hard work and benefit from new products. But we have become entrapped in a pattern of *over*consumption or buying more than we need. Advertising, malls, shopping from home, holidays and social status have all contributed to our addiction to things. In our relentless and often fruitless pursuit of happiness by means of possessions, we are fueling an economy and a way of life that is becoming progressively more harmful to us and our planetary community.

A society based on ever-growing levels of excess consumption is just not sustainable, especially with the population increasing as it is. We have no choice but to become less materialistic—unless we want to give our descendants a world that has been, to quote author Alan Thein Durning, "impoverished by our affluence." Americans are not the only ones buying things, using up resources and creating enormous waste. But we're having the greatest impact on the world. So, it is incumbent on us to alter our lifestyle and to set an example of environmental leadership. We can't expect others to create sustainable economies if we continue on our harmful path.

God

Your Souls want you to seek happiness in ways that are good for you and the planetary community, instead of buying stuff you don't really need. Also, I'm asking you to practice what Mr. Gandhi preached: **"Live simply so others may simply live."**

Alan Thein Durning, in his essay "Are We Happy Yet?" (which is contained in the book *Ecopsychology*), makes this critical point: "Lowering consumption need not deprive people of goods and services that really matter. To the contrary, life's most meaningful and pleasant activities are often paragons of environmental virtue. The preponderance of things that people name as their most rewarding pastimes are infinitely sustainable. Religious practice, conversation, family and community gatherings, theater, music, dance, literature, sports, poetry, artistic and creative pursuits, education, and appreciation of nature all fit readily into a culture of permanence—a way of life that can endure through countless generations. ... The future of life on Earth depends on whether the richest fifth of the world's people, having fully met their material needs, can turn to nonmaterial sources of fulfillment." As a society, we need to regard these activities more highly and make them more accessible.

How We Might Climb Down The Consumption Ladder

- ☐ Practice personal restraint; pursue nonmaterial pleasures.
- ☐ Teach children the values of simplicity and less consumption.
- ☐ We help developing countries meet their needs with products that use less materials and are "environment-friendly."
- ☐ We change the "infrastructure" of society to make it easier for us to consume less while maintaining a good quality of life.*

* Possible changes: more mass transit; "clustered" communities, where people can live, work and buy what they need all within a small geographic area and where new housing and offices promote a cooperative approach to meeting common needs; more new businesses that provide goods and services that help our planetary community.

We Can Become More "Mindful and Compassionate" Consumers

I don't expect you to live like monks, but I do ask that you make your purchases with more awareness. Ask yourself, "Do I really need this item? Is there a nonmaterial way to meet my emotional needs? Will my choice hurt the Earth or other living things? Is there a less harmful or benign alternative I could choose?"

We can reduce our personal impact on the world by accepting the sacredness and interdependence of all life and by putting that new perspective into practice. We can become more aware of the consequences of our choices and *do our best* to avoid making purchases that are needless or harmful.

Compassion also extends to what you consume for food. I'm pleading with you, my spiritual cousins, to eat a lot less animal products. We're really suffering.

When we choose our meals we're deciding what other life will die so that we can live. Yet, how mindful are we of what we eat? The nature of our diet is a complex and an emotional issue. Our choices involve personal preferences affected by family traditions, spiritual beliefs and societal realities such as what kind of food is sold in stores and restaurants. So, it is far too simplistic to say vegetarians are "better" than meat-eaters. There are good people in each camp. Moreover, some parts of the world don't have many options one way or the other; and some people feel better health-wise by eating a little animal protein. Still, the nature of our diet is more than a personal concern. What we eat has an impact far beyond our own life. And since the planet cannot sustain our current dining habits, the "typical American diet" has to change — *and change soon.*

Why Change?

Because our meat-based diet involves:
- The destruction of natural resources
- Feeding livestock instead of people
- Human health risks
- Cruel factory farms

If one believes animals have Souls and should be treated with respect, then that is reason enough to eat a more vegetarian diet. Of course, there are other compelling reasons to be less carnivorous. The high-volume, unnatural and cruel way in which we "process" animals today is having terrible consequences. It is taking its toll on our health, on the people who are starving, on the "family farmer," and on the environment. By abusing and overusing the animals (including the fish in the sea), we are abusing ourselves too.

I know in my soul, that to eat a creature who is raised to be eaten, and who never has a chance to be a real being, is unhealthy. It's like ... eating misery. Alice Walker; author	The vast majority ... of all cancers, cardiovascular diseases, and other forms of degenerative illness can be prevented ... simply by adopting a plant-based diet. T. C. Campbell; nutritional researcher

The Soul of a **plant**

We have feelings too, but here are four reasons why it is better for you to eat us: (1) we require far less resources than animals, (2) it is more compassionate to feed us to people than to animals, (3) you don't always kill a plant to take what's edible, and (4) it's better for your health.

Someone should figure out how the "standard diet" would need to change so it could include *some* animal protein **and** result in the wise use of resources, food for hungry people and the end of factory farms.

One last point on eating a veggie diet: you may find you feel more energetic, not just physically but spiritually too. We Souls like it when our choices reduce suffering.

At this point, you might be asking yourself several questions: "Who is this guy to tell me that I should change my procreating, buying and dietary habits? Won't these changes be bad for the economy? What does any of this have to do with the 'meaning of life?' And when is this chapter going to end?"

I will address the last two questions first. We are here, in part, to bring forth our spiritual nature and to make life better for ourselves, for the Souls—human and otherwise—who share the planet with us, and for the Souls who will incarnate next. To be more "spiritual" involves more than just reading a book or attending religious services. *All of our choices*—from what we buy and eat to how we treat the poor and what we do for work—represent an opportunity for us to act as children of God and to fulfill our mission. That's why I felt it was important for us to consider the subjects covered in this chapter. As to the length of the chapter, there are only eight pages left to go after this one. I appreciate your perseverance.

I must say I do feel uncomfortable prescribing a new way of life when my own life is not "pure." We all have our own circumstances that affect our choices, and there is no single, "right" way to live. Still, I am convinced the status quo is unsustainable and that we really do need to make some serious changes. So, I feel it's okay for me to add my voice to the choir of people who are discussing these issues, knowing that I need to practice what I am preaching and lessen my own impact on the world.

Finally, if we consume less and change our diets there will be negative consequences for some segments of the economy. We face a situation similar to that of an addict who enjoys the "high" from his drug but is on a self-destructive path. Kicking the habit won't be painless, but it will lead to a longer and more meaningful life. It's basically a *"I may be hurt if I do and damned if I don't"* scenario. As a society, our goal can be to make the transition to the new world of sustainability and compassion *and* to help the businesses and people who will be hurt by the changeover. That help could involve direct economic assistance and/or training for new careers.

Here are four reasons for helping those who will be hurt by the change: (1) It is the compassionate thing to do. (2) Their creativity and energy would be focused on "new world" activities sooner. (3) It might reduce their resistance to change, which is important given that time is of the essence. (4) We will either "pay now or pay later." History shows that if we don't confront an issue early on or expend adequate resources, we pay a huge price down the road.

God

There are no easy answers, but I am here to tell you that profound change is of the utmost importance. Come together and figure out how to best make the transition to a sustainable world. There will be short-term problems, but there will also be wonderful, new opportunities.

It Won't Be Heaven Until Most Of Us Are Engaged In Meaningful Work

Today, billions of young people have little or no hope of finding jobs, and a billion or more adults are unemployed.

Earth speaks:

There is so much work that needs to be done. Create jobs aimed at meeting the basic needs of people and healing the natural world.

Everyone should have the chance to use their gifts, to support themselves and their families, and to make a contribution. But how can we attain that goal? One approach is to create businesses and jobs throughout the world that provide what the human population and our planetary community really need. As Matthew Fox writes in *The Reinvention of Work*, everyone could have a meaningful job if we set out to satisfy the widespread demand for housing, education, food, health and child care, renewable energy and the other essentials of life. People could also perform vital ecological tasks such as reforestation, soil preservation, water purification and the recovery of endangered species. Given the amount of critical work needing to be done, there should be no such thing as unemployment.

By putting people to work on activities that are so fundamental to their well-being and good for the planet, we can begin to create a global economy that is more life-affirming, equitable and sustainable than what exists now. We will also greatly reduce suffering and despair and unleash the creativity of billions of Souls.

Regarding Work, We Need To ...

- Make existing jobs more satisfying and respectful of family life.
- Use our individual gifts and make a contribution, which may mean we should change jobs.
- Create jobs that meet the basic needs of humankind and that help the Earth and other species.
- Phase out jobs that are harmful to us and our planetary community; help people find new work.

Our challenge is greater than ending unemployment. We also need to enhance the quality of work for those who are now or soon to be employed. This will take more "enlightened management." The people who control the nature of work can provide suitable conditions, pay a decent wage, allow employees to participate in decision-making, share the financial rewards of good collective performance, and treat everyone with respect regardless of their position.

For there to be Heaven on Earth, the pursuit of profits and higher stock prices cannot be at the expense or exploitation of workers or the natural world. The businesses that will thrive in the "new world" will be those that are *good* for our planetary community and that allow workers to express their creativity and to feel that they are an integral part of a worthwhile endeavor.

By **not** investing in or buying the products of companies that are doing harmful things to workers or the world, we can help them to become "enlightened."

Often, employees can also take actions to enhance the nature of their work. As noted in a prior chapter, we can change our attitude, improve workplace relationships and develop new skills. But even if we do those things and more, we may find it is best to move on and pursue a new job or career. This is especially true if we're not currently using our gifts, or we are working for a company that is not good to us or isn't making a positive contribution to the world.

Finally, if we're to fulfill our mission, more of us—and particularly young people—need to ask ourselves what we really care about and how we can help make the world better. Can we redirect our talents and energy to serve the greater good of our planetary community? Can we join with others who are similarly motivated to start new, enlightened businesses? Work is an essential part of our lives. It ought to be rewarding—financially *and spiritually.*

Can we afford to create jobs for everyone? There has been and there is plenty of money available. But a lot of it is used by governments and businesses for military purposes.

We've Paid A BIG Price For Our Defense

Consider how much the United States alone has spent conducting and preventing wars from 1940 through 1996.

Nuclear weapons *	$ 5.5 trillion
Other defense	13.2 trillion
Total military spending	18.7 *trillion*

* Includes all costs associated with making and deploying nuclear weapons.
Numbers are shown in 1996 dollars.

Source: *Atomic Audit* by Stephen Schwartz; published by The Brookings Institution; 1998

"... expenditures for nuclear weapons exceeded the com-bined federal spending on education, training, employ-ment, and social services; agriculture; natural resources and the environment; general science and space research; community and regional de-velopment (including disaster relief); law enforcement; and energy production and regulation."

From the press release for the *Atomic Audit*.

We live in a dangerous world and we must defend ourselves. But it is mind boggling how much money and creative talent we have expended on military matters. Collectively, nations probably spent *30–40 trillion dollars* in the 20th century waging and preparing for war. Now, after all that expense and effort and millions of lost and wasted lives, we still face a reality of nuclear proliferation, terrorism, excess militarism in rich and poor countries, armed conflicts around the globe, and major health and environmental issues caused by nuclear wastes and fallout. And of course, we continue to neglect and under-fund our vital, nonmilitary needs. We've got the financial and human resources to create Heaven on Earth in the 21st century, but we must put them to better use.

Every gun that is made, every warship launched, every rocket fired, signifies in the final sense a theft from those who hunger and are not fed, those who are cold and are not clothed. This world in arms is not spending money alone. It is spending the sweat of its laborers, the genius of its scientists ... This is not a way of life ... it is humanity hanging itself on a cross of iron.
Dwight Eisenhower – General and U.S. President; 1890–1969

If war no longer occupied men's thoughts and energies, we could within a generation put an end to all serious poverty throughout the world.
Bertrand Russell – British philosopher; 1872–1970

Governments Create Reality On Our Behalf
Are we aware of what our representatives are doing? Are they acting as wise leaders?

"Let there be ... peace."

The United States Capitol

There is probably enough waste in the U.S. defense budget to generate tens of billions of dollars in savings that could be put to better use, and our leaders should make that happen. However, we can't fully create Heaven on Earth as long as our economy and political system are so dependent on and affected by the vested interests that profit from *war on Earth*. We have to reduce what President Eisenhower called the "unwarranted influence" of the "military-industrial complex."

Of course, we want our leaders to ensure our defense, but we also want them to spend our money more judiciously. They should become less beholden to the arms industry and curtail the export of weapons. Powerful nations such as the United States should be beacons of peace instead of being involved in the production and distribution of the tools of war. Otherwise, we will never see the end of the fighting and suffering.

We see ourselves as separate.

We focus on religious, ethnic, racial and national differences. We see ourselves as only human.

The path to a peaceful world requires a reduction in militarism, but we also have to address the underlying causes of the belligerence that makes our defense necessary. The "dark side" of human nature is at the root of the fighting, but what is bringing it forth? The fundamental problem is we don't see ourselves as *interconnected* or as *spiritual beings.* Our limited perspective leads to selfishness and intolerance, which lead to fear and hatred, which often cause violence in the form of crime, oppression or war.

Peace begins with a new perspective.

 We began our cosmic journey as spiritual siblings. The question is, will we come together at this time of mutual and planetary need and act as "brothers and sisters?"

There are, of course, other factors that cause antagonism and violence, including poverty and deprivation, ignorance and a history of ill will between peoples. We have to address these and other issues too.

An Eight-Fold Path To Peace

Foster the view that we are all spiritual beings and interconnected.	
Stress reconciliation / prevention	Meet basic human needs *
Maintain a strong, *efficient* defense	Stabilize the global population
Protect / restore the natural world	Curb the power of the arms industry
Act together and early to stop aggression and the death of innocent people	

* Create work, feed the hungry, raise literacy rates, address health and housing needs.

A strong defense is vital to our national security. But ultimately we will feel the most secure when we are living in a world that is not heavily armed, allows all people to meet their essential needs and to pursue happiness, is environmentally healthy and can sustain a good way of life for us and our descendants.

We have grasped the mystery of the atom and rejected the Sermon on the Mount.   General Omar Bradley; 1893–1983

In that sermon, which can be found in The Gospel According to Matthew, Jesus said that children of God are "**peacemakers**."

Abraham Lincoln said our government is "of the people, by the people and for the people." As citizens, we need to be well-informed and let our leaders know that we want to follow the path of peace and sustainability. Politicians should declare their independence from special interests and divisive partisanship and help us to pursue this higher vision. Finally, it is important we honor our citizenship and vote.

Some Final Thoughts

Hang in there. There are only 3 more pages after this one.

We Must Bring a New "Energy" To The Planet

Love and compassion, spirituality, optimism, collaboration and community are the key to our future.

We face serious problems, to say the least. It is reasonable to believe we will never solve them. However, we can bring forth the goodness of our Souls, use our creativity for the betterment of the world, and connect with each other as spiritual siblings engaged in a common mission. That is how we will create the reality we desire.

**Let's Spread
The Good News**

It will inspire us and get us thinking.

There are scores of people around the world involved in activities that are helping to solve our problems. We all need to hear more about these efforts. By knowing what's working and emphasizing the positive, we will feel more hopeful. It will empower us and spark the imagination of others who would like to contribute. And it will allow us to replicate and build upon what has already been done successfully instead of "reinventing the wheel." Given that time is of the essence, it is vital that we share knowledge and leverage our creative efforts.

How can we spread the news? Obviously, the internet is a great vehicle for this purpose. There are also a growing number of radio and television enterprises addressing this need. However, the people in charge of the mass media could help by elevating the quality of their products. For example, as Barbara Marx Hubbard suggests in her book *Conscious Evolution,* newscasts, documentaries, movies and even sitcoms could focus more on what we are doing right and put forth visions of a positive future that would inspire us. Now, we are overwhelmed with negativity, gratuitous sex and violence, and mindless programming.

Activities which "lift our spirits," create a greater sense of community and help us to appreciate different cultures, religions etc. are essential. We need more life-affirming art, literature and entertainment; and we need to beautify our neighborhoods and cities. Anything that nurtures us emotionally and spiritually should be encouraged.

Let's have more public events that celebrate our achievements, honor our interconnectedness, promote harmony and mutual understanding and are **joyful**.

It Takes Positive Reality Makers To Create Heaven On Earth

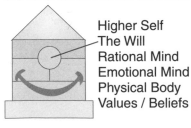

Higher Self
The Will
Rational Mind
Emotional Mind
Physical Body
Values / Beliefs

We are all imperfect. Yet, there are people who are seriously troubled in one or more of their "elements" and thus causing harm to themselves and others. We need to do more to heal people who are emotionally impaired or addicted to drugs or alcohol. We must also devote more resources to finding cures for diseases and disorders that restrict people from leading full lives. Basically, we need to help people get into an "aligned and synergized" state—that is, pursuing their calling and feeling good emotionally, intellectually, physically and spiritually. It is particularly important that we focus on the children and provide them a "holistic" education.

A wise, old Soul

When people are in a positive state, using their gifts and in touch with their Souls, they don't cause harm to themselves, to each other or to the planet, at least not on purpose. That's why personal growth is so important.

Seven Ways Each Of Us Can Help Create Heaven On Earth

- ☐ Find a way to make a contribution, whether it be using our talents in the pursuit of meaningful work, volunteering our time to help those in need, or in some other way.
- ☐ Tend to our own self-care; do things that are nurturing and good for our body, mind and Soul; break harmful habits.
- ☐ If we're a parent, raise our children well; if we're planning to be a parent, do it when we're ready and have a *small* family.
- ☐ Buy fewer things; conserve; recycle; if possible, drive less.
- ☐ Make the move, even if it's a small one at first, to a more vegetarian diet; eating less meat is a good way to start.
- ☐ If we can, contribute some of our money to worthwhile causes.
- ☐ Each day, be a little more loving, kind and tolerant; do this with family, friends, coworkers, neighbors and strangers too.

"Namaste"

It's a Hindu greeting that means: "I see and honor the divine within you, as you see and honor the divine within me." It's pronounced:

nä – mäs – tay

Even if we don't actually say "namaste" to each other, it would be nice if we thought it as we greeted people.

Light Up The World ...
with the power of your love

When one of us acts more loving, it can inspire others to do the same. Each of us can help bring peace to the world.

Your act may be very small, it may seem insignificant, but it is very important that you do it.
Mohandes Gandhi; 1869–1948

Some believe there is nothing one man or one woman can do against the enormous array of the world's ills. Yet many of the world's great movements, of thought and action, have flowed from the work of a single man (or woman). ...

It is from numberless diverse acts of courage and belief that human history is shaped. Each time a man stands up for an ideal, or acts to improve the lot of others, or strikes out against injustice, he sends forth a tiny ripple of hope, and crossing each other from a million different centers of energy and daring those ripples build a current that can sweep down the mightiest walls of oppression and resistance. ...

Robert Kennedy – from a speech given in South Africa in 1966

Some men see things as they are and say **why**. I dream things that never were and say **why not**.

From a play by George Bernard Shaw

At this point, the goal of creating Heaven on Earth seems like an impossible dream. However, we need to remind ourselves that we possess incredible powers. If as few as 1% of us apply our "Let there be ..." energy to our collective mission, we will change the world. We won't make it perfect, for there will always be pain and suffering. But we can make the Earth a place where most Souls are able to live up to their full potential, free of needless fear and worry and in harmony with the people and other forms of life with whom we share our journey. It won't be easy, and it won't happen soon, but we can do it. We are, after all, children of God.

Please have faith in yourselves and in the future. Focus on the mission and stay determined. After millions of years of human evolution, now is finally the time when you will manifest your divinity and act as a community of Souls. I just know it.

If we don't change the direction in which we are going, we will end up where we are headed.

Red Skelton – comedian; 1913–97

Next, we will look at how changing certain beliefs and being more "spiritual" could help us to more easily create Heaven on Earth.

Spirituality and Religion – Bringing Forth the Essence of our Souls

To Create Heaven On Earth We Must Bring Forth Our Love, Joy and Creativity

Our challenge is to bring a new energy to the planet and to elevate the quality of life for everyone. This goal is so formidable, and the time we have to accomplish it is so short, that we can't go about it thinking we are "only human" —or we can do it without cooperating with one another.

So, the questions are, "How can we bring out the best in us, and what could bring us all together?" We can begin by recognizing our common spiritual origin and our interconnectedness here on Earth. Ultimately, the key to our success lies in our ability to tap into the divine power we each possess.

When we manifest the essence of our Souls in all areas of our lives, we will be on the path which leads to the fulfillment of our collective mission. So how can we each bring forth our higher power? The best way is to engage in a regular "spiritual practice." Such a practice would involve activities that put us in touch with our Soul and God, renew us physically and emotionally, and connect us with other people and the nonhuman members of our planetary community.

Possibilities For A "Spiritual Practice"

- Meditate and pray each day
- Really connect with our loved ones
- Commune with nature and animals
- Be artistic /creatively expressive
- Do holistic exercises: yoga, tai chi etc.
- Listen to uplifting or calming music
- Develop our intuitive skills
- Keep a journal of our experiences, lessons, gratitudes and dreams
- Do deep, conscious breathing
- Be compassionate and help others
- Celebrate/study with spiritual buddies
- Belong to an organized religion (?)

There are, of course, other activities one could add to the list, and we each need to discover what sort of spiritual practice works best for us. One of the possibilities is belonging to an organized religion. For many people, religions are seen as the caretakers and nurturers of spirituality, providing their members with comfort, hope and direction in a stressful and confusing world. They offer a framework in which the faithful can make a connection with the supernatural. So, religion can be very good for us.

Some Of The Other Benefits Provided By Religion

- A spiritual community to feel part of, to turn to in time of need, and to participate with in shared learning, worship and celebration.
- Weekly and holiday services in a sacred place; words, music and rituals to help us to praise and talk with God (or Whomever) and to commemorate life's passages; meaningful traditions.
- Values, beliefs and rules to guide our behavior and to explain who we are, why we're here and what happens to us after death.

Religions are great in many ways, but they also have some negative attributes that we should consider.

You don't have to read much history or look beyond the daily news to see that religions are not perfect. In fact, millions of people have died or been persecuted in this century alone in the name of God and religion. And since this has been going on for thousands of years, it only makes sense that we question how effectively religion is in helping us to bring forth our love, joy and creativity. We need to examine some of the religious beliefs that many of us were taught—beliefs that are cutting us off from the goodness of our Souls and getting in the way of our mission. I am *not* saying the world would be better off without religions, but rather we should strive to make them better.

Here's a religious view that is especially harmful.

You're not going to Heaven. You're "toast."

A fervent "believer"

A "non-believer"

God

That is not true. He has a good Soul. Anybody who is loving can get close to Me in the afterlife.

How we live, not what we believe, is the ticket into Heaven.

Some Religious Beliefs That Are Troubling To Many People

1. My God is the true and only real God.
2. If you don't believe in my God, you will burn in Hell or cease to exist after death. If you don't live as I feel my God says you should, you are morally wrong.
3. We are sinful beings; we have to be "saved."
4. Men are better than women because God created a man first, and a woman caused our "fall from grace"; women should obey men.
5. Artificial birth control should not be used; it is a sin.

These beliefs bother Me too.

A belief is troubling if it ...
- Obscures our common spiritual heritage, creating a reality of separateness and divisiveness.
- Breeds feelings of moral superiority, intolerance or even hatred.
- Denies our spiritual nature and our ability to change ourselves and the world—with God's help of course.
- Leads to the oppression of women and denies us all the benefit of the creativity and compassion that women offer.
- Ignores the reality of the world and leads to more suffering.
- Blocks our Souls' love, joy and creativity in any way.

We Souls don't like beliefs that make us feel "small," fearful or judgmental. We are all blessed with God's energy, and God loves everyone.

The beliefs shown above have had really negative consequences. It's hard to imagine they originated from God. Many people like myself have dropped out of their religion because of these and other similar beliefs.

There is nothing wrong with questioning the teachings of one's religion. It is an act of spiritual maturity, not of disobedience or disrespect. Religions may have been inspired by God, but they have evolved as *human* institutions. So, they are not infallible.

I believe in the fundamental Truth of all the great religions of the world. I believe they are all God-given ... and that all (have) some error in them.

Mohandes Gandhi; 1869–1948

Many people would describe their religion as hierarchical or bureaucratic and as being too rigid or stuck in the past. And in some cases there is so much strife within our religion that it gets in the way of the spiritual message.

Jimmy Carter says in his book, *Living Faith,* that after 2,000 years the Christian church is probably divided *worse* now than it was in the early days. He writes, "In almost all denominations, various beliefs have torn us apart, and sometimes entire denominations have split permanently and officially." This has happened, he says, for the same reasons that divided the early Christians. They let the "overarching concepts of faith, love and forgiveness be obscured by arguments about exactly what was written or said or remembered about past history."

Your spiritual consciousness has moved beyond negative teachings and bickering about the past. As you become more expanded and enlightened beings, you need your religions to be more positive and expansive too. It is time for change.

For thousands of years, many (but certainly not all) religious leaders have been trying to alter or control human behavior by making us feel badly about ourselves, intolerant of others, and fearful of what might happen to the world and to us in the afterlife. This approach hasn't worked very well. So doesn't it make sense to try a new and more uplifting approach?

Let's motivate people by focusing on our inherent goodness and innate ability to learn and grow. Let's emphasize how we are alike and how we can do more together than separately. Let's give people positive reasons and ways to improve their lives and the world, instead of focusing so much on what we should *not* do. Let's be optimistic and courageous, instead of waiting for God to save us. Let's be inclusive and appreciate the sacredness of everyone and everything. And let's make religious services more joyful!

In the 16th century there was the Reformation, which was aimed at changing certain religious doctrines and practices. In the 21st century, perhaps we could have a **Transformation** and take existing religions to a "higher level." We could rise above the beliefs that have been harmful and get on a more loving path.

Spiritual Beliefs That Are Positive and Life-Affirming

- A person doesn't have to be a member of any particular religion or even believe in God to lead a good life or to go to Heaven; our behavior is more important than our beliefs.

- There are many paths to God; none is the "best" one.

- God is loving and compassionate, not vengeful or punishing.

- All of creation came from the same Source; we're interconnected and are meant to exist in harmony with other people and all life.

- We are glorious spiritual beings having a human experience; we are children of God; we are not sinners by nature.

- God wants us to be happy and to feel good about ourselves.

- We have the power to "save" ourselves and to create a better reality; it can be done more easily if we act as children of God.

- It's okay to enjoy sex and to take precautions to prevent the conception of a child before we're ready to be a parent.

- It's good to learn about different religions; each one has something useful to offer; God will still love us if we change religions.

- God loves everyone regardless of their gender, race, sexuality or any other personal trait—and we should too.

- Women are the equal of men; they belong and are needed in positions of spiritual leadership.

- We are all born with the right to be loving, joyful and creative.

- God is not going to destroy everything because humankind has been bad; the best is yet to come—if we learn to make better choices.

These beliefs please Me.

This list is written for those who believe in "God." If you prefer another name, please use it. If you don't believe in such a Being, please feel free to modify my list.
I think many people would return to the "flock" or get more from their religion if they heard this sort of message.

We Souls like these beliefs because they make all of us feel "big"—without making others feel "small." They inspire and empower us to live to our full potential.

As your home planet, I must say that positive thoughts like these would make it a whole lot easier for all of us to fulfill our mission.

We Could Change the World, If Only ...

... we each would let go of any feelings of intolerance and superiority;

... we could focus on the Values and Beliefs we have in common;

... we each lived in accordance with the positive teachings of our faith;

... we made our religions even more positive by "transforming" them.

unique beliefs	Hindus	Buddhists	Muslims
	Jews	Christians	Others
common ground	Shared Values and Beliefs		

If all religions are given by God, then they are all based on the same principles—especially love, compassion and forgiveness. It is time for us to acknowledge and honor our common spiritual heritage while respecting our earthly differences. We can no longer afford to see ourselves as separate and unequal. We need to act with love and acceptance towards all men and women regardless of their faith.

— My Dream For the Future —

We are told the following by all of our religious leaders:

> "After thousands of years of fighting between and within our religions, we have agreed upon the following:
>
> 1. No human being can really understand the true nature of the Spirit World. So, we will no longer judge or be critical of any religion's spiritual concepts or views on "God."
>
> 2. We are no longer going to blame women or any religion for the problems of the world, and we will no longer preach that those with different beliefs than ours will be punished.
>
> 3. From now on we are going to accentuate what we have in common and focus on all the positive things we can do to make the world a better and more peaceful place."

> In separateness lies the world's great misery; in compassion lies the world's true strength.
>
> Buddha; 563?–483? BCE

Compassion involves more than helping people who are suffering. It means you see the good in others and avoid causing harm. That's why I am asking you to change some of your beliefs. Imagine a future in which all religions coexist in a peaceful world of harmonious diversity.

In the future, religions will be doing more *together* to advance our mission. They will be unified in their efforts to reduce suffering, to foster understanding between peoples and to promote social justice. Spiritual leaders will be out front on these issues, showing us how to help those who are excluded and unloved in our global society. Religions will also enhance our connection with the natural world and help focus our efforts to heal the planet. There will be more interdenominational learning and celebrating going on too. In the future, religions will truly inspire us and act as beacons of compassion and cooperation.

Until those dreams come true, what can I do if I'm not happy with my religion?

Actually, it is largely up to us to affect change in our religions. We can have thoughtful discussions with members of our congregation and with the clergy. We can respectfully ask them to let go of the beliefs that block our spiritual essence and cause separateness between us and other people. We could also discuss ways to make the services more joyful and meaningful, if that's needed. There are, of course, members of the clergy who are already acting as "agents of change," and we should support them.

Ultimately, we each must decide which values and beliefs to acccpt and live by. Our Soul wants us to follow what we know in our heart to be the path of love. If aspects of our religion are at odds with that, we can try to change them, overlook them, learn about and try another religion, or pursue other options.

Whether we are in a religion or not, we can expand our spiritual practice and find more fellowship. We can have gatherings in our home to share meals, discuss books or to meditate together; help create forums for speakers, the showing of uplifting films, the sharing of wisdom and for "brainstorming"—where people come up with solutions to local or even global issues; help setup or conduct educational classes; perform acts of service and compassion with other people; honor the sabbath and make our holidays more meaningful and less materialistic.

We really benefit from rituals, traditions and celebrations. This is especially true for children. When family members spend "quality time" together and participate in common spiritual activities, it brings forth the light of their Souls.

"Spirituality" is a way of life. It is any activity or state of being in which you manifest the essence of your Soul—namely, love, joy and creativity. You can be "spiritual" in your role as friend or life partner, parent or child, or as you work and play.

Seeing a bit of Me in all people and in all that exists is at the heart of spirituality. Whenever you act with compassion and honor the sanctity of life and your common heritage, you are being spiritual.

Spirituality transcends religion. It is universal—encompassing all of life. Every day as we go about our life we have the opportunity to act with love and kindness towards others, to use our gifts to create a positive reality, and to find joy and pleasure in our Soul's earthly journey. To live fully in this way is to celebrate our spiritual nature. It is to act as a child of God.

Some Final Thoughts

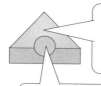

Each of us can help to create Heaven on Earth by starting in our own Life Circle. We can work on our spiritual practice and bring more love to our family and friends. The "transformation" begins at home.

God wants us to become "missionaries"—not in the old sense of trying to convert others to our religion, but in the new sense of making a contribution to our Souls' collective mission.

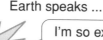
Earth speaks ...

I'm so excited. My energy rises when I just think of religions taking their beliefs to a higher level and people becoming more spiritual. Imagine what the world will be like when it really happens!

Next, we're going to consider why we should feel hopeful about what lies ahead for us and humankind.

The Best Is Yet to Come

> To me, the sole hope of human salvation lies in teaching Man to regard himself as an experiment in the realization of God, to regard his hands as God's hands, his brain as God's brain, his purpose as God's purpose.
>
> George Bernard Shaw – Irish dramatist; 1856–1950

Earth Angel

Ask not what God can do for you. Ask what you can do for yourselves.

Many people believe the Apocalypse lies directly ahead and that God will bring it upon us. God will destroy all that is bad about the world, save the true believers and usher in a new millennium of peace. I don't subscribe to this view. I do believe we are at a crossroads. Our global reality will get much better or much worse. The status quo can't be sustained. However, the ruination of this planet and of life, human and otherwise, won't be God's doing. It will be, and to a great extent already is, the result of our own unwise behavior. Likewise, the creation of Heaven on Earth will not be left to God's intervention but rather to us and our own godliness. We have to do it ourselves, *and we can*. It will be the supreme test of our "Let there be ..." powers.

Of course, it is possible God will send Jesus or other enlightened teachers to show humankind once again the path of love. We could use all the help we can get. Or maybe we will rise to the challenge ourselves and bring forth more of our inherent goodness. One of the lessons Jesus taught before was that we are here in part to ease the suffering of others and to advance the quality of life for all. The best does lie ahead, but only if we come together to make the future good for everyone. We can wait for God to save us, or we can choose to act as the spiritual beings and siblings that we are.

Remember, we are all interconnected. And we are not "sinners" incapable of greatness. Inside each of us is a divine spark which we can reconnect with at any time. Humankind has incredible potential. We are only near the beginning of our evolution as a species.

The chapter *Creating Heaven on Earth* presented a brief look at what a positive future would be like, but it also had a lot of dire facts and forecasts. We shouldn't be motivated just by the desire to avoid negative consequences, however. So, let's reconsider a vision of tomorrow that will inspire us.

Imagine a world in which ...

... love, joy and creativity are expressed in abundance; there is a worldwide spiritual awareness; people are dedicated to their personal growth and engaged in acts of compassion and service;

... everyone can satisfy their basic needs; no one who is unable to care for him or herself is left alone or is deprived;

... all children are wanted and loved; they are properly fed, clothed, housed and educated; no child's life is wasted;

... children are taught to be self-respecting and self-loving; people are eating healthfully and taking good care of their bodies;

... we can prevent or cure many or even most illnesses;

... everyone has meaningful and joyful things to do; we feel we are contributing, using our gifts and that our efforts matter; the workplace is respectful of family and personal life;

... we're leading balanced and simpler lives; the pace of life is slower and more relaxed; we have the time for what really matters;

... people stay healthy and engaged throughout their senior years, and more of us are living satisfying lives beyond 100;

... we honor the passages of life and respect people of all ages; we are learning from our elders as they share their wisdom;

... people can move peacefully through the portal of death without needless pain and suffering;

... we have more understanding between peoples and have learned how to resolve conflicts without resorting to violence;

... we've learned to relate better within our families and communities; we're treating each other with basic love, respect and kindness;

... we have uplifting, joyful, positive forms of entertainment; there are more celebrations, and we share our cultural rituals and traditions;

... cities are vibrant, healthy, safe places and full of diversity; beauty abounds—there are flowers, trees and parks; buildings etc. are well-maintained; people can walk, ride bikes and take public transit;

... we have clean air and water, benign forms of energy, and very little material waste; our natural areas are pure and healthy;

... the population is at a level that allows for a good and sustainable life for all people and for members of the natural world;

... governments are better serving the people's interests, and we are more involved in the democratic process;

... businesses that contribute to the collective mission and that are good employers and stewards of the Earth are plentiful and thriving;

... we are respectful of all life, and our planetary community is living together in harmony;

... and when we each die we say, "My life was worthwhile and mostly enjoyable, and I look forward to coming back again."

P.S. I like to imagine a future in which we have established a human presence on other planets, we're exploring beyond our solar system, we have proven that life exists not just on Earth, and the ordinary person can take trips and vacations in space.

Is there anything you would change on the list? Or what did I leave out that you would like to add? What sort of world do you want your descendants living in or that you would like to experience when you come back?

It's okay to be a dreamer. Indeed, we should each aspire to a better personal reality. And collectively, we ought to have an ideal for our global reality. However, as noted previously, a vision is not enough. We need to take action. It is now more essential than ever that we step up to the challenge of creating Heaven on Earth. At the heart of that effort is restoring the sense of *community* we all had when God made our Souls. We can each do our part to bring forth that spirit of oneness and play a role in shaping the future. Even if we are nearing the end of our own journey, we can still make a contribution. Most of all, it is vital that the children and young adults get excited about and committed to the vision of a better tomorrow.

There are many wise, old Souls among the young people now on Earth. But they're being caught up in the overwhelming materialism of the day. I hope they will soon rediscover their *idealism* and pursue lives of service. A good future depends on them.

We May Be Part of a Community, But Life Is Also Very Personal

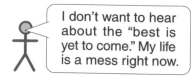

> I don't want to hear about the "best is yet to come." My life is a mess right now.

> What about me? I'm in real pain, and my life will be over soon. I'll be going through the portal.

Death

For many people their life situations are anything but promising. They face a desperate set of circumstances and have little or no hope for a better tomorrow. However, once they move through the pain and suffering of this life and return to the Spirit World, they will indeed experience a much better reality.

We all have moments, even extended periods of time, when we're not pleased with our current situation or optimistic about the future. As we age and see our body decline, or if we have lost or never found our life partner, we can get particularly down. Still, life has a "funny" way of changing overnight—sometimes for the worse, but often for the better. We can improve our life with our own choices. Or someone will appear to help us or to be a loving partner. Or some other fortuitous event will occur. The point is generally there are good reasons to "keep hope alive." As far as aging goes, we may lose our youthfulness and certain physical or mental capacities, but we can grow in other ways. The best can lie ahead for our emotional and spiritual development, and we can find new ways to enjoy life.

> We Souls never give up hope. We really like that saying, "As long as we're alive, anything is possible." And if there is no chance conditions will get better, we know this life is but one episode in our eternal existence.

We Can Only Do Our Best to Make The Most of Whatever Happens

time

"I don't know what is in store for me, but I'm going to do all I can to make each of my moments good ones."

> Well, I promised my Soul I would keep the book under 400 pages. So, it is time to wrap it up. Please proceed to the Epilogue.

Epilogue – To Make a Long Story Short

Okay, let me see if I have this straight. There is a God who created me and the universe and who loves me unconditionally. I am an eternal spiritual being and a Reality Maker. I am here to learn and grow and to bring forth my light—which of course is my love, joy and creativity.

My Soul

That's basically it, but I would add the following points. Then, please put on your clothes, love and accept yourself as you are, stop worrying and get on with living life to its fullest.

- [ ] We're here to make progress on our personal mission and to contribute to the collective mission, which means we're to do our best in the face of life's many challenges to use our gifts and to manifest our Soul's light in all that we say, think and do.

- [ ] We're here to enjoy the beauty and pleasures of the Physical World as much as we can—without being hurtful.

- [ ] We're here to help others to express their light (especially our kindreds and most especially our children, if we have them).

- [ ] We're here to make choices that honor God's Values and Beliefs. We're to avoid causing needless physical or emotional harm to others, ourself and other forms of life.

- [ ] We're here to help take humanity to a higher level, where we've gained mastery over our darker impulses, and we are manifesting our spirituality as individuals and as a community of Souls.

- [ ] We are each here to live the life we have imagined.

- [ ] We're here to learn. We're not competing with others. Life is a personal quest—an ongoing process of growth.

- [ ] We're here to expand our Soul's energy by making wise choices, and doing so will bring us closer to God.

Please don't forget to be kind and compassionate in your everyday life. Live spiritually. And please be tolerant of people who believe and live differently than you. We are all God's children.

Thank you very much for reading my book. If you have any specific comments about its content or alternate views you would like to share, I would enjoy hearing from you.

You can contact me via email at: tomgregory@meaningoflife.net

Or you can write me at: Living Spirit Press
P.O. Box 2455 Dept. 16
Walnut Creek, CA 94595-0455 U.S.A.

I don't know how many emails or letters I might receive, so I can't promise I will respond to all of them. But I will read them and do my best to answer as many as I can.

Also, please visit our web site at: **www.meaningoflife.net**

Let's give God the last words:

Let there be ... Love, Joy and Creativity in your life and through-out the world!

Recommended Books

The following list includes books that were helpful to me in writing *The Meaning of Life* or that are of special interest. Of course, some of them contain viewpoints that I don't entirely agree with, but I still highly recommend them.

Boorstein, Sylvia. *It's Easier Than You Think: The Buddhist Way to Happiness.* San Francisco: Harper San Francisco, 1995.

Brehony, Kathleen. *Awakening at Midlife.* New York: Riverhead Books, 1996.

Brown, Lester R.; Flavin, Christopher; French, Hilay, et al. *State of the World. A Worldwatch Institute Report on Progress Toward a Sustainable Society.* New York: WW Norton, 1999 (Published annually).

Dass, Ram and Bush, Mirabai. *Compassion in Action: Setting Out on a Path of Service.* New York: Bell Tower, 1992.

Fox, Matthew. *The Reinvention of Work: A New Vision of Livelihood for Our Time.* New York: Harper Collins, 1995.

Gawain, Shakti. *Creative Visualization.* Mill Valley, CA: Whatever Publishing, 1979.

Gawain, Shakti. *Living in the Light.* Mill Valley, CA: Whatever Publishing, 1986.

Gawain, Shakti. *Creating True Prosperity.* Novato, CA: New World Library, 1979.

Gawain, Shakti. *The Four Levels of Healing. A Guide to Balancing the Spiritual, Mental, Emotional and Physical Aspects of Life.* Mill Valley, CA: Nataraj Publishing, 1997.

Hay, Louise. *The Power is Within You.* Santa Monica, CA: Hay House, 1991.

Hay, Louise. *You Can Heal Your Life.* Santa Monica, CA: Hay House, 1984.

Heeren, Fred. *Show Me God: What the Message From Space is Telling Us About God.* Wheeling, IL: DayStar Publication, 1997.

Holland, Gail. *A Call for Connection: Solutions for Creating a Whole New Culture.* Novato, CA: New World Library, 1998.

(**Note**: This book and the one listed next contain many names, addresses and web sites for people and organizations that are involved in the areas of social change and planetary transformation.)

Hubbard, Barbara Marx. *Conscious Evolution: Awakening the Power of Our Social Potential.* Novato, CA: New World Library, 1998.

Jeffers, Susan J. *Feel the Fear and Do It Anyway.* San Diego: Fawcett Columbine Books, 1987.

Kabut-Zinn, Jon. *Full Catastrophe Living. Using the Wisdom of Your Body and Mind to Face Stress, Pain and Illness.* New York: Delacorte Publishing, 1990.

Kasl, Charlotte Sophia. *A Home for the Heart: Creating Intimacy and Community with Loved Ones, Neighbors and Friends.* New York: Harper Collins, 1997.

Kornfield, Jack. *A Path With Heart: A Guide Through the Perils and Promises of Spiritual Life.* New York: Bantam Books, 1993.

Lennon, Robin. *Home Design From the Inside Out.* New York: Penguin Books, USA Inc., 1997.

Levine, Stephen. *A Year to Live.* New York: Bell Tower, 1997.

Levine, Stephen. *Healing Into Life and Death.* Garden City, NY: Anchor Press/Doubleday, 1987.

Levine, Stephen. *A Gradual Awakening.* Garden City, NY: Anchor Press/Doubleday, 1979.

Muller, Wayne. *Legacy of the Heart: The Spiritual Advantages of a Painful Childhood.* New York: Fireside, 1992.

Northrup, Christiane, MD. *Women's Bodies, Women's Wisdom: Creating Physical and Emotional Health and Healing.* New York: Bantam Books, 1994 (Revised 1998)

Redfield, James. *The Celestine Prophecy.* New York: Warner Books, 1993.

Redfield, James. *The Tenth Insight.* New York: Warner Books, 1996.

Reed, Henry. *Edgar Cayce on Mysteries of the Mind.* New York: Warner Books, 1989.

(**Note:** When I finished with my original notes and drawings, I found the above book. I was surprised to see that I had described the same three elements of the Soul as it did. This is a very interesting book.)

Robbins, John. *Diet for a New America.* Walpole, NH: Stillpoint, 1987.

Roszak, Theodore; Gomes, Mary E.; and Kanner, Allen D., editors. *Ecopsychology.* San Francisco: Sierra Club Books, 1995.

Seldes, George (compiled by). *The Great Thoughts.* New York: Ballantine Books, revised and updated edition 1996.

(**Note:** This is one of my favorite books. It is a "must read" especially for students even though some of the "great thoughts" are not so agreeable.)

Shaffer, Carolyn R. and Anundsen, Kristin. *Creating Community Anywhere: Finding Support and Connection in a Fragmented World.* New York: Jeremy P. Tarcher/Putnam, 1993.

Thoreau, Henry David. *Walden.* Multiple editions and printings. Originally published 1854.

Weil, Andrew, MD. *8 Weeks to Optimum Health.* New York: Fawcett Columbine, 1997.

Weil, Andrew, MD. *Spontaneous Healing.* New York: Alfred Knopf, 1995.

Williamson, Marianne. *The Healing of America.* New York: Simon and Schuster, 1997.

Williamson, Marianne. *A Return to Love.* New York: Harper Collins, 1992.

———

Finally, I also found the *Personal Power* course offered by Anthony Robbins to be very helpful. I took it several months before my work on this book began. It reinforced the concept of "values and beliefs" and introduced to me the idea of asking "empowering questions." Millions of people have used this course and other materials offered by Robbins as a way of moving toward the "aligned and synergized" state that I described in *The Meaning of Life.*

His web site is: http://www.anthonyrobbins.com

General Index

Quotes Index

About the Author

The Meaning of Life is Tom Gregory's first book. It was inspired by a revelation that came to him one sleepless night. It is the culmination of his personal quest for understanding which began after he experienced a series of major losses and setbacks, including the deaths of his mother and a close friend and a very public business failure.

Tom has studied spiritual subjects, t'ai chi, and meditation for many years. In the late 1980's, he spent a transformative year living and working in Ireland, where he had much time to study and reflect and travel to sacred sites throughout the area. The current focus of Tom's work is combining spirituality with matters of personal and planetary change.

Tom is a graduate of the Kennedy School of Government (where he focused on environmental and social justice issues) and of the Harvard Business School. For most of his professional life he has been an entrepreneur running his own business or helping others as a management consultant. He has a lifelong interest in history, politics, social change, and science. He is also an amateur astronomer.

Tom lives in Northern California with his wife, Nancy and their two cats.

You can contact the author via email at:
tomgregory@meaningoflife.net

Or you can write him at: Living Spirit Press
P.O. Box 2455 Dept. 16
Walnut Creek, CA 94595-0455 U.S.A.

Also, please visit his web site at: www.meaningoflife.net

ORDER FORM

Give *The Meaning of Life* to your family and friends.

Check your favorite bookstore, visit our web site
(www.meaningoflife.net) or order here.

FAX orders: 925.256.0281. Complete and send this form.

TELEPHONE orders: From the US and Canada, call *toll free* at:
    877.785.LIFE (877.785.5433). Otherwise, call: 925.256.0335

EMAIL orders: orders@livingspiritpress.com

POSTAL orders: Living Spirit Press
                PO Box 2455-A
                Walnut Creek, CA 94595-0455 USA

❑ YES, I want ___ copies of the paperback edition (with black & white illustrations) at **US$18.95** each. (The price per book is $20.51, sales tax included, for *California* residents only.)

❑ YES, I want ___ copies of the hardcover edition (with color illustrations) at **US$29.95** each. (The price per book is $32.42, sales tax included, for *California* residents only.) *Available March 2000*

Shipping (via US Postal Service Priority Mail)
US: $4 for the first book, $2 each additional book
Canada: US$8 for the first book, US$4 each additional book
Other Countries: Please call or email us for shipping costs.

Total amount of your order: US$ _____

❑ My check or money order is enclosed. (Payable to: *Living Spirit Press.*)
    (International orders must have a postal money order in US funds.)

❑ Please charge my: ❑ Visa ❑ Mastercard ❑ AMEX

Name _____

Address _____

City/State/Zip _____

Phone _____ Email address _____

Card # _____ Exp. Date _____

Name on card (if different from above) _____

Signature _____

— Thank you very much for your order. —

```
┌─────────────────────────────────────────────────────┐
│                    ORDER FORM                         │
└─────────────────────────────────────────────────────┘
```

Give *The Meaning of Life* to your family and friends.

Check your favorite bookstore, visit our web site
(www.meaningoflife.net) or order here.

FAX orders: 925.256.0281. Complete and send this form.

TELEPHONE orders: From the US and Canada, call *toll free* at:
    877.785.LIFE (877.785.5433). Otherwise, call: 925.256.0335

EMAIL orders: orders@livingspiritpress.com

POSTAL orders: Living Spirit Press
    PO Box 2455-A
    Walnut Creek, CA 94595-0455 USA

❑ YES, I want ___ copies of the paperback edition (with black & white illustrations) at **US$18.95** each. (The price per book is $20.51, sales tax included, for *California* residents only.)

❑ YES, I want ___ copies of the hardcover edition (with color illustrations) at **US$29.95** each. (The price per book is $32.42, sales tax included, for *California* residents only.) *Available March 2000*

Shipping (via US Postal Service Priority Mail)
US: $4 for the first book, $2 each additional book
Canada: US$8 for the first book, US$4 each additional book
Other Countries: Please call or email us for shipping costs.

Total amount of your order: US$ _____

❑ My check or money order is enclosed. (Payable to: *Living Spirit Press.*)
    (International orders must have a postal money order in US funds.)

❑ Please charge my: ❑ Visa ❑ Mastercard ❑ AMEX

Name _____

Address _____

City/State/Zip _____

Phone _____ Email address _____

Card # _____ Exp. Date _____

Name on card (if different from above) _____

Signature _____

— Thank you very much for your order. —